M000213446

PRAISE FOR *THE END OF BURNOUT*

"In this profound, humane, and timely book, Jonathan Malesic diagnoses our burned-out condition with more clarity than anyone before him. But just as importantly, he shows us a path through and out of the crisis—toward a thrilling yet achievable vision of life with our jobs no longer at the center."

OLIVER BURKEMAN, author of *Four Thousand Weeks: Time Management for Mortals*

"*The End of Burnout* is compassionate and wry, addictive, and propulsive. It doesn't just identify the causes of burnout; it offers us compelling examples of what the alternative offers and what it can look like. It's one thing to identify burnout in your own life. It's another to actively seek out the ways to embrace a posture that counters it. This book, one of very few that offer you a graspable glimpse of a different way of a life, feels like a revelation."

ANNE HELEN PETERSEN, author of *Can't Even: How Millennials Became the Burnout Generation*

"Jonathan Malesic has written a moving account of an underacknowledged cultural and spiritual malady. He weaves psychology, theology, philosophy, and real-world experience into a convincing argument that we must attend to the prevalence of burnout if—for no other reason—it undermines our ability to seek the good life."

SIVA VAIDHYANATHAN, author of *The Googlization of Everything (And Why We Should Worry)*

The End of Burnout

The End of Burnout

WHY WORK DRAINS US AND HOW TO BUILD BETTER LIVES

Jonathan Malesic

UNIVERSITY OF CALIFORNIA PRESS

University of California Press
Oakland, California

© 2022 by Jonathan Malesic

First Paperback Printing 2022

Library of Congress Cataloging-in-Publication Data

Names: Malesic, Jonathan, 1975- author.
Title: The end of burnout : why work drains us and how to build better
 lives / Jonathan Malesic.
Description: Oakland, California : University of California Press, [2022] |
 Includes bibliographical references and index.
Identifiers: LCCN 2021012142 (print) | LCCN 2021012143 (ebook) |
 ISBN 9780520344075 (cloth) | ISBN 978-0-520-39152-9 (pbk.: alk.
 paper) | ISBN 9780520975347 (ebook)
Subjects: LCSH: Burn out (Psychology)
Classification: LCC BF481 .M275 2022 (print) | LCC BF481 (ebook) |
 DDC 158.7/23—dc23
LC record available at https://lccn.loc.gov/2021012142
LC ebook record available at https://lccn.loc.gov/2021012143

Manufactured in the United States of America

31 30 29 28 27 26 25 24 23 22
10 9 8 7 6 5 4 3 2 1

"You don't have to like it. That's why it's called work."

GEORGE MALESIC (1933–2018)

Contents

Acknowledgments

I would like to thank the many friends, colleagues, and mentors whose intellectual, editorial, and emotional support helped make this book better: Beth Admiraal, Abbey Arnett, Garrett Barr, Dan Clasby, Jason Danner, Barb Fenner, Mark Fenner, Robin Field, Amy Freund, Tony Grasso, Kendra Greene, Erin Greer, Charles Hatfield, Annelise Heinz, Dan Issing, Farrell Kelly, Kurtley Knight, Katie Krummeck, Vincent Lloyd, Tom Mackaman, Nicole Mares, Charles Marsh, Chuck Mathewes, Jenny McBride, Michael McGregor, Noreen O'Connor, Regan Reitsma, Cris Scarboro, Joel Shuman, Ross Sloan, Jessie Starling, Whitney Stewart, Janice Thompson, Brian Till, Shilyh Warren, Ben Wright, and Willie Young.

I thank my critique partners Elizabeth Barbour, Ceal Klingler, Christina Larocco, Robin Macdonald, Danielle Metcalfe-Chenail, Martha Wolfe, and Vonetta Young. Their careful and loving attention to my work over the last several years improved this project, and my writing in general, immeasurably. I thank Anne Gray Fischer and Will Myers for reading and talking about this book so often, so willingly, and with such intelligence and humor.

I thank Thomas Hagenbuch and Emily Zurek not only for our years-long dialogue about work but as representatives of hundreds of students who have helped me clarify my thinking on this topic.

I thank all those who shared their stories with me, both those named in the book and not, as well as the Monastery of Christ in the Desert, St. Benedict's Monastery, St. John's Abbey, and CitySquare.

I thank the Collegeville Institute for twice hosting me for writing workshops, and the National Endowment for the Humanities and the Louisville Institute for funding this project early on.

I thank the newspaper, magazine, and journal editors who sharpened my words and thoughts in earlier stages of this project: Elizabeth Bruenig, Evan Derkacz, Aline Kalbian, Martin Kavka, Ryan Kearney, Laura Marsh, B.D. McClay, John Nagy, Tim Reidy, Matt Sitman, Jay Tolson, and Kerry Weber.

I thank the band The War on Drugs, whose album "Lost in the Dream" was the soundtrack for my work.

I thank the University of California Press for bringing this book to you. I thank especially Naomi Schneider for seeing the book in my writing on burnout, as well as Summer Farah, Teresa Iafolla, Benjy Mailings, Francisco Reinking, and all those staff members whose labor I did not get to see firsthand. I thank Catherine Osborne, who copyedited the manuscript, and Shannon M.T. Li, who indexed it. I thank the scholars, including Anna Katharina Schaffner, who, at the press's invitation, offered thoughtful comments on a draft of this manuscript.

I thank my family for their enduring support: my mother Carol, my sisters Lisa and Nicole, and my brother Jeff. I thank those whom we lost during my work on this book: Tony, Nana, and my father George.

I thank the following publications for permission to use material I wrote that was originally published in their pages: "Taming the Demon," *Commonweal,* February 8, 2019; "When Work and Meaning Part Ways," *The Hedgehog Review* 20, no. 3 (Fall 2018); "Millennials Don't Have a Monopoly on Burnout," *The New Republic,* January 10, 2019; "Imagining a Better Life After Coronavirus," *The New Republic,* April 1, 2020.

I thank all those I have forgotten to thank here.

Above all, I thank Ashley Barnes. In our life together, burnout has been not just an intellectual problem but an existential one, too. She helps me solve it every day. Without her, none of this would have been possible.

Introduction

Several years ago, instead of spending my mornings getting ready for my job as a college professor, I would lie in bed for hours, repeatedly watching the video to "Don't Give Up," the English pop star Peter Gabriel's 1986 duet with Kate Bush. In the video, the two singers embrace for six minutes as the sun is eclipsed behind them. Gabriel's lyrical expression of despair and desolation echoed my inner monologue. It didn't matter how many times I heard Bush compassionately repeat the song's title and her assurance that this suffering would pass. The words never rang true.

My first class was at two in the afternoon; I'd make it there barely on time and barely prepared, then go right back home when it was over. At night, I ate ice cream and drank malty, high-alcohol beer—often together, as a float. I gained thirty pounds.

By any objective standard, I had a fantastic job. I exercised high-level skills and training in something I was good at: teaching religion, ethics, and theology. I worked with intelligent, friendly colleagues. My salary was more than adequate; my benefits, excellent. I had great autonomy in determining how to teach my classes and pursue research projects. And with tenure, I had a level of job security unheard of outside academia and increasingly rare within it. Still, I was miserable, and it was clear my job was at the center of that feeling. I wanted to give up. I had burned out.

At the time, I thought something was wrong just with me. Why did I hate such a good job? But as I eventually realized, the problem of burnout is much bigger than one worker's despair. Residents of the United States, Canada, and other wealthy countries have built a whole culture of burnout around our work. But burnout doesn't have to be our fate.

The End of Burnout springs from my desire to understand why millions of workers across all industries find themselves drained of the strength they need to do their jobs, and why that makes them feel like they have failed at life. I define burnout as the experience of being pulled between expectation and reality at work. And I argue that burnout is a cultural phenomenon that expanded in the past five decades but that has deep historical roots in our belief that work will be a means not just to a paycheck but to dignity, character, and a sense of purpose. In fact, despite widespread concern about burnout, burnout culture has persisted *because* we cherish these ideals; we fear losing the meaning that work promises. And yet the working conditions that are typical in the United States and other rich, postindustrial countries prevent us from attaining the very things we seek.

I hope this book will help our culture recognize that work doesn't dignify us or form our character or give our lives purpose. *We* dignify work, *we* shape its character, and *we* give it purpose within our lives. Once we realize this, we can devote less of ourselves to our jobs, improve our labor conditions, and value those of us who do not work for pay. Together, we can end burnout culture and flourish in ways that do not depend on work. In fact, many people already embrace an alternative vision of work's role in a well-lived life. And they often do so at the margins of burnout culture. This book will introduce you to them.

The End of Burnout appears in the wake of the Covid-19 pandemic, which upended work around the world. In the United States, the mass unemployment caused by society-wide quarantine demonstrated once and for all that our ideals for work were a lie. People's dignity, their worth as humans, had nothing to do with their employment status. A waitress who lost her job due to the pandemic had no less dignity than she did before stay-at-home orders forced her restaurant to close. The pandemic has, in this sense, given us an opportunity to make a decisive break from the ethos that has governed our work and caused our burnout over the past fifty years. It's a chance to remake work and reimagine its place in our lives. If we don't take this opportunity, we will slip back into the patterns that created the burnout culture in the first place.

Burnout represents a strange puzzle for the way we ordinarily think about problems with work. The fact that it can happen to tenured college professors means it isn't only about poor conditions of employment. It isn't something we can eradicate just with better pay, benefits, and security across the board. Working conditions matter, and I do think workers deserve better, but they tell no more than half the story.

Burnout isn't only a problem of labor economics. It's an ailment of the soul. We burn out in large part because we believe work is the sure path to social, moral, and spiritual flourishing. Work simply can't deliver what we want from it, and the gap between our ideals and our on-the-job reality leads us to exhaustion, cynicism, and despair. Additionally, our individualistic approach to work keeps us from talking about burnout or uniting in solidarity to improve our conditions. We blame ourselves when work doesn't live up to our expectations. We suffer alone, only exacerbating our plight. That's why the cure for burnout has to be cultural and collective, focused on offering each other the compassion and respect our work does not.

Before we get to solutions, though, we need to understand the experience of burnout. Stories about burnout lack an inherent drama. They're not like stories about a great discovery or catastrophe or love affair. There's no clear threshold from ordinary, functional worker to crumpled husk tumbling through your workday. There probably is a first morning you wake up and think, "Not this again," but it passes unnoticed. By that point, it's too late anyway. Your chance to avoid burnout has already passed. You were just doing your job the way you're expected to, and day by day, your ability to do it withered. At some point, you realize you can barely do it at all. You're too tired, too embittered, too useless.

I'll begin by telling you how all of that happened to me.

· · ·

I dreamed of being a college professor almost as soon as I met my own professors. I wanted to be like them, reading strange books by Nietzsche and Annie Dillard and asking challenging questions in class. One of my favorites taught theology and lived on campus as a faculty advisor. On Friday afternoons he opened his small, cinderblock apartment to students. I was a regular. I sat on the burgundy upholstered institutional furniture and, over coffee, chatted with him about heady topics like the theological implications of the universe's expansion. He also showed movies in the residence hall's TV lounge, mostly foreign and art films from when he was our age: *My Dinner with Andre, Crimes and Misdemeanors, Au Revoir les Enfants*. We all had lengthy discussions afterward. To my eyes, this man lived the good life. He lived for knowledge and art and wisdom and got paid to pursue them and hand them on to a young generation eager for them. Well, I was eager for them, anyway. He had turned late-night dorm-room conversations into a profession. I did all I could to follow his lead.

Over the next decade, I did the things you need to do to live that life. I went to graduate school, finished my dissertation, and went on the always-difficult academic job market. After a few tries, I succeeded: I landed a full-time, tenure-track position teaching theology at a small Catholic college. This was my shot at my dream. My girlfriend and I packed up my dozens of boxes of books and my tweed jackets and moved me from Virginia, where I had gone to grad school, to northeast Pennsylvania. Then we moved her to Berkeley, California so she could go to grad school, in pursuit of her own dream of being a college professor.

With a long-distance relationship, I threw myself into the work. I assigned Nietzsche and Annie Dillard and asked challenging questions in class. I published, I served on faculty committees, I worked late at the office. I was determined to be inspiring, like my professors were, and not like the dinosaurs who lectured from the same yellowed notes year after year. The biggest problem I faced was students' indifference to my subject matter. They all *had* to take theology, but hardly any *wanted* to take it. So I came up with some techniques—tricks, really—to get students to put in a little more effort to learn than they would otherwise. It sort of worked. I even tricked a few students into becoming theology majors. I showed movies in class—*The Apostle, Higher Ground, Crimes and Misdemeanors*—and had a few rangy conversations about them with students. I was living my dream.

After six years, I earned tenure. By this time, my girlfriend had become my wife and moved back east. She finished her PhD and got a job in rural western Massachusetts. I had a sabbatical, so I followed her there for a year. Day after day, I wrote and exercised in the morning, and in the afternoon I either read in a café or went for a bike ride past hillside pastures and disused water mills. I couldn't have been more content.

But then I had to return to my job, and my wife and I went back to long-distance. To see each other, we drove four and a half hours, two or three weekends a month. Once again, I threw myself into the work. But it was much harder this time. For one thing, I was no longer new to the job. I didn't have to impress anyone for my tenure application. More important, though, the college faced two crises: one pertaining to its finances, the other to its accreditation. People got laid off. Salaries and budgets were frozen. There were concerns about enrollment. Would tuition payments be enough to keep the college out of the red? And there was much more work to do, to satisfy the accrediting agency. Everyone seemed to walk around the campus in a constant state of worry.

The stress got to me, too, despite my job security. I was working harder than ever—not just teaching and doing research, but heading up committees and leading the college's center for teaching excellence—but I felt I was not getting much recognition from the college's leaders. I wasn't getting affirmation of my work from the students, either. It seemed like they were learning nothing from me. Peers, including my department chair, continued to compliment my teaching. I didn't believe it; I saw my daily failure in the classroom firsthand, in every blank face of every student who wanted to be anywhere but at a desk listening to me.

It feels like an admission of shameful weakness, a pseudo-problem of privilege, to say that the thing I most needed was acknowledgment that my work meant something to someone. Don't people put up with far worse than a lack of recognition? I made decent money. I got to do interesting work. I didn't have a boss looking over my shoulder. Why couldn't I just shut up and do my job like everyone else? What was *wrong* with me?

My temper grew shorter. I started returning students' papers later and later. Class preparation became increasingly difficult. I faced a mental block every night as I tried to remember my pedagogical tricks. I had forgotten everything I knew about good teaching. And I watched "Don't Give Up" over and over.

It no longer felt like I was living a dream. It wasn't the life I'd imagined two decades before. After two years of progressive misery, I took a semester of unpaid leave and returned to the bucolic site of my sabbatical to live under the same roof as my wife again. I hoped some rest would help. I came back to Pennsylvania for the spring semester, but nothing had changed. The job was the same. I was the same. In fact, things were about to get even worse.

.   .   .

The classroom is silent as the projector's light shines straight into my eyes. My department chair sits at a desk in one corner, taking notes. It's the day of my annual teaching observation, and none of the twenty students in my social ethics class makes a move in response to the harrowing video to Kendrick Lamar's song "Alright." There's the scene of the white cops, wearing mustaches and shades, shuffling down the street, the car on their shoulders like a coffin, as Kendrick rocks in the driver's seat and someone empties a bottle out of a rear window. There are scenes of black men, including Kendrick himself, being gunned down by police in the street. Maybe no one says anything because the video is too new, too weird, too confrontational for the students. Every second of silence is emotional torture.

Eventually, a brave, sincere girl in the front row raises her hand. She mentions how disturbed she was by the video's language and images. We talk, her voice cracking. But the conversation doesn't go far. I ask the class more questions: "Did anything you saw in the video connect to anything we've talked about in the class so far? What about the scene where Kendrick stands on the telephone wires like Jesus on the parapet of the temple? If he's Jesus, then who is 'Lucy,' tempting him with money and cars?"

Nothing. No one says a word. I feel the adrenaline rise up my back.

Fine. Onto the next thing on the lesson plan, an 1891 document by Pope Leo XIII on labor in the industrial economy. Who can say what Leo thinks about private property? Who caught a biblical reference in there? The students don't budge. Who has a question? Anyone?

I do, but I don't voice it: *Who has a single thought in their head? Not one goddamned person?* The adrenaline surges to the back of my skull, telling me it's time for fight or flight.

Do I lash out at the students for ignoring the reading? For being lazy, for not even trying? Do I shame them, maybe remind them, like a pedantic prick, that it's their education at stake, not mine? Do I tell them that everyone who didn't read has to leave? Then wait, repeat the words to show I'm serious, and stare them down while they put away their notebooks and pull on their coats?

Or do *I* pack up and walk out? That's a gambit even my extremely sympathetic department chair could not ignore in her observation report. It would, however, get me out. I would live.

My jaw clamps shut. My face reddens. I don't fight. I don't run. I breathe deep and force myself into a professional composure. I stand at the podium and deliver a condescending lecture on the homework reading assignment. I don't bother asking the students to participate.

I have never felt so stupid in my entire life, never so humiliated in my eleven-year teaching career. I can't even get twenty-year-olds to have an opinion about a music video.

Mercifully, the class period's time runs out. The students zip their backpacks and leave. As my department chair walks past me to the door, she says things didn't go as badly as I thought they did. But I know it's over.

I have arrived at the antithesis of the good life I had glimpsed when I was a student. The professor whose life I envied was never pedantic. In class, he sat with us in a circle and nodded his head as we spoke, inviting us to "say more" when we haltingly tested our new ideas. He was affably erudite. I am angrily dogmatic. My dream of being a college professor, which had sustained me through grad school, the job market, and the slow climb to tenure, has fallen apart.

A week later, I decide to quit.

. . .

In the United States and other rich countries, burnout is much discussed but little understood. We speak about it imprecisely, which only contributes to burnout culture's persistence. I feel like I have read the same unhelpful article about burnout dozens of times in business magazines and on popular websites. The writers often call attention to the way burnout causes workers to lose sleep, disengage from work, and become more likely to get heart disease, depression, and anxiety.[1] Many point out that workplace stress costs Americans up to $190 billion a year in excess health-care costs and untold amounts of lost productivity.[2] In addition to providing these facts, the authors also dole out dubious advice. One typical article recommends that, to avoid burnout, you should do three things:

> First, find ways to serve every day. . . . Second, choose organizations to work for with the right mission and culture that fits who you are. Third, 'entrepreneur' your job: take ownership of your situation and creatively find ways to integrate your values, strengths, and passions into your work—while also meeting your performance expectations—so that you achieve not only success but also significance.[3]

These suggestions are comically out of touch, betraying an ignorance of both the psychological literature on burnout and the reality of working life. Authors like these don't just put all responsibility for burnout on the shoulders of the worker; they also posit that workers have total control over where they can find a job and what aspects of it they can "take ownership of." This article was published during the depths of the Great Recession in 2008, in a month when US employers shed more than a half million jobs.[4] I wish I could say it's an outlier, but it represents the common public wisdom on burnout, absolving companies and their managers of any fault for the stress their workers experience.[5]

The dreary familiarity of most writing on burnout shows how our collective thinking about this problem is stuck. We keep reading and writing the same story, despite the harm that story is causing us. Many authors tell people who already feel worn out and ineffectual that they can change their situation if they just try hard enough. What's more, by making it individuals' responsibility to deal with their own burnout, the advice leaves untouched the inhumane ethical and economic system that causes burnout in the first place. Our thinking is stuck because we don't recognize how deeply burnout is embedded in our cultural values. Or else we're afraid to admit it. Insofar as the system that works people to the point of burnout is profitable, the people who profit from it have little incentive to alter it. In an individualistic culture where work is a moral duty, it's up to you to ensure you're in good working order. And many workers who boast of their hustle embrace that duty, no matter the damage it does. In a perverse way, many of us love burnout culture. Deep down, we want to burn out.

This book aims to pull our thinking about burnout out of its five-decade rut. It identifies burnout as a cultural problem, not an individual one. It traces the history of burnout and names the trends that brought it to cultural prominence in the 1970s. It synthesizes scientific findings to define burnout as the experience of having to stretch across the gap between your ideals about work and the reality of your job. It shows how these ideals have only grown in recent decades as our working conditions have decayed. Then it offers a new way of thinking about work that can end burnout culture. It proposes a new set of ideals that elevate human dignity, compassion, and leisure activity, which together can displace work from the center of our lives. And it dives deep into the communities, workplaces, and individuals who are resisting burnout culture and stand as an avant-garde for the rest of us to create a new way of living and working.

The bad advice about burnout assumes—as we all often do—that the institutions and systems of culture are immutable, almost God-given. But, of course, they aren't. We have changed how we work before, with cultural shifts often playing a significant role in reform efforts. Child labor went from being commonplace to illegal during just a few decades in the early twentieth century; at the same time, parents began viewing children not as economically useful, but as "priceless," too morally and emotionally valuable to perform dangerous labor.[6] And we have changed other norms and institutions since then, often at a rapid pace. Same-sex couples can now legally marry. Transgender people are gaining recognition and acceptance. It may be hard to dismantle social structures and create something new, but it's clearly not impossible. After all, human beings built these structures to begin with. Why can't we build something better?

. . .

Burnout is a complex phenomenon, an inner experience that affects our behavior both on the job and off. Its causes range from our highest ideals to our effort to support our families, from global economic forces to our daily interactions with that one annoying customer. My quest to understand burnout in all its complexity led me to read numerous psychology papers, as well as works of sociology, political science, and theology. I interviewed dozens of workers and spent several days in a remote canyon in the New Mexico desert. I also looked deep into my own life, dredging up emails and notes I wrote throughout my academic career. There is science writing and history in this book, cultural analysis and philosophy, immersive reporting and memoir.

Part I is about how we created our burnout culture over the past fifty years. In chapter 1, I survey burnout's place in our public conversation and find an ill-informed cacophony of viewpoints on it. Scientists, clinicians, marketers, employers, and workers all have competing interests at stake when they use the term burnout. And so there is little consensus on what the term even means. This makes burnout a cultural buzzword, an often-empty signifier onto which we can project virtually any agenda. Our imprecise language about burnout raises questions about whether we truly want to solve the problem at all.

Burnout is a modern phenomenon, but it has historical antecedents, including acedia, melancholia, and neurasthenia. I explore this history in chapter 2. Like burnout, these bygone sicknesses of the soul were points of both pride and shame that reflected cultural priorities. Burnout itself first came to public attention in the United States in the 1970s, when two psychologists, working independently, simultaneously described a new ailment afflicting idealistic workers like free-clinic volunteers, poverty attorneys, and counselors. Burnout appeared at a crucial moment when Americans' way of work was changing dramatically, becoming at once more intense and more precarious.

In chapter 3 I dive into the psychological research on burnout to make sense of how it can be both so widespread and such a varied phenomenon. As the gap between your ideals and your reality at work widens, it becomes harder to keep yourself in one piece. That said, there is not just one way to undergo burnout. Burnout is a spectrum, on which there are several distinct modes of experience, which we can call burnout profiles.

On a larger scale, burnout *culture* results from the growing gap between working conditions and societal ideals for work. Chapter

4 is about how those conditions have eroded since the 1970s. Outsourcing and temping have expanded, while the growing service sector has made increasing demands on workers' time and emotions, exposing more of who we are to workplace stress. These factors contribute to shortfalls regarding the fairness, autonomy, community, and values people experience at work. In this respect, burnout culture is an ethical failure—a failure to honor workers' humanity.

In chapter 5 I survey the other side of the gap, our ever-growing ideals for work. These ideals make a promise: engage with your work, and you will earn more than a salary. You will earn social dignity, moral character, and spiritual purpose. But the promise is false. Engagement actually leads to "total work," a condition where work is the highest human endeavor, diminishing our dignity, character, and spiritual aspiration. Our work ethic's ultimate virtue is martyrdom, a willing acceptance of burnout for the sake of those ideals. The true beneficiaries of this sacrifice, though, are employers.

Part II is about how we can create a new culture, with work no longer at the center of our lives' meaning. Preventing and healing burnout will demand that we collectively lower our ideals for work and improve conditions so that they match workers' human dignity. In chapter 6, disparate thinkers, including a pope, a transcendentalist, and a Marxist feminist, become guides to how we might reorient work around people's inherent worth by limiting work's reach into our lives and subordinating it to higher ends, discovered within communities of mutual recognition.

In chapter 7, I look for people outside the mainstream who embody the work ideals and conditions we will need if we are going to eradicate burnout culture. Benedictine monasteries offer one model from which we can draw secular lessons. The monks at an isolated monastery in New Mexico take a radical approach. They labor just three hours a day, so they can spend much more time in communal prayer. Other Benedictine communities, including two in Minnesota, represent a more accessible example. They work longer hours in direct response to worldly need, yet they still maintain practices to honor each other's worth and keep from identifying themselves with their jobs.

My search for models of anti-burnout culture leads me in chapter 8 to a nonprofit organization in Dallas, Texas that aims to recognize the full humanity of those who undertake the difficult work of fighting poverty. I also encounter people who seek identity and meaning after work, in their hobbies. And I find, in listening to artists with disabilities, that people who cannot find dignity through paid employment find it in self-acceptance, ritual, and community, often online. Regardless of our ability to work, we will only heal the wounds of burnout culture through compassionate solidarity with all others as burnouts-in-the-making.

In the book's conclusion, I argue that we now have an opportunity to align our work with more humane ideals. The Covid-19 pandemic changed work for nearly everyone. Despite the losses it imposed on so many lives and communities, it has given us a chance to reorder work's place in our lives and culture.

.   .   .

I have a few caveats concerning what this book is not about. First, it is not a self-help book for individuals, but rather for an entire culture. The examples of people who are resisting burnout culture, the subjects of chapters 7 and 8, may inspire readers to make changes in their lives, but I am convinced that beating burnout is necessarily a collective effort. Second, the core of the argument is not that burnout is the direct result of capitalism—or even "late" capitalism. Reforming our economic priorities could certainly improve some conditions of our jobs, but overthrowing capitalism (even if that were possible) would not end burnout once and for all. Capitalism alone didn't cause our ideals to diverge from our reality at work. Still, the profit motive leads employers to put constant pressure on workers to produce more with fewer resources, adding to employees' anxiety and stress. Third, this book is mainly about burnout in paid employment. It does not cover parental burnout, for instance.[7] This is not to say that parenting isn't difficult, or that it does not have work-like characteristics. But the scientific research on parental burnout is limited, and the dissimilarities between parenting and paid employment are great.[8] Parents don't worry about getting fired, and they don't have a human resources office where they can take their complaints. In fact, a crucial step in breaking down burnout culture must be to recognize that unpaid activities like parenting, school, and relationships have a value altogether different from the value of paid work.

It may be impossible to eliminate burnout entirely. As long as we toil, there will be pain. But we can surely ease it. Burnout arises from the contradictions between our ideals and our organizations, but it's also a product of the unhealthy interpersonal relations we have at work. Burnout stems from the demands we place on others, the recognition we fail to give, the discord between our words and actions. It is ultimately the result of a failure to honor each other's human dignity. The question, in the end, cannot just be "how I can prevent *my* burnout?"; it has to be, "how I can prevent *yours*?" The answer will entail not just creating better workplaces, but also becoming better people.

I *Burnout Culture*

1 Everyone Is Burned Out, But No One Knows What That Means

In the weeks following my decision to quit my job as a tenured college professor, the word *burnout* occurred to me as a possible way to explain the angry dread I felt toward my career. A scholar at heart, I spent my lame-duck semester at the college swimming through research on this topic to understand my own life. The name that came up again and again in my reading was Christina Maslach, a psychologist at the University of California, Berkeley. My college had a copy of Maslach's starkly-titled 1982 book *Burnout: The Cost of Caring* in the basement of its authentically unrenovated midcentury library, so I checked it out.

It was as if Maslach had written my professional biography. The book focuses on workers in human-service professions: counselors, social workers, police and corrections officers, and teachers like me. She finds that those who burn out tend to be idealistic. "[N]oble ideals can pose problems for a provider when ideals are all he or she has to guide the direction of work," she writes, "because then, no matter how hard the person works, each day is doomed to be a failure."[1]

Maslach recognizes the importance of having psychological needs met at work: "The person who lacks close relationships with friends or family will be far more dependent on clients and colleagues for signs of appreciation."[2] I certainly was. At the time when my workload was greatest, my wife was living two hundred miles away. We both lived far from our parents and siblings. And all my friends were work friends; when we got together, we often complained about work. My students' perpetual disinterest felt like a rebuke to everything that mattered to me.

Reading Maslach's work, though, I felt understood. Her writing was filled with compassion for the burned-out workers she and her colleagues studied. She didn't blame us for our unhappiness. She praised our idealism, and while she thought we needed to be more honest with ourselves about the difficult reality of our professions, she didn't see us as inadequate, just inadequately trained to deal with professional challenges.[3] Maslach's occasional collaborators Ayala Pines and Elliot Aronson agree. They discovered that people found comfort in knowing that their suffering had a name, that there was not "something uniquely wrong with *them*."[4] As Maslach and Michael Leiter argue in their 1997 book *The Truth About Burnout*—a book I heavily underlined and annotated during my final weeks of teaching at the college—burnout was caused by institutions, not individuals. "[B]urnout is not a problem of the people themselves but of the *social environment* in which people work," they write. "When the workplace does not recognize the human side of work, then the risk of burnout grows, carrying a high price with it."[5]

Individuals aren't to blame for burnout, but they certainly feel its negative effects. Maslach sees burnout as having three dimensions: exhaustion, cynicism (sometimes called depersonalization), and a sense of ineffectiveness or diminished accomplishment.[6] You're burned out at work when you are constantly drained of energy (exhaustion), when you see your clients or students as problems rather than people you're meant to help (cynicism), and when you feel that your work accomplishes nothing (ineffectiveness). I felt all of these intensely. I woke up tired, dreading the work ahead. I fought hard to contain my frustration with students and administrators who didn't seem to care. And I thought my effort and talent amounted to nothing. The students just wouldn't learn. My career was a waste.

There was a deep irony to my experience of burnout, a "cruel optimism," to borrow a term from the literary critic Lauren Berlant. Cruel optimism is "when the object that draws your attachment actively impedes the aim that brought you to it initially."[7] I was pursuing worthy goals in my career—learning, teaching others, contributing to a community of fellow scholars—but the pursuit itself exhausted me, made me cynical, and threw me into despair. And in doing so, it undermined my ability to attain those very goals.

As I kept reading articles about this condition I now claimed as my own, I followed the footnotes in one paper to the next one I would read, and the next, and the next. One thing that came up in most of them was something called the Maslach Burnout Inventory, a psychometric test developed by Christina Maslach that has become standard in burnout research. I decided to take the version of the test written specifically for educators. It cost $15 and took five minutes to complete online, a small price to pay for scientific confirmation of whether I really was burned out. The twenty-two-question test asked me to say how often I had various feelings about my job and students, from "I feel emotionally drained from my work" (a measure of exhaustion) to "I don't really care what happens to some students" (a measure of depersonalization or cynicism) and "I feel exhilarated after working closely with my students" (a measure of personal accomplishment or effectiveness). I answered honestly but worried that if I "failed," if the test said I wasn't burned out, then I would have to keep searching for what had derailed my career and nearly ruined my life.

I passed with flying colors. I had scored in the ninety-eighth percentile for exhaustion and the seventeenth percentile for personal accomplishment, which meant I was among the most emotionally drained educators who have taken the MBI and that I felt less effective than five out of six test-takers. (Personal accomplishment is scored on a reverse scale; the lower your score, the greater your sense of ineffectiveness.) To my surprise, I was only in the forty-fourth percentile for depersonalization, a shade below the average but nevertheless at a level some researchers deemed a high score. Still: below average for cynicism? I had been writing long, angry all-faculty emails late at night; what were the *truly* cynical doing? Regardless, I had scored very high on the key dimension of exhaustion. As someone who thrives on the validation of standardized tests, I felt proud, just like I did when I got my GRE scores to get into graduate school.

The research I was reading, along with the fact that there was a test for the three dimensions of burnout, meant that I was not alone in my condition. But how many workers are burned out? And what is their experience like? The same as mine, or different? These are harder questions to answer than you would think. But they lead directly into our culture's conflicted feelings toward burnout.

. . .

Burnout is certainly the subject of considerable public discussion. Based on what you can read about it on popular websites, in magazines, and in trade publications, every profession is susceptible to burnout. While writing this book, I received a daily email that notified me of articles on burnout published across the internet. Each message included dozens of links. On just one day, there were stories about burnout among physicians, nurses, teachers, parents, dentists, police, climate activists, campus safety officers, attorneys, neurointerventionalists, people with security clearances, tennis players, graduate students, librarians, musicians, freelancers, volunteers, and comedian Dave Chappelle.

Many of the headlines claim a high prevalence of burnout within the occupations. For instance, the article on neurointerventionalists—physicians who operate on strokes and other vascular blockages—said that 56 percent of doctors in that specialty met the criteria for burnout.[8] One research team says 28 percent of the general working public is burned out, as are 44 percent of physicians.[9] Another, 23 percent of workers.[10] Keep reading, and you'll find numbers that strain the limits of plausibility. According to one survey, "77 percent of respondents say they have experienced employee burnout at their current job, with more than half citing more than one occurrence."[11] Another claims—astonishingly—that 96 percent of millennials are affected by burnout.[12]

Each headline, taken individually, tells a simple and alarming story: a significant portion of workers have this condition that is somehow built into their jobs yet impairs their ability to do their jobs. The articles often frame burnout as a clear and definitive state, like having strep throat. "A Startling 79% of Primary Care Physicians *Are Burned Out,* New Report Finds," reads a typical headline.[13] The precise percentages make it seem like there is a bright line between healthy and unhealthy workers. When it comes to your job, you're like a light bulb; either you are still burning, or you're burned out. There is nothing in between. And if you are burned out, then it's all you can do to drag yourself through your workday. You're the working dead.

Taken together, though, the articles say something more complex and less conclusive. Yes, burnout is widespread, but the figures that get cited in making this point are not compatible. It can't be true that basically all millennials are burned out, while only a quarter of all workers are, because, at the time these surveys were published, millennials were more than a third of all workers.[14] And surely some older workers suffer from burnout, too.

A look behind the numbers reveals that the researchers who produced them are all working with different definitions of burnout. The studies are not talking about the same thing—a problem that some burnout researchers themselves acknowledge.[15] Few studies rely on the full twenty-two-question Maslach Burnout Inventory that I took. And even researchers who do use the MBI apply it in disparate ways. One meta-analysis found that out of 156 studies that used the MBI to examine physician burnout, there were forty-seven different definitions of burnout and at least two dozen definitions each of emotional exhaustion, cynicism, and ineffectiveness. It's no wonder these studies produced widely divergent results, from 0 percent of physicians experiencing burnout, up to 80 percent.[16] It is as if everyone has been trying to build a house, but no one can agree on how to measure the boards, and we keep on cutting and hammering anyway.

In addition, the MBI measures exhaustion, cynicism, and ineffectiveness on a scale, yet many studies set a distinct threshold for burnout. Below it, you are not burned out; above it, you are. It's like having a lamp on a dimmer, but you declare that it isn't really "on" if it falls below some arbitrary level of brightness, even though it still lights up the room. On top of that difficulty with burnout research, many studies rely on ordinary people's subjective definitions of burnout. If a survey-taker asks us, "Do you experience burnout," and I think burnout is a complete inability to function, while you think of it as needing a nap on Saturday afternoon, then our responses will mean very different things, yet both of our definitions will make their way into the data. If the studies' respondents don't agree about the meaning of burnout, and study designers don't agree, then all of these numbers, supposedly measuring the same thing, are really just comparing apples to oranges to compost piles.

For example, a Mayo Clinic study that compared burnout rates between physicians and the general workforce classified someone as burned out if they responded that the statement, "I feel burned out from my work" applied to them at least a few times a month, or if "I have become more callous toward people since I took this job" applied to them once a month or more.[17] Someone did not need to say yes to both questions in order to count as having burnout symptoms. The two questions are certainly easier to ask than the twenty-two on the MBI. And there is in fact a strong correlation between answers to these single questions and the emotional exhaustion and depersonalization dimensions of the full MBI.[18] But the Mayo Clinic study didn't take the third dimension, personal accomplishment (or its inverse, ineffectiveness), into account at all. And the first question—the measure for emotional exhaustion—invites respondents to rely on their individual definitions of "burnout."

To be sure, it is a major societal problem if, as the Mayo Clinic found, 30 to 40 percent of doctors are frequently exhausted or depersonalize their patients—that is, treat them like less than full human beings. But it's not the same as saying a large minority of physicians can barely complete their daily work obligations. Or that they need talk therapy or pharmaceutical treatment. And the trouble is, absent a clear definition of burnout, we don't know what those figures suggest about the magnitude of the burnout crisis in medicine. Likewise, the survey that claimed virtually all millennials were burned out, conducted via Amazon's Mechanical Turk platform, may point to a widespread problem, but only if the researchers used reliable means to obtain their result. In that survey, participants were asked a question—"Do you believe that burnout or mental exhaustion affects your everyday life?"—that is absurdly broad and falsely assumes agreement about what burnout even is. The results are meaningless. We would not deem someone clinically depressed if they responded yes to a single question like, "Do you ever feel depressed?" Yet that is exactly how marketers, pollsters, and even some academic researchers are trying to establish that burnout is a societal epidemic.

Compounding our trouble with defining burnout is the fact that, like any widely-perceived ailment, burnout is potentially big business. Marketers hype burnout's status as a work-related syndrome recognized by the World Health Organization while simultaneously relying on subjective definitions of it. By applying this veneer of scientific respectability over a broad and fuzzy set of experiences, they can create a burnout emergency—and an entire market of people who stand in need of a cure, from wellness regimens to well-curated "content."

For instance, the media conglomerate Meredith Corporation released a survey titled "Burnout Flashpoint" in conjunction with the Harris polling company in 2019. Nineteen percent of women respondents claimed to be more burned out than they were five years earlier. That sounds like a significant problem, but it is a much smaller percentage than those who said they were more "stressed" (36 percent) or more "tired" (33 percent) than they were in the past.[19] Still, "burnout" was the headline term, not "being tired." "Tired" doesn't sell. Burnout: that's the cultural phenomenon. That's the zeitgeist. So that must be the problem we face.

And with that problem comes opportunity for anyone who can claim to have a solution. "More than ever," the Meredith report claims, "women are looking to brands to be their ally in combatting burnout (not adding to it)."[20] It hardly needs to be said that Meredith's "content studio" offers the kind of services to help brands become the allies women want. Along the same lines, the consulting firm Deloitte found, in its 2018 Workplace Burnout Survey, that the vast majority of workers have experienced burnout and that "employers may be missing the mark when it comes to developing well-being programs that their employees find valuable to address stress in the workplace."[21] But there's good news: Deloitte's human capital consulting services can help with that.

. . .

The fact that burnout is a contested term, whereas strep throat is not, tells us something important about burnout culture: there are different interests at stake in this definition. Workers, employers, researchers, marketers, and clinicians all want the term to do different things, whether it is to validate their experience (as I did), identify deadwood to cull from the company, or define a new area of therapeutic practice. The term burnout *matters* to us, and yet we cannot settle on a definition of it. In that context, the sensationalized research findings don't just report on the condition; they invite readers to claim they're burned out, too. If you read that a huge percentage of people like you—who share your profession, your gender, your age cohort—are undergoing burnout, then, to fit in, don't you have to say you are as well? This is the paradox of burnout culture. Burnout is a negative condition, and yet many workers want to apply it to themselves.

You can see the paradox in the public conversation over millennial-generation burnout. In early 2019, the journalist Anne Helen Petersen published an essay in *BuzzFeed News* about burnout as the explanation for why millennials—in their twenties and thirties at the time—seemingly couldn't fulfill ordinary tasks, including something as important as registering to vote. It wasn't that they were lazy. In Petersen's account, millennials have been under pressure to perform for their entire lives, they're deep in educational loan debt, and they've experienced a precarious job market, leading them to hustle past the point of exhaustion. Burnout, to Petersen, is "not a temporary affliction: It's the millennial condition. It's our base temperature. It's our background music. It's the way things are. It's our lives."[22]

Petersen's essay was a sensation, read millions of times and discussed widely on radio shows and podcasts. In the days following the essay's appearance, I eagerly watched the social media conversation unfold, as this topic that sat at the intersection of my personal and professional lives was suddenly getting the attention it deserved. I suspect the essay was so popular because it gave a name—and with it, legitimacy—to what readers had experienced. It told millennials and others that what they were undergoing was in fact a large-scale problem, not their individual fault. That's why Maslach's definition of burnout resonated so much with me in the final weeks of my academic career. I knew I wasn't alone.

The article may also have been popular because it didn't just name an experience; it elevated those who had that experience. It justified their inability to function as the price they paid for being ideal workers. It gave them status in the moral system of American work culture. Petersen defines burnout as something more than exhaustion: "Exhaustion means going to the point where you can't go any further; burnout means reaching that point and pushing yourself to keep going, whether for days or weeks or years."[23] According to this definition, burnout isn't a failure of productivity but the continuation of productivity despite lacking the strength it takes to produce. The burned-out worker is, in this sense, a kind of hero. And to be sure, Petersen emphasizes that through her own growing exhaustion, she continued to work both hard and effectively: "While writing this piece, I was orchestrating a move, planning travel, picking up prescriptions, walking my dog, trying to exercise, making dinner, attempting to participate in work conversations on Slack, posting photos to social media, and reading the news. . . . I was on the treadmill of the to-do list: one damn thing after another."[24]

So far as she says in the essay, though, Petersen kept getting her work done, and she betrays no cynicism about her job. Granted, other things fell by the wayside, by her account. She gives the name "errand paralysis" to the sense that small tasks like corresponding with friends or scheduling a doctor's appointment were too daunting even to attempt. Still, errand paralysis is not unique to people suffering from work-related stress. It's ubiquitous. I am no longer burned out, and *I* keep putting off doctor's appointments. I find it hard to make time to email people I care about. Errand paralysis is a feature of everyday life.

I don't doubt that Petersen felt severe stress around her work. I'm sure I would, too, if I had covered a Senate campaign across Texas—as she had—and then moved house while taking on new projects. But Petersen's apparent effectiveness raises an important question: Is it burnout if you're still performing your job at a high level?

Petersen's article prompted responses that questioned parts of her argument even while affirming the prevalence and depth of burnout among young workers. One prominent focus for these responses had to do with the relationship between burnout and race.[25] Specifically, writers thought Petersen's argument grew out of a position of white privilege, and that the experience of burnout for people of color was more acute. In an essay titled "This Is What Black Burnout Feels Like," the poet and academic Tiana Clark wrote that burnout is nothing new to African Americans, who have endured a "litany of inherited trauma—or should I say inherited burnout? I'm thinking about slave ships, sharecropping, the school-to-prison pipeline, a steady state of mental collapse." Where Petersen called burnout the millennial "base temperature," Clark says that "No matter the movement or era, being burned out has been the steady state of black people in this country for hundreds of years."[26]

Clark's account of her own life, including her "dead black batteries," does sound like someone working hard to keep up with both her own ambitions and other people's (possibly racist) expectations of her. She writes of being wiped out at the end of a day of teaching. She writes of bearing a heavier load of committee work than her white colleagues. She enumerates the costs of her labor, borne largely by her body: "I grind my teeth at night. I lose sleep. I stop working out. I work while my head is pounding. I develop PCOS [polycystic ovary syndrome]. I cancel therapy. I can't keep up. I stop reaching out to friends."[27]

But like Petersen, Clark doesn't sound so exhausted that she can't do her job. She doesn't sound cynical about it. She certainly doesn't sound like she has lost a sense of accomplishment. She sounds justifiably proud of her considerable professional achievements: a rare tenure-track position in poetry, a couple of published collections, awards, speaking invitations. As with Petersen, I can't fully know Clark's subjective experience. I have to take her word for it. And what I gather is that she's exhausted, but she's getting it done.

In fact, even as she writes about being burned out, Clark takes pride in being in-demand. Her work "continually feels like both a sprint and a marathon. Why? Because, Jay-Z said it best: *I'm a hustler, baby!*"[28] Petersen's and Clark's accounts tell me that when you say you're burned out, you aren't only admitting to failure. You're also claiming to fulfill the American ideal of constant work.

.   .   .

All the inconsistency and subjectivity in defining burnout, along with burnout's potential to signal status and virtue in a work-obsessed culture, invites doubt about whether burnout is a real condition at all. Burnout has no clinical definition in most countries, which means it has as much medical status as being an artist or a Chicago Cubs fan. You're burned out if you say you're burned out. But should we give credence to unverifiable claims, including my own?

Because there is so little consensus for how to define burnout, some critics allege burnout research is just groping blindly in the dark. The clinical psychologist Linda V. Heinemann and sociologist Torsten Heinemann wonder if all the burnout researchers "are actually investigating the same phenomenon."[29] Even some researchers warn of the term's overuse and imprecision. Ayala Pines and Elliot Aronson observed in 1988 that over the previous several years, "the term 'burnout' has become extremely popular—perhaps too popular; it has been so loosely used that it has become almost meaningless." They caution that burnout "is not synonymous with job stress, fatigue, alienation, or depression. To use the term loosely is to diminish its usefulness."[30]

Culturally, the burnout syndrome has expanded to fit the baggy terms we clothed it in. The Heinemanns argue that burnout's imprecise definition allowed it to become "a cover-up diagnosis that allows people to call in sick without being stigmatised as mentally ill, and with the opportunity successfully to return to the workplace." This was especially true in Germany, where burnout was widely discussed in the popular press in the 2010s as a *Volkskrankheit,* a society-wide disease.[31] In the early part of that decade, German magazines and newspapers ran hundreds of articles on burnout, often focusing on admissions of burnout by celebrities and professional athletes.[32] As burnout attracted more public attention, the Heinemanns claim, journalists described it as a growing societal problem, something that could strike any ambitious worker. A tighter definition would have constricted the narrative. Burnout thus became "an umbrella term" for many varieties of work-related malaise.[33] One German scientific paper from 2011 refers to burnout as "a fashionable diagnosis" in dire need of a sharper definition.[34] Another notes that Germans' propensity to label a depressive episode "burnout" increased dramatically between 2001 and 2011.[35] The German psychiatrist Ulrich Hegerl even warns that focusing too much on burnout can be deadly. "Speaking of burnout is entirely unhelpful," he told the magazine *Der Spiegel* in 2011, "because it can mean everyday exhaustion as well as a severe, life-threatening depressive episode. Ultimately, the concept of burnout trivializes depression."[36]

A skeptic might reasonably say that because subjective claims to burnout are both widespread and clinically meaningless, it's fair to suppose that many of the people telling pollsters and journalists they're burned out would not score high on the Maslach Burnout Inventory for exhaustion, cynicism, and ineffectiveness. In a society that overvalues work, you can gain status by saying you have this condition that signals your tireless devotion to labor. It costs nothing to do so. If many who claim burnout don't "really" suffer from the syndrome, then there may be no epidemic of burnout after all.

Skepticism toward burnout is nearly as old as Maslach's pioneering work in the 1970s. In a 1981 essay titled "The Burnout of Almost Everyone," the *Time* magazine columnist Lance Morrow drafted burnout into the culture war, using it to criticize the shallow narcissism that carried over from the "Me Decade." Morrow writes that burnout had "become faddish and indiscriminate, an item of psychobabble, the psychic equivalent, in its ubiquitousness, of jogging." He saw widespread claims to burnout as evidence of a softened national psyche. "The era of 'grace under pressure' vanished in the early '60s," he writes. In the 1980s, "too many people become a little too easily thwarted."[37]

The psychiatrist Richard Friedman made a similar argument in the *New York Times* in 2019, following the World Health Organization's decision to label burnout an "occupational phenomenon," though not itself a medical condition. Friedman criticizes the overly broad diagnostic tests used in workplaces to identify people who are "at risk of burnout." He writes, "If almost everyone suffers from burnout, then no one does, and the concept loses all credibility." In Friedman's view, which is informed by his experience counseling a whole generation of medical students, many workers are misinterpreting ordinary, expected stress as a debilitating condition. This leads him to conclude that it would be a mistake to "medicalize everyday stress and discomfort as burnout."[38]

It's certainly true that more people say they're burned out than actually would be, if we had reliable, agreed-upon criteria for burnout. But Friedman's skeptical argument doesn't do what he thinks it does. In fact, he makes a good case for the exact opposite point. If the problem is overdiagnosis of burnout, and the reason for overdiagnosis is that there are no diagnostic criteria for burnout, then we can fix the problem by establishing criteria—in other words, by medicalizing it. A precise diagnostic checklist for burnout would surely rule many people out, but it would also rule people in who don't realize their work is grinding them down. And even if we found that a smaller number of people were clinically burned out, we could then mobilize the whole medical apparatus—including prescriptions, insurance, and disability coverage—to help the ones who remain. A more limited definition of burnout could also respond to Ulrich Hegerl's concern that our elevation of burnout trivializes depression. If clinicians can distinguish between the two disorders, then they can better identify people whose condition extends beyond job-specific malaise and into the all-pervading affliction of depression.

An expansive definition of burnout also allows commentators to diagnose whole populations with this syndrome and then attach virtually any social or political program to it as the cure. When this happens, burnout becomes just "what's wrong with society." Is burnout the poisoned fruit of racism, patriarchy, or capitalism? Is claiming burnout for a group—for mothers, for women generally, for African Americans, for millennials—the same as saying, simply, that this group is disadvantaged? Tiana Clark writes of the "inherited burnout" of black people in America, from enslavement to Jim Crow and beyond, but burnout seems like much too mild a term for systemic oppression and violence on that scale. Is burnout the appropriate word to use when talking about historic injustice? Or, on a smaller scale, do we use burnout as a placeholder concept for the effect of social marginalization on the individual? If so, then how do we make sense of the fact that doctors, or college professors for that matter, who by and large are not oppressed, appear to experience burnout at such high rates?

Trying to understand this slippery term has only led to further questions. The one thing we can be sure of, it seems, is that we are a whole society of burnouts, whatever that means.

. . .

My stance toward the term *burnout* is as ambivalent as our culture's. I am certain that burnout is a real thing. I experienced it. And what I experienced was much more than the ordinary tiredness I would feel at the end of a busy week, or the exhaustion of finishing a semester in a dead sprint of grading exams. Rest did not cure the deep sense of despair I felt over my students' apparent inability to learn from me. Even the two extended periods I took away from the job—a yearlong paid sabbatical and, later, a semester of unpaid leave—only paused my burnout. Both times, I came back to work and was exhausted, angry, and miserable within weeks. My burnout picked up right where it left off.

I am also fairly confident that what I experienced was not depression. The psychotherapist I saw for several months said no one in her profession would diagnose me as clinically depressed.

My doctor, for his part, gave me a diagnosis of adjustment disorder with depressed mood and prescribed a selective serotonin reuptake inhibitor. The medication seemed to shorten my bouts of anger, but I didn't feel a lot better in general. I went off it before I took unpaid leave. It was only after I left the college for good that I began to improve. Whatever my condition was, it was tied to my job.

While I know burnout is real, I share skeptics' concern that we too casually apply the term, that we are too ready to diagnose ourselves with this ailment. When I read about some new scourge like bridesmaid burnout or Burning Man burnout or—heaven help us— TV-show-binge-watching burnout, I think we have spread the definition too thin.[39] If everything is burnout, then nothing is. Paradoxically, when we try to demonstrate burnout's significance by showing that it's everywhere, we ultimately make it invisible, as it dissipates into the haze of our everyday frustrations.

The fact that *talking* about burnout is a phenomenon in its own right signals that burnout is not just a psychological matter but a cultural one, too. To understand that culture, we need to know its history, including how the emergence of burnout as a topic of concern reflects changes in our economy and our vision of a well-lived life. That is our next step.

2 *Burnout*

The First 2,000 Years

When I retrace the course of my academic career, I realize that as my professional misery grew, my body was sending me signals that something was wrong. In the week before classes began one January, I started to notice a sharp, intermittent pain in my torso. It felt like a quick stab between my ribs. I would lie awake at night both anticipating the next shock and hoping it wouldn't arrive. The pain was most often on my left side, which led me to worry about my heart. They say if you have chest pain (*was* this chest pain?), you should go to the hospital. So I did. The EKG and chest X-ray didn't show anything unusual. The doctor suggested the pain might have come from stress or perhaps "viral syndrome"—in other words, some hard-to-identify, mostly-untreatable source endemic to modern life. It was an unsatisfying diagnosis. I complained about it to a friend who studies Victorian British history; she joked that the doctor might as well have chalked up my condition to miasma, as a nineteenth-century physician would. She suggested that maybe I had walked past a graveyard.

Because medical knowledge changes quickly, the boundaries around health and sickness are often unstable. This is even more true for psychological conditions, which exist in the shadowy labyrinth known as the mind. A broken bone is a broken bone, but what we think about anxiety, for instance, has changed tremendously in the past century. The list of discredited mental illnesses, like lunacy or hysteria, is long and growing.

We want to trust in the objective, timeless knowledge of expert physicians, but their diagnoses are cultural facts as much as scientific ones. Ailments don't only exist in a body or a mind; they also exist in society and reflect what we expect from ourselves and from it. A failure to meet those expectations is a disorder. That is, something—whether it's a balky knee or acid reflux or an unwelcome thought—is out of order, not in the place we think it belongs. And because what counts as "order" changes over time, so does what counts as disordered. That means one culture's disease is a perfectly normal condition somewhere else. And medical problems become moral ones, or the responsibility for treating them passes, over time, from physicians to psychologists. Homosexuality, for instance, has been at different times a sin, a crime, a mental illness, and now, an orientation. Likewise, alcohol dependence changed from being a moral failing to a physical disease in a matter of decades.

Present-day discussions of burnout show that its definition is contested. In that respect, it is typical of exhaustion disorders throughout history. Burnout seems perfectly suited to our age, but we are hardly the first human beings to feel chronically drained and unable to fulfill our duties. "Exhaustion is intricately bound up not just with our private inner lives and our physical health," writes Anna Katharina Schaffner in her 2016 book *Exhaustion: A History,* "but also with wider social developments, in particular with more general cultural attitudes toward work and rest."[1] All humans have felt worn out, but each era seems to be worn out in its own way. I wanted to know how burnout became the characteristic way we're exhausted in hyperactive, work-obsessed twenty-first-century society. But the roots of our burnout culture run much deeper into the past.

. . .

"Vanity of vanities! All is vanity. What do people gain from all the toil at which they toil under the sun?"[2] This complaint about the ineffectiveness of work comes from the book of Ecclesiastes, composed around 300 BCE. The speaker in the book, known simply as Qoheleth ("teacher," in Hebrew), complains that the fleeting nature of life renders all our work meaningless. It's just "chasing after wind."[3] Qoheleth is a connoisseur of the good things in life—the pleasures of food, drink, sex, art, and learning—but he despairs over the fact that none of them is a safeguard against death. To make matters worse, even good work is often undone. "Wisdom is better than weapons of war," he says, "but one bungler destroys much good."[4] In light of this sad fact, Qoheleth enjoins his death-bound readers to live for the moment, including in their labor: "Whatever your hand finds to do, do with your might; for there is no work or thought or knowledge or wisdom in Sheol, to which you are going."[5]

Qoheleth sounds melancholic, afflicted with an excess of black bile, one of the four humors of Hippocratic medicine. He is tired and pessimistic, standing at a reflective distance from even his own life. Ever since its origins in fourth-century BCE Greek philosophy, melancholia has been associated with "exceptionality, artistic inclinations, and 'brain work,'" Schaffner writes.[6] Like burnout, melancholia could be a mark of honor, though not on account of the sufferer's hard work. Useful labor was less honorable than pure thought, according to Aristotle.[7] Melancholia was the hazard of those who nobly pursued the life of the mind.

Centuries later, Christian brain-workers battled a different exhaustion disorder as they faced not the fleeting nature of our days but their apparently interminable length. The earliest monks named it acedia ("without care," in Greek) and numbered it among the eight "bad thoughts" that haunted them in their caves in the deserts of northern Egypt. They also called it the "noonday demon," because it visited around midday, when the sun was high and supper still a few hours off. The demon "makes it seem that the sun barely moves, if at all, and that the day is fifty hours long," wrote the monk Evagrius Ponticus in the late fourth century CE. It makes the monk restless, looking around for someone to talk to. Next, the demon "instills in the heart of the monk a hatred for the place, a hatred for his very life itself, a hatred for manual labor." It gets him thinking about other, easier means of pleasing God or finding worldly success. Ultimately, it gets him thinking about his life as it was before he went to the desert—his family, his former occupation—and presents the path ahead, the monk's own life, as an interminable bore.[8]

The noonday demon's goal is to get its victim to give up monastic life. To counter the temptation, Evagrius's disciple John Cassian prescribed labor. He offers the example of a venerable monk, Abbot Paul, who lived in a remote place and spent his days gathering palm leaves—raw material for making baskets—and stored them in his cave. "And when his cave was filled with a whole year's work," Cassian writes, "he would burn up what he had so carefully toiled over . . . proving that without manual labor a monk can neither stay in one spot nor ever mount to the summit of perfection."[9]

This account suggests acedia is the inverse of both the burnout's ineffectiveness and Qoheleth's despair; the futility of Abbot Paul's work was its whole point. Anything to keep the demon at bay.

Medieval theologians transformed the eight bad thoughts into the seven deadly sins and turned acedia into sloth, a morally culpable state. It's too bad the term acedia disappeared from Western culture, since it so perfectly captures the anxious distractibility typical of workers today. In the desert of the open-plan office—or the improvised home office, a laptop on a kitchen table—our temptations are often online, just a click away from our work. We are not being especially productive, but we aren't being lazy, either. We're *at work,* after all. As a result, I don't think we could cure acedia today by imitating Abbot Paul's pointless labor. We're already pointlessly laboring enough. Like bacteria that evolve antibiotic resistance, the noonday demon has, over seventeen centuries, found a way past our traditional defense.

In the early modern period, melancholia transformed into the characteristic affliction of intellectuals in the new humanist age. Nevertheless, melancholy was a varied phenomenon, even a questionable one, as theorists and artists acknowledged at the time.[10] Shakespeare's embittered philosophizer Jaques in *As You Like It* observes that there are as many types of melancholy as there are professions. He claims to have "a melancholy of mine own, compounded of many simples, extracted from many objects, and indeed the sundry contemplation of my travels, in which my often rumination wraps me in a most humorous sadness."[11] Melancholy was also the condition of Hamlet, paralyzed by his ability to understand all the circumstances and options around him. Albrecht Dürer's 1514 engraving *Melancholia I* shows a winged female figure supporting her head with one hand, idly toying with a compass in

the other. She is surrounded by scientific, geometrical, and industrial equipment, all of it in disuse. Her dog hasn't been fed in days.
The figure is "weighed down by the boundless possibilities and
responsibilities that come with her newly gained status as a self-
reflexive subject," Schaffner writes in *Exhaustion*. "Indeed, the
birth of the modern subject in the fifteenth century might be seen
as entailing a sense that exhaustion is a necessary correlative of
self-consciousness as such."[12] By the industrious nineteenth century, melancholy was more firmly associated with idleness, and its
surest cure, for men at least, was work.[13]

Each of these disorders—ancient melancholia, acedia, and
modern melancholy—afflicted the elite, who found they could not
fulfill their religious duties or secular ambitions. They were diseases of the avant-garde, the archetypal men (and occasionally
women) of the age. These disorders were the underbelly of their
eras' notion of the good life, whether that life was one of pleasure
or holiness or knowledge. But unlike burnout, they were not a form
of ironic self-defeat, whereby zealously pursuing the good undercuts your ability to achieve it. Constant work ultimately makes it
impossible to work. But a monk who prayed all day long would, in
principle, never fall victim to acedia. And while burnout emerges
from social conditions at work, melancholy had natural causes. A
melancholic had a humor imbalance or was born under Saturn; the
fault was in their stars.

· · ·

The history of science is filled with simultaneous discoveries, when
two or more researchers, working independently, gain a similar
new insight. Some famous examples include the invention of

calculus, the discovery of oxygen, and the formulation of the theory of evolution. Less famous is the diagnosis of neurasthenia, a state of exhaustion brought on by excessive pressure on the nervous system, which two American physicians—George M. Beard in New York City and Edwin H. Van Deusen in Kalamazoo, Michigan—first described in articles published in 1869.[14] In subsequent decades, neurasthenia became not just a widespread medical phenomenon but a cultural obsession, a word equally ubiquitous in fashionable banter and popular advertising. The psychologist and philosopher William James even called the disease "Americanitis," owing to its prevalence in the United States.[15] It was, for a while, the national ailment.

Neurasthenia, like melancholy before it and burnout after, was a contested phenomenon. At stake in the contest was the character of a still-young country asserting its economic power. While James saw neurasthenia as scientifically valid (indeed, he experienced it), a writer for *The Century* magazine argued in 1896 that Americans were too vigorous to exhibit the degenerate exhaustion of the neurasthenic. A typical "American is energetic, pushing, restless, impatient; he may move more briskly, his apprehension may be quicker, he may have a keener wit, and he certainly is in more of a hurry, and perhaps lives under a greater strain and with less ease, than the European," he wrote.[16] In 1925, the psychiatrist William S. Sadler drew the opposite conclusion from Americans' busyness. Americans weren't immune to neurasthenia at all, he claimed. Rather, "the hurry, bustle, and incessant drive of the American temperament" brought it upon them. Sadler blamed Americanitis for the alarming death rate of Americans in their forties due to "heart disease, apoplexy, Bright's disease, high blood pressure." He estimated the disorder's toll at 240,000 lives a year.[17]

One reason for the popularity of neurasthenia as a diagnosis was that its symptoms were exceptionally broad, encompassing everything from indigestion and drug sensitivity to tooth decay and baldness.[18] The frontispiece to Beard's 1881 book, *American Nervousness*, the first major treatise on neurasthenia, features a chart of the "Evolution of Nervousness" from such mild complaints as nervous dyspepsia, nearsightedness, sleeplessness, and hay fever up to various forms of nervous exhaustion (neurasthenia proper) and beyond to the serious conditions of inebriety, epilepsy, and insanity.[19] All of these ailments were connected, like the roots and branches of a tree. Neurasthenia was the trunk.

Despite its link to seemingly common disorders, a neurasthenia diagnosis also carried an element of prestige. Schaffner writes that because Beard "believed that exhaustion was caused by the very processes that characterized the modern age ... being exhausted could be seen as a positive quality."[20] The neurasthenic was a quintessentially modern man or woman, in tune with the spirit of the times. And because civilization itself caused neurasthenia, its sufferers were innocent victims. They were no sinful layabouts.

Like those who suffered from acedia and melancholy, neurasthenics were the elite. Beard wrote that the disorder

> is developed, fostered, and perpetuated with the progress of civilization, with the advance of culture and refinement, and the corresponding preponderance of labor of the brain over that of the muscles. As would logically be expected, it is oftener met with in cities than in the country, is more marked and more frequent at the desk, the pulpit, and in the counting-room than in the shop or on the farm.[21]

The neurasthenic was more likely to have fine physical features, be highly intelligent, and exhibit vigorous emotions, according to Beard. Neurasthenic traits are found among "the civilized, refined, and educated, rather than of the barbarous and low-born and untrained."[22] Numerous authors of *fin-de-siècle* literature, including Marcel Proust, Oscar Wilde, Henry James, and Virginia Woolf, received the diagnosis and, in turn, placed neurasthenic characters in their novels.[23] Beard observed that intellectuals could work whenever they liked and could optimize their workdays: "literary and professional men especially, are so far masters of their time that they can select the hours and days for their most exacting and important work; and when from any cause indisposed to hard thinking, can rest and recreate, or limit themselves to mechanical details."[24] Beard's account conjures for me the image of a buzzy, twenty-first-century tech startup office, where employees work and play into the night, thanks to Lego blocks on conference tables and craft beer on tap. You never know when inspiration will strike, so you'd better not leave.

As that list of neurasthenic authors indicates, nervous exhaustion eventually crossed the Atlantic to Europe. It would also spread to the American middle and lower classes, becoming a near-universal affliction. Beard, however, thought blacks, Southern whites, and Catholics were less susceptible than their Northern white Protestant contemporaries.[25] In this way, neurasthenia was a national disease not just because it was so widespread and reflected the country's self-understanding as dynamic and industrious. It also reflected the unjust racial, religious, class, and gender hierarchies of the society and told a story about whose effort was driving the nation to prosperity, who deserved to reap its benefits, and who did not.

Beard's theory of neurasthenia drew inspiration from a burgeoning technology that was synonymous with the new, 24/7 era in American society: the electric light bulb. Writing just two years after Thomas Edison's invention first sparked to life, Beard compares the nervous system to an electrical circuit meant to illuminate a series of lamps that represent the often-oppressive achievements of modern culture: printing, the steam engine, the telegraph, democratic politics, new religious movements, poverty and philanthropy, and scientific education. The lamps burn bright, but they also drain the power source. Most individuals will strain their nerve force to remain connected to all of them. "[W]hen new functions are interposed in the circuit, as modern civilization is constantly requiring us to do," Beard writes,

> there comes a period, sooner or later, varying in different individuals, and at different times of life, when the amount of force is insufficient to keep all the lamps actively burning; those that are weakest go out entirely, or, as more frequently happens, burn faint and feebly—they do not expire, but give an insufficient and unstable light—this is the philosophy of modern nervousness.[26]

In other words, an overloaded nervous system will burn out.

Other accounts of neurasthenia read almost exactly like present-day laments over the always-on hyperconnectivity of our day. In 1884, the German psychiatrist Wilhelm Erb attributed the neurasthenia epidemic to "the excessive increase in traffic and the wire-networks of our telegraphs and telephones," to globalization, and to "the worrying repercussions of serious political, industrial, and financial crises," all of which a growing share of the population feels it must keep constantly in mind. These facts of modern life "overheat people's heads and force their spirits to undertake ever new exertions while robbing them of the time for rest, sleep, and stillness; life in big cities has become ever more refined and restless."[27] We make similar complaints today. Our technology, from washing machines to instant messaging, frees us from so many tedious tasks, but we strain to keep up with everything we "have to" do. No matter the century, greater ease seems, paradoxically, always to beget new difficulties.

Treatments for neurasthenia ranged as widely as its symptoms and causes. Hydrotherapy, gold cures, and (for men) vigorous exercise all earned doctors' approval.[28] Women were more likely to receive the "rest cure," a method of total confinement developed by physician S. Weir Mitchell and criticized in Charlotte Perkins Gilman's proto-feminist 1892 short story, "The Yellow Wallpaper."[29] Such remedies were big business. Numerous pop-up drug companies hawked patent medicines—proprietary tonics and elixirs—through the new medium of the direct mail catalog. Electrotherapy was popular, too; neurasthenics could purchase electrified belts that were meant to recharge their nervous systems.[30] A 1902 Sears, Roebuck catalog ad featured a drawing of a shirtless, handlebar-mustached strongman wearing one such belt. The ad touted its ability to cure not only nervousness but also male sexual dysfunction. Hanging from the belt was a genital attachment, which "encircles the organ, carries the vitalizing, soothing current direct to these delicate nerves and fibers, strengthens and enlarges this part in a most wonderful manner."[31] Other commentators suggested larger-scale solutions; only a return to traditional values, including traditional gender roles, could heal the neurasthenic society. Richard von Krafft-Ebing, a German psychiatrist, saw neurasthenia as a sign of civilizational decline. The exhausted antihero of

Joris-Karl Huysmans's 1884 novel *Against Nature* yearns for a lost Catholic faith.[32] Nervousness, then, was the site of a cultural war.

After a few decades as the quintessential modern illness, neurasthenia itself burned out. People stretched the diagnosis too far, attempting to cover too many complaints. One physician grumbled in 1905 that neurasthenia had been so "elaborated and broadened and abused that to-day it means almost anything and with equal truth almost nothing."[33] Doctors never settled on a bodily cause. Beard's "nerve force" didn't hold up to biological scrutiny, especially after the discovery of hormones and vitamins.[34] The American Medical Association and the US government cracked down on patent medicine advertisements. And in the early decades of the twentieth century, psychoanalytic explanations for mental disorders ascended to prominence.[35] People did not cease being exhausted in the 1920s. But significant legal, medical, and social changes caused the signature disease of the era to disappear.

. . .

The first public hint of burnout's emergence in English-speaking culture was Graham Greene's 1960 novel, *A Burnt-Out Case*. The novel represents a crucial step in the history of exhaustion disorders, because, much more than neurasthenia, the condition it describes has to do with the protagonist's career. It is about an occupational disorder.

In the novel, a famous European architect named Querry, having suddenly left his practice, shows up one evening at a remote leprosy hospital run by an order of Catholic priests and sisters in far-inland Congo. Querry announces to the leprosery's lone doctor, "I am one of the mutilated," and like a desert hermit tormented by acedia, he seeks a cure in the form of simple work tending to the patients. The doctor is not convinced by Querry's self-diagnosis. "Perhaps your mutilations haven't gone far enough yet," he says. "When a man comes here too late the disease has to burn itself out."[36] That is, the disease needs to run its course, taking everything it can from the victim: limbs, fingers, toes, nose. But once it does, the patient is no longer contagious and can go back about his or her life—damaged, to be sure, but a threat to no one.

The priests and the doctor see Querry as a man of vocation like them. But he won't have it. He writes in his journal, "I've come to the end of desire and to the end of a vocation. Don't try to bind me in a loveless marriage and to make me imitate what I used to perform with passion."[37] He compares his talent to obsolete currency. Later, he tells an English journalist who has tracked him down in the jungle, "Men with vocations are different from the others. They have more to lose."[38] Eventually, Querry does lose everything that can be taken, particularly his lust and ambition, and he finds himself designing new buildings for the leprosery, reminting his talents for a new purpose.

Querry is a different kind of worker than the iconic figures of midcentury capitalism: the nine-to-five corporate bureaucrat or assembly line laborer, both of whom are, in cultural memory at least, replaceable cogs in the machinery of postwar prosperity. Querry, by contrast, is committed and creative. He's independent, unlike the company man in the denim shirt or gray flannel suit. He identifies with his work and is identified by it; everyone in the novel is shocked that someone so renowned for his career would give it up. He embodies both a new ideal of work as an all-consuming vocation and a rejection of that ideal.

In Greene's self-consciously Catholic outlook, the loss Querry undergoes is ultimately a gain. Callings can be dangerous, both to the self and to others. It's the curse of the talented, those who don't merely shuffle through bland afternoons in drab institutions. The burnout of Querry's vocation liberates him. One priest suggests that Querry has "been given the grace of aridity," a reference to the sixteenth-century mystic St. John of the Cross's dark night of the soul, which purges the person's senses in preparation for a higher level of divine contemplation.[39] Burning out—all the way out—clears the path to Querry's greater calling.

· · ·

In the song "Shelter from the Storm," recorded in 1974, Bob Dylan reels off a long litany of troubles. Among them: being "burned out from exhaustion." The line, which appeared on the chart-topping album *Blood on the Tracks,* distilled a significant cultural moment. The mid-1970s was when burnout as we know it first gained scientific legitimacy and broad public attention. And like Dylan's career a decade earlier, burnout's origin story is tangled up in the counterculture of Lower Manhattan.

In the early 1970s, Herbert Freudenberger, a psychologist in New York City, would regularly put ten hours a day into his private practice and then head downtown for a second shift at the St. Mark's Free Clinic, which served the medical needs of young people living in the East Village—helping them with everything from drug addiction to pregnancy to dental cavities—in examination rooms decorated with rock 'n roll posters.[40] Freudenberger had helped found the clinic in 1970 after spending the summer of 1968 at the Haight-Ashbury Free Clinic in San Francisco, ministering to hippies. Freudenberger iden-

tified strongly with his patients at the St. Mark's clinic. "Their problems, their battles, became mine," he later wrote. After the clinic
closed for the night, he and the volunteer staff would hold meetings
until the wee hours. Freudenberger would then head back uptown,
get a few hours of sleep, and do it all again the next day.[41]

Of course, he couldn't do it forever. After about a year on this
schedule, Freudenberger broke down. His daughter Lisa recalls
him being unable to get out of bed on a morning the family was
supposed to leave for vacation.[42] The term "burn-out" was already
in circulation in his professional world. An official at a rehabilitation center for young adult offenders in Southern California mentioned it as a "phenomenon" among treatment staff in a 1969
paper.[43] St. Mark's Free Clinic workers used the term to describe
themselves, but they may have picked it up from the East Village
streets where their patients spent their days and nights. One sense
of the term referred to heroin users' veins. Inject into a spot long
enough, and it becomes useless, burned out.[44] In a 1980 book,
Freudenberger compared "Burn-Outs" like himself to burned-out
buildings: "What had once been a throbbing, vital structure is now
deserted. Where there had once been activity, there are now only
crumbling reminders of energy and life."[45]

To understand what had happened to him, Freudenberger
turned his psychoanalytic training on himself; he spoke into a tape
recorder, then played the tape back, as if he were his own patient.[46]
And in 1974, he published a paper titled "Staff Burn-Out" in an academic journal. In the paper, Freudenberger asks, "Who is Prone to
Burn-Out?" His answer is unambiguous: "The dedicated and the
committed."[47] Free Clinic staff offered "our talents, our skills, we
put in long hours with a bare minimum of financial compensation,"
Freudenberger writes. "But it is precisely because we are dedicated

that we walk into a burn-out trap. We work too long and too intensely. We feel a pressure from within to work and help and we feel a pressure from the outside to give. When the staff member then feels an additional pressure from the administrator to give even more, he is under a three-pronged attack."[48]

Freudenberger's first-person account resonates strongly with my experience. I know that three-pronged attack: students' and colleagues' demands, my own expectations of myself, that email from the dean requesting a meeting about the curriculum. Maybe that's where those inexplicable sharp pains came from that one week before classes started. Freudenberger's analysis of burnout is an unscientific, ad-hoc explanation, not rigorously worked out. He doesn't have a survey or a scale for measuring burnout, only limited observations that, for instance, people typically burned out after about a year of working at the clinic. His language merges psychoanalytic jargon with counterculture lingo. He drops seventies slang like "speed freaks" and "self con" and uses "bad rap" as a verb.[49] In a similar paper published the following year, he emphasizes that it's important to identify "what kind of trip one may be on—a self-fulfilling ego trip, a self-aggrandizement ego trip," or some other trip entirely.[50] Freudenberger's list of burnout symptoms is as wide and loose as George Beard's list for neurasthenia: "exhaustion, being unable to shake a lingering cold, suffering from frequent headaches and gastrointestinal disturbances, sleeplessness and shortness of breath," as well as "quickness to anger," paranoia, overconfidence, cynicism, and isolation. The burned-out clinic worker may "get into pot and hash quite heavily."[51] Despite its lack of rigor, though, the 1974 paper appeals to me because of Freudenberger's obvious passion for his work and compassion for those he works with. His argument is little more than a conjecture, a guess evidently born of late-night bitch sessions. But it's a guess that, decades later, still feels basically right.

. . .

Around the time Freudenberger was pulling double shifts in New York, Christina Maslach was on the other side of the country, trying to convince psychologist Philip Zimbardo to put a stop to his now-infamous Stanford Prison Experiment. In the summer of 1971, Maslach had just completed her PhD at Stanford and was dating Zimbardo, though she had no part in designing the study. In the experiment, students were asked to play roles as inmates and guards in a mocked-up prison for a planned two weeks. It was meant to be a study in depersonalization: how people come to see others as less than human. The students soon fell deep into their new identities, with "guards" punishing "prisoners" deemed unruly by physically humiliating them, seizing their mattresses, and placing them in solitary confinement.

The prison experiment demonstrated the process of depersonalization so well, it had to be cut short. When Maslach visited the prison site on its fifth day, she was horrified by the brutality ordinary-seeming college students could inflict on each other. She got sick to her stomach as she watched "guards" lead a procession of "prisoners," who were shackled together and made to wear bags over their heads, down a hallway.[52] When she spoke with Zimbardo that evening, she later recounted, "I started to scream, I started to yell, 'I think it is terrible what you are doing to those boys!' I cried." Zimbardo ended the experiment the next morning. Out of fifty people who visited the prison site, Zimbardo said, Maslach alone was the voice of ethics and compassion.[53]

Maslach soon began studying depersonalization in the less dire conditions of human-service work. (She and Zimbardo married in 1972.) She wanted to understand "how people who are responsible for the care and treatment of others can come to view those they care for in object-like ways."[54] She found that "detached concern" is a crucial mode for caregivers, though different professions approach it in different ways. While the norms of health-care work demand an attitude that combines sympathetic concern with clinical objectivity, human-service workers typically engage emotionally with their clients, only to find that, over time, the work drains them. Their detachment is a protective strategy. "If the detachment becomes too extreme," Maslach writes in a 1973 report, "the service professional experiences 'burn-out,' a phrase which is used by poverty lawyers to describe the loss of any human feeling for their clients."[55] Maslach's report preceded Freudenberger's paper by only a few months. Like neurasthenia a century before, burnout was a simultaneous discovery whose influence soon grew well beyond research papers and became a cultural buzzword.

Several key elements of Maslach's influential model of burnout as exhaustion, cynicism, and ineffectiveness are present in the 1973 report, but she hadn't pulled them together yet into a coherent theory. The dimension of ineffectiveness, for instance, is already there. Maslach notes that psychiatric nurses and social-service workers often encounter clients whose conditions do not improve, leading practitioners "to feel somewhat ineffective, impotent, and even unnecessary."[56] The concept of emotional exhaustion is still inchoate. And Maslach mostly equates "burn-out" with depersonalization. *Burnout* is not yet the term for the entire syndrome. Considering that this report is arguably the first-ever psychological study of occupational burnout, it is surprising to see Maslach claim that in one profession, poverty law, "'burn-out' is beginning to occur at faster rates."[57] This means that for the entire five decades we have been talking about burnout, we have perceived it as getting worse.

Freudenberger and Maslach are not only, as co-discoverers, the Newton and Leibniz of burnout, but also its Lennon and McCartney, playing complementary roles in popularizing the concept. Freudenberger is chiefly a clinician, not a scholar, and his work relies on case studies of his patients rather than experimental observation. It comes across as free-wheeling and anecdotal—which is a big part of its charm. Freudenberger's accessible diagnosis of a vague modern problem even earned him spots on the TV talk shows "Donahue" and "Oprah."[58] Maslach, ensconced in the psychology department at University of California, Berkeley, is a consummate researcher, though an unusually compassionate one. In the early 1980s she developed her burnout inventory, applying the scientific method to innumerable participants in hundreds of studies, all carried out with a large cast of coauthors. She has remained a vital figure in burnout research ever since.

Maslach and Freudenberger also have complementary views of how and why people burn out. We need both of their perspectives to give a complete account of burnout's causes and effects. Freudenberger focuses on the dedicated individual worker who throws everything into the work, hits an obstacle, and then works even harder, right up to the point of breakdown. He emphasizes the role of *ideals* in causing burnout. Maslach emphasizes working *conditions*. She agrees with Freudenberger that devoted workers are at risk of burning out, but by the 1990s she had developed a comprehensive theory of burnout as a failure of institutions.[59] When your employer doesn't reward you enough, or when unfairness is rampant, or when you have no community among your coworkers, your ability and willingness to keep doing the job disintegrate.

. . .

It can't just be coincidence that Freudenberger and Maslach independently "discovered" burnout in 1973–74. Something was happening in American society that they both detected, despite being on opposite coasts and using different methods to read the signs of the times. Bob Dylan picked up on it, too. So did Neil Young in early 1974, singing of "burn-outs" aimlessly dragging their feet in his song, "Ambulance Blues." What was going on that made burnout just the right word to make sense of this cultural moment?

The broken idealism of the 1960s may have played a role. The counterculture of the era—including, surely, people Freudenberger worked with at the St. Mark's Free Clinic—imagined ways of living that did not place nine-to-five work at the center. But by the 1970s, it had made little dent in the establishment. Thousands of optimistic and well-educated people went into human-service careers, motivated to win the "War on Poverty," only to discover how intractable society's problems were, and how much time they would spend ensnared in bureaucracy.[60] At the same time, universal basic income became a much-discussed, and apparently attainable goal. In 1964, a socialist publication proposed that societal wealth be shared without regard for work.[61] A few years later, feminist and welfare-rights activists appeared in prominent political and media venues, calling for a "guaranteed adequate income" as a way to combat both patriarchy and the work ethic.[62] Thinkers as divergent as Milton Friedman and Martin Luther King, Jr. also advocated a basic income, and cities and states ran experiments to test the policy. Even President Richard Nixon supported a proposal that would have provided a minimum income to all American families. His Family Assistance Plan passed the House of Representatives with a large majority. But this measure that would have freed some workers from the most miserable, underpaid jobs never fully materialized. The bill failed in the Senate and thus never came to Nixon's desk for approval.[63]

As important as those disappointed ideals may be to the emergence of burnout in the early 1970s, there was a still bigger factor involved. Burnout first came to public attention at a critical transition point in the history of work in America. With decades of hindsight, historians now see 1974 as "a watershed between eras," as Jefferson Cowie puts it in *Stayin' Alive,* his book on the 1970s working class.[64] Prior to 1974, the New Deal consensus on labor still reigned; if productivity increased, so would workers' wages. Accordingly, the real wages of rank-and-file workers steadily rose, reaching their peak in 1973.[65] It was the heyday of the working class—the white working class, anyway, which enjoyed the full benefits of government programs and union representation. Prosperity seemed to be broadly within reach. The working class even dominated the television dial, led by Archie Bunker on "All in the Family." This did not mean an absence of conflict, though. A younger generation of union members wanted to fight against the fast pace and deadening repetition of work on the lines. Their elders argued that they already had favorable contracts, so why did they want to agitate against boredom?[66] Still, an internal debate over the quality of work signals a labor movement with real power.

It wouldn't last. After 1974, the midcentury golden age crumbled. The ignominious ends of the Nixon presidency and the Vietnam War shook Americans' faith in their political institutions.

American manufacturing and organized labor drowned in a toxic brew of global competition, the "oil shock" resulting from an OPEC embargo, and rapid inflation. For the first time since World War II, workers' productivity gains detached from their wages. Since 1974, labor productivity has kept increasing, but workers' compensation has not. Real wages for nonsupervisory employees actually declined in the 1970s and 80s, and, aside from a temporary uptick caused by the Covid-19 pandemic's effect on the workforce, they still have still not recovered.[67] "The continuous readjustment of expectations—*downward:* that was a key experience of the 1970s," writes the historian Rick Perlstein.[68]

The problems facing the United States in the 1970s weren't just political or economic. They were emotional. Historians and contemporary observers called the events of the middle of the decade a national "nervous breakdown," "a collective sadness."[69] The decade ended with President Jimmy Carter diagnosing the whole country with a chronic spiritual sickness in a televised address that has come to be known as the "malaise speech." In it, Carter spoke of having just spent ten days talking to Americans about their concerns. He recited a long list of their complaints about his leadership and the state of the country, from his aloofness to the oil shortage. Then he addressed what he saw as "a fundamental threat to American democracy." That threat: "a crisis of confidence. . . . We can see this crisis in the growing doubt about the meaning of our own lives and in the loss of a unity of purpose for our nation." Carter saw the crisis also in reduced voter participation, reduced labor productivity, and reduced faith in the future. In other words, America had become a burnt-out case: exhausted, cynical, and consumed by a feeling of uselessness.[70]

At the dawn of the 1980s, burnout became a key term to describe the condition of frazzled, defeated American workers. Maslach soon developed her theory of burnout's institutional causes, and Freudenberger's 1980 book *Burn-Out: The High Cost of High Achievement* became a popular self-help guide. In 1981, the president of the air-traffic controllers' union cited "early burnout" as the first reason union members were going on strike for higher wages and a shorter workweek.[71] I see the strike as a moment of optimism in the fight against burnout; it must have seemed possible to cure the condition through collective action. When President Ronald Reagan fired eleven thousand controllers for refusing his return-to-work order, that hope was ruined. Reagan's decision sent a message that workers still hear today: they will deal with burnout on their own, or not at all. A year later, the term had apparently become so commonplace that William Safire declared in his *New York Times* "On Language" column that it was itself "undergoing linguistic burnout."[72]

· · ·

Even as research on burnout grew in the 1990s and 2000s, extending beyond human services to encompass white- and blue-collar workers alike, the term went into a two-decade dormant period in the United States. Meanwhile, like neurasthenia had a century before, it traveled overseas. Maslach and two coauthors observed in a 2009 paper that "roughly speaking, the order in which the interest in burnout seems to have spread corresponds with the economic development of the countries involved."[73] That is, burnout began as a concern of wealthy North American and European countries, then propagated to Latin America, Africa, and Asia. (I admit, I hear in this claim a faint echo of George Beard's contention that northern white Protestants were more susceptible to neurasthenia than other regional, racial, and religious groups.) In 2019, burnout was classified as a "syndrome," though not an illness, in the World Health Organization's main compendium of diagnoses, the International Classification of Diseases.[74] That was also when neurasthenia finally disappeared from the ICD. In a few European countries, including Sweden, burnout is an official diagnosis that can entitle its sufferers to paid time off and other sickness benefits.[75] In Finland, burned-out workers can qualify for paid rehabilitation workshops that feature ten days of intensive individual and group activities, including counseling, exercise, and nutrition classes.[76]

Even though awareness of burnout has grown beyond its original American context over the past five decades, public understanding of the condition has progressed little. Even the scientific understanding is, in some ways, frustratingly stagnant. There is still little consensus on how to measure burnout and no widely-acknowledged means to diagnose it. Burnout has no status as a disorder in the American Psychiatric Association's Diagnostic and Statistical Manual. We still hear echoes of Freudenberger's vague, catch-all list of symptoms decades later. In 1980, Freudenberger attributed burnout to the fast pace of social and economic change, from the sexual revolution to consumerism. "At the same time," he writes, "TV has exposed us to alluring pictures of people leading the 'good life.'"[77] Substitute Instagram for television in that sentence, and it could have been published yesterday on some life-optimizing wellness website.

A front-page *New York Times* story on burnout from 1999, the height of a tech boom, also sounds familiar. Its author, Leslie

Kaufman, focused on a Hewlett-Packard regional sales office where more than half the workers reported "experiencing excessive pressure" at work. To alleviate this pressure and retain employees, managers at HP and other companies were trying some new remedies: "everything from limiting work to 40 hours a week to discouraging employees from checking their E-mail and phone messages over the weekend." We still face exactly the same problems, and we still propose some of the same solutions. The article notes that flextime and telecommuting had been tried and did not work. "The movement to do something about the problem is inchoate," Kaufman notes. "[M]any companies are talking about it but do not know how to move from their old ways."[78] More than two decades later, companies are still talking about burnout, and they still don't know how to change.

All this history leads me to a depressingly clear conclusion: we have been having the same conversation about burnout for fifty years. Add in the history of neurasthenia, and it has been a century and a half. If you count melancholia and acedia, then it's been more than two millennia. As we talk about exhaustion from our work and culture today, we don't just sound like Freudenberger, Maslach, and their critics in the 1970s and 80s, with their focus on well-educated, elite workers, their sense of cultural acceleration, and their tendency to draw all afflictions under a single, vague umbrella. We also sound like George Beard and S. Weir Mitchell theorizing neurasthenia in the 1880s. Early burnout researchers echoed their belief that to be exhausted was to be a modern person, an avatar of the age. Now, according to the public discussion, burnout is the mark of an entire generation, a generation that has been synonymous with technology, transformation, and the cultural cutting edge.

I have mixed feelings about the fact that we have been talking in circles around burnout for so long. On the one hand, I want to set the conversation on a new course. I don't want to repeat the mistakes of the past—the elixirs, the calls to rugged individualism, the lamentations about technology, the empty vows to change how we do business. I don't want to become the George Beard of our moment, quacking on about easily-debunkable pseudoscience. I want burnout research to become much more systematic, with an aim to establish diagnostic criteria for this condition that caused me so much misery and cost me my career. I want the marketing nonsense to give way to more reasonable, yet compassionate, voices. I don't think we will be able to help burned-out workers until our conversation becomes more sober, more exacting, and less alarmist.

On the other hand, I fear that the burnout conversation hasn't changed because it can't change. Burnout is as embedded in our culture as acedia was in desert monasticism, and as neurasthenia was in the electric age—perhaps so embedded that we can't alter the conditions that cause burnout from within our culture. It would be like using your right hand to perform surgery on itself. I despair when I read headlines like "How to Grow Your Startup Without Risking Burnout."[79] You can't. To participate in the work culture of our era *just is* to risk burnout. You may as well try to swim without getting wet. When we cease to burn out, we will cease to be who we are. We will lose the cultural assumptions that orient our lives: assumptions about what is worth pursuing, whom to model our lives after, and how to spend our time. That may be why, despite decades of stress and complaint, we have failed to end burnout culture. On some level, we don't want to end it.

Together, this hope and fear can foster a sense of resolve. I do believe we can refashion our identities, with work no longer at the center. We *can* end burnout culture. But first, we need a much more precise vocabulary for this affliction that sits at the core of our social, moral, and spiritual lives.

3   The Burnout Spectrum

No one starts burned out. When I began my job as a theology professor, I had boundless energy and optimism. I was beginning my dream job, after all. I finally had the opportunity to get students as excited as I was about the search for truth and the cultivation of the mind. My first semester, I had class every morning at eight o'clock. Even though I came in to work earlier than my colleagues, I stayed later than nearly all of them. Nevertheless, I managed to keep some limits on my work. I tried to leave it at the office on weekends; most of the time, I succeeded.

My first professional crisis hit me midway through the semester, when I graded the first paper in one of my classes. I had assigned the students to write an essay analyzing the theme of friendship in Augustine's *Confessions,* a dense but beautiful memoir marked by long theological passages. (Looking back, I realize this assignment was *perhaps* a bit heavy for college sophomores.) One student's paper stood out as unusual, its language strikingly different from the typical undergrad's error-prone but workmanlike prose. Whole paragraphs in this paper sounded like they were written by a pipe-smoking Oxford don in the 1950s. The student correctly used the word "implacable" in a sentence.

But then the paper shifted abruptly to the kind of inane rhetorical questions someone would ask if they wanted to seem smarter than they actually were. Strangest of all, the student used "friendship" as a verb numerous times, as in, "we should friendship God because he friendships us." Huh? After puzzling over the paper and showing it to some colleagues, who were equally baffled by it, I surmised that the student had patched together pieces of other people's writing on the topic of Augustine and love, and then performed a find-and-replace in their own document to change "love" to "friendship." And of course, the student did not then proofread the paper. Once I figured out what had happened, I was furious. Then I grew despondent as I discovered that several other students had plagiarized their papers, too.

A few weeks later, my students averaged a D on their midterm exam. Weren't they learning anything? Weren't they even trying? I wrote to a friend about having "the angst of thinking that education is an impossible lie." The following year, nearly half the students in one class plagiarized their papers. Each one of these classroom challenges felt like an affront to my ideals.

It's true that teaching wasn't all bad. I saw students learn every semester; they laughed politely at my small repertoire of theology jokes. But their plagiarism and apathy weighed on me enough that at two o'clock one morning, while I was in the midst of applying for tenure, six years into my job, I also wrote myself an "anti-tenure letter," making the case for my incompetence. I wrote that I had come to hate the fact that my job was "to get people to do things they do not remotely want to do: read, discuss new and challenging ideas, and write." I wrote that I could imagine ways to break through "the impasse" in the classroom, but I didn't have the courage to attempt them. "I simply lack the energy or initiative or desire to do the things it would take to teach something to the many who are not inclined to learn."

I now recognize in that one sentence all three of the classic symptoms of burnout: exhaustion, cynicism, and a feeling of ineffectiveness. But this was years before I quit. Despite that late-night moment of despair, I wasn't struggling to get out of bed. I wasn't trying to eat and drink my bad feelings away. I received tenure. I kept going. I kept reminding myself: *This is my dream job*.

I think it's fair to say I was undergoing burnout during the period I wrote the anti-tenure letter. But that experience wasn't final; I wasn't "burned out" like a dead lightbulb or firewood reduced to ash. Something changed over the next few years that made quitting seem like the only way to survive. If we can understand how workers experience that change from mild frustration to miserable futility, we will have the solid definition of burnout our public conversation so badly needs.

. . .

The variety of people's experience with burnout is oceanically broad, and its depth varies from shallow continental shoals to unfathomable trenches. In some cases, it can look like clinical depression; in others, it resembles compassion fatigue, a condition that usually appears (and dissipates) more suddenly than burnout.[1] Our definition of burnout needs to take these differences into account. Huge percentages of workers across the globe either exhibit the symptoms of burnout or call themselves burned out, but by all appearances, most manage to keep going. Meanwhile, a smaller percentage can barely function at work. They undergo chronic exhaustion; diminished performance and commitment to work; and reduced cognitive abilities like executive function, attention, and memory.[2] They might fall into substance abuse and addiction. Some, including an alarming number of doctors in the United States, even contemplate suicide.[3] Not everyone who calls themselves burned out reaches such depths, but the millions of people who use the term are saying *something* when they use it. *Something* is wrong with their relationship to work.

To balance the need for breadth (everyone feels a bit burned out) and depth (some are so burned out, they can no longer do their jobs), we ought to think of burnout not as a *state* but as a *spectrum*. In most public discussion of burnout, we talk about workers who "are burned out," as if that status were black and white. A black-and-white view cannot account for the variety of burnout experience, though. If there is a clear line between burned out and not, as there is with a lightbulb, then we have no good way to categorize people who say they are burned out but still manage to do their work competently. Thinking about burnout as a spectrum solves this problem; those who claim burnout but are not debilitated by it are simply dealing with a partial or less-severe form of it. They are experiencing burnout without *being* burned out. Burnout hasn't had the last word.

Psychologists already treat other conditions—such as autism—as spectrums, classifying together several related disorders of varying intensity. Some, including the aptly-named Swiss researcher Jules Angst, view depression as a spectrum, too. In a 1997 paper, Angst and his coauthor Kathleen Merikangas report that, over a fifteen-year period, young adults shifted along a spectrum of depressive states. That is, they would exhibit more or fewer of the depression criteria over time, and would often pass back and forth across the threshold for major depressive disorder.[4] They found that people who experienced one of the "subthreshold" depressive states were at much higher risk of developing major depression later.[5] This research implies a hopeful result; recognizing these lower-level states might make it possible for people who have a few depressive symptoms to get treatment before they develop more.

The notion of a depression or burnout spectrum also better reflects people's experience of these disorders than a single-threshold, all-or-nothing model does. All thresholds are arbitrary, including the lines separating the different categories of "subthreshold depression." We don't know where the line is, on the Maslach Burnout Inventory or some other measure, between "burned out" and "not burned out," because there isn't one. Different experiences of burnout severity blend into each other, just as the colors we call "red" gradually become more orange in a rainbow. We can draw a line, and we may need to in clinical settings where it is important to make clear diagnoses. But a finer-grained classification may allow for more nuanced treatments. Angst and Merikangas suggest that everyone experiences mild and fleeting depressive states in their lives.[6] If we likewise recognize the existence of a low-grade experience of burnout, then we might expect most people to land on the burnout spectrum at some point, even if not everyone "advances" to higher levels of exhaustion, cynicism, and inefficacy. All work opens us up to the possibility of burnout, though any individual may only experience it partially, as just a single dimension that can, over time, become a fuller expression of the disorder.

One worker whose experience illustrates the shifting character of burnout is Liz Curfman, a licensed social worker who works for a Dallas nonprofit that serves the children of refugees. Curfman told me that people in her field "wear burnout like a badge." For her, though, burnout takes a particular shape. Throughout her career, she said, job stress made her susceptible to cynicism. At one of her previous employers, her team was applying for renewal of a crucial grant that paid their salaries. With her job on the line, she recalls feeling great anxiety that led her to gossip about coworkers—a type of depersonalization. "I was so cynical, and I was ready to point out the parts where other people had failed," she said. After the grant was renewed, Curfman's cynicism evolved into feelings of ineffectiveness. She wondered if her work, coordinating AmeriCorps members, was making a difference. "Let's just get this over with," she would say when trying out a new solution to a problem at her job. "It's not going to matter anyway."

Later, in another organization, Curfman's cynicism returned. "I was not the very kind, gracious person you're talking to now," she joked. "I was prickly—very pugnacious, ready at every turn to pick a fight." The organization put her on two weeks' paid leave to rest and gain perspective on her work. At first, Curfman was offended: "I was like, 'How dare you?'" But the time off helped her realize how much she was struggling and how poorly she and her superiors were communicating their expectations of each other. She came back to work with greater knowledge of what she needed in order to perform well.

Curfman didn't talk in terms of exhaustion during our hourlong conversation, but other workers certainly do. In fact, we often equate exhaustion with burnout. If we think of burnout as a spectrum of conditions, not an all-or-nothing disorder, then it makes sense that workers could have exhaustion without depersonalization or ineffectiveness. Any of us who undergoes a partial experience of burnout is on the spectrum, just not all the way at the far end. As depleted or cynical or useless as we feel due to our work, things can still get a lot worse.

· · ·

My experience of burnout ebbed and flowed for several years before becoming a permanent condition. Like Liz Curfman, I developed cynicism and feelings of ineffectiveness without severe exhaustion. Exhaustion came later. I usually taught four general-education classes per semester—classes the college required the students to take, regardless of their major. Students voiced their resentment in course evaluations. "Strict grader and very picky for such a meaningless class," read a typical comment. To find professional satisfaction, I invested time in other parts of the job: committees, conferences, publications. But it took a toll. As I wrote in a note to myself around the time I also wrote my anti-tenure letter, "All of this wears me out. It's not an intellectual challenge. (It's a challenge, just not an intellectual one.) And it isn't really rewarding, since most students don't seem to profit from it, and those few who do, don't give me any thanks."

That parenthetical aside about teaching not being an intellectual challenge jumps out at me now. It tells me I went into the job expecting one thing but got something else. I wanted to live the sort of life I imagined my own professors lived. By going into academia, I thought I was becoming a citizen in the republic of letters. But in reality, it was still just a job, with a bureaucracy and a schedule and boring things that need to get done by five o'clock. And the students didn't think of their learning as a lofty, intellectual pursuit. To them, education was a means to becoming an accountant or an athletic trainer or a teacher. They weren't in it for the sheer pleasure of theological thought, as I had been. I don't blame them. Still, I couldn't help expecting them to be like me.

That gap between our ideals for work and the reality of our job is burnout's origin point. We burn out when what we actually do at work falls short of what we hoped to do. Those ideals and expectations are not only personal, but cultural. In the cultures of wealthy nations, we want more than just a salary from our jobs. We want dignity. We want to grow as persons. We might even want some transcendent purpose. And we don't get these things, in part because work has become emotionally more demanding and materially less rewarding over the past several decades. (I will say much more about these diminished working conditions and disappointed ideals in chapters 4 and 5.) I imagined the life of a college professor as one of nonstop intellectual conversation with brilliant colleagues and eager students. The reality was that teaching was difficult, recognition was uncommon, and I spent a lot of time in tedious meetings or alone in my office, paranoid about students' plagiarism.

The idea that burnout results from a gap between ideals and reality is common in the research literature.[7] Christina Maslach and her coauthor Michael Leiter call burnout "the index of the dislocation between what people are and what they have to do."[8] I take them to mean that burnout signals how much your job requirements differ from your self-understanding. In one of Maslach's earliest articles on burnout, published in 1976, she connected the problem to parts of people's job they were not prepared to undertake. A poverty lawyer told her, "I was trained in law, but not in how to work with the people who would be my clients. And it was that difficulty in dealing with people and their problems, hour after hour, that became the problem for me, not legal matters per se." There was a huge empty space between this person's ideal of the work as being about "legal matters" and the reality of solving non-legal human problems, making him or her ripe for burnout.[9]

The experience of burnout is like trying to stand on a pair of stilts that are falling away from each other. The two stilts represent our ideals and the reality of our jobs. If we're lucky, they line up pretty closely with each other, and it's easy to hold onto both and walk forward without stretching or fumbling. But that is rarely the case. As the stilts move apart, they form a widening V shape. If they aren't very high, if your job doesn't demand too much of you, then a few degrees of separation between ideal and reality won't loosen your grip. But if the stilts are very high, if your job is as demanding as an emergency-department nurse's, then even a small departure of reality from your ideals will strain you greatly. Over time, your strength gives out, and you either let go of one of the stilts, or you snap altogether. In any case, a person who is pulled between them will have less available slack in their lives to flourish in a full sense.

Low-level or temporary forms of burnout occur in periods when the two stilts first drift apart, drawing you between them. The pain is real, as is the difficulty of maintaining a firm grip. The exhaustion, cynicism, and ineffectiveness you feel are symptoms, like fever is a symptom. They signal that something is wrong, that you are off balance. You stretch for a week or even a month, but then the project ends, or you meet the deadline, and the poles draw closer again. The tension relaxes, and you can solidify your hold on both ideals and reality. But then you face a new challenge, and the V gets wider again, and this time, it doesn't close up after a few weeks. You just keep stretching and stretching, trying to hold it together. Your palms get sweaty. You can feel yourself fraying. You know the stilts are *supposed* to stay together; it's what your parents and teachers and graduation speakers always told you. So what's wrong with *you*, that you're having such a hard time hanging on? But the poles never do return to alignment, and after a month, or a year, or longer, you reach the point where something has to give.

When I read my old notes to myself, I see the effects of my struggle to maintain high ideals for the work—to ignite young minds to new ways of thinking—in the face of the students' actual indifference to what I had to offer them. I felt the strain often as I tried to live in this contradiction between what I imagined my job would be and what it really was. The same feelings come up again and again in my notes. Those moments are when the gap got wider. But the gap must have narrowed, too, enabling me to relax and recover. I wasn't under constant tension. All that stretching, though, caused me to lose elasticity. Years later, when the poles moved apart again for an extended time, I finally broke.

．　●　．

It's tempting to say that everyone experiences the stress of burnout differently. But in fact, people and their jobs aren't *that* different from each other. If burnout manifests chiefly as cynicism for one person, then it probably does for others, too. So if we can identify a few categories of typical burnout experience, we may also be able to develop a few ways to help people who undergo each type of burnout along the spectrum.

That is the thinking behind researchers' recent focus on burnout "profiles," or characteristic experiences of burnout.[10] Since there are three separate dimensions to burnout, you might expect to find people who score particularly high on one of them but not the others—someone who is exhausted but not cynical or plagued by feelings of ineffectiveness—as well as people who score high on all three. Maslach and Leiter, for instance, view burnout in terms of five profiles: one where you score low on all three dimensions, one where you score high on all three, and then one each for a high score on exhaustion alone, cynicism alone, and ineffectiveness alone. Although I'm referring to "high" and "low" scores, this type of analysis does not rely on arbitrary cutoff scores to establish whether someone fits one profile or another. Rather, it looks for patterns in people's responses to the Maslach Burnout Inventory, clusters of frequent scores on the scale.[11] Those clusters are the profiles, the most common ways people experience burnout.

Returning to our metaphor of walking on stilts, the five burnout profiles correspond approximately to five different ways of dealing with the task of holding both your ideals for work and the reality of your job upright. One way is the easiest: there is already close alignment between ideal and reality, and you can hold both stilts and walk without serious struggle. That's what Leiter and Maslach call "engaged," but I think a better term is, simply, *no burnout*. (I'm convinced that "employee engagement" as a work ideal itself contributes to burnout; I will say more about that in chapter 5.) The other four profiles appear when the poles start falling away from each other. At that point, depending on our circumstances and psychological makeup, we can respond in four different ways. I want to be clear, though, that these are not *chosen* responses. You can't decide *how* you're going to burn out any more than you can decide *whether* you're going to burn out. The four responses are involuntary, four different ways our bodies and minds react to a particular kind of stress.

The first way we might deal with on-the-job reality that diverges from our ideals is to try to hold onto both poles for dear life as they pull us across the space between them. By sheer force of will, or denial, we cling to our expectations for what our work ought to be, even as its reality looks less and less like them, whether due to an excessive workload or inadequate support or burdensome emotional demands. When we're stretched like this, but still holding onto both stilts, exhaustion dominates our experience, and we are *overextended.*

The second way is to abandon our ideals and submit to that compromised reality. When we do this, we depersonalize our coworkers and clients. Or we care only about our paychecks after giving up on the social mission of our jobs. Workers who fit this profile might include the medical technician who reduces patients to their conditions—the viral infection in bed 27—or the teacher who thinks working in the school would be great if it weren't for all the students. This profile also includes a worker like Liz Curfman said she had been, lashing out at coworkers and talking about them behind their backs. When ideals no longer matter to our work, including the ideal of treating others as complete human beings, we are *cynical.*

The third approach is to ignore or rebel against the reality while maintaining our ideals. We become disappointed or angry because our work doesn't measure up to what we expect of it. Or else we detach ourselves from it, doing as little as possible: *Why bother? I'm just going to fail anyway.* We feel ineffective and worthless. We see the ideal and believe we could never attain it. We are *frustrated.*

Finally, we can let go of both ideal and reality. Or, if we're stretched for long enough, we're torn apart. We're off the stilts, unable to do more than the bare minimum. Every effort is exhausting. Our job is just a chore, with no redeeming value. We feel used up, empty. We are *burned out.*

Researchers have identified how many workers fit into each of these five profiles at any given time. Multiple studies of hospital employees in the United States and Canada, including both clinical staff, like doctors and nurses, and administrative and trade workers, show that about 40 to 45 percent fit the profile I am calling *no burnout,* 20 to 25 percent fit the *frustrated* profile with high scores on inefficacy only, 15 percent are *overextended* due to high levels of exhaustion, 10 percent have high depersonalization scores and are thus *cynical,* and 5 to 10 percent fit the *burned-out* profile with high scores on all three dimensions.[12] Other studies that define the profiles differently support the finding that the no-burnout profile comprises about 40 percent of workers, with 5 to 10 percent classically burned out.[13]

With these numbers, we finally have an answer to an important question: How many workers are burned out? A bit more than half are on the burnout spectrum, exhibiting one of its profiles due to high scores on one or more of burnout's three dimensions. And a smaller share, up to one in ten, score high on all three and fit the classic burnout profile. These estimates make intuitive sense. Just look around your workplace; chances are, a lot of people seem to be doing fine, a lot are unhappy or visibly overburdened, and a few are truly struggling to hold it together.

The number of workers who exhibit the burned-out profile is smaller than the numbers who "are burned out" that you read about in splashy news articles and marketing reports. But that does not diminish burnout's significance as a problem in our workplaces and culture. In fact, the percentage of workers who fit the burned-out profile is similar to the percentage of adults who have clinical depression, 8.1 percent in the United States, and we rightly see depression as a serious problem.[14] If half of workers are on the burnout spectrum at any given time, then it is safe to say that the vast majority experience one of the profiles at some point in their careers. And a significant minority are likely to fall into the burned-out profile at least once. No, not everyone is burned out right now. But most of us have felt the strain of our reality at work diverging from our ideals, and we have stumbled. And many of us have fallen hard.

· · ·

The profiles reveal nuances of the burnout experience that a one-dimensional, burned-out-or-not model would miss. They can help clinicians identify partial forms of burnout and then prescribe remedies that suit the sufferer's specific needs. The profiles can also help us see how people in a specific workplace or profession experience burnout differently than other workers do. A study of French psychologists, for instance, identified four clusters of Maslach Burnout Inventory scores among members of the profession; the cynical, high-depersonalization profile was missing. As the authors note, "It is indeed quite difficult to imagine an energetic psychologist who thinks he is efficient while being cynical and distant toward his patients."[15] In other words, the burnout profiles confirm the suspicion that people in this line of work are more likely to experience burnout as overextension or frustration than as cynicism, and so there is no need to develop treatments specifically aimed at cynical *psychologues.*

My MBI scores—high on exhaustion, moderate-to-high on depersonalization, and low on personal accomplishment—suggest I was not an obvious match for any one of the five profiles. Just by making an eyeball comparison between my scores and the charts in Leiter and Maslach's paper, though, it looks like I could have fit the overextended, frustrated, or burned-out profiles. I was certainly exhausted and overextended, but due to my low sense of accomplishment—remember, I wrote myself a letter arguing I didn't deserve tenure—whatever happened to me was more than overextension.

Our cultural conversation about burnout focuses almost solely on exhaustion. Even some researchers make this mistake. But research on the profiles confirms that exhaustion does not tell the whole story. Leiter and Maslach warn that when researchers use the exhaustion dimension of the MBI as a proxy for burnout, they may be counting many people as burned out who are in fact "only" over-extended. The experience of being overextended is simply not the same as the experience of other burnout profiles on the spectrum. In Leiter and Maslach's studies, people who scored high only on exhaustion tended to have very negative views toward their work-load but not toward other areas of their work. People with the burned-out profile, by contrast, had negative views toward *all* areas of work.[16] This finding is good news; if an evaluation can identify workers who fit the overextended profile, then their employer can reduce their workload and, one hopes, spare them from greater strain over time. Along the same lines, the burnout profiles can help identify workers whose job stress leads them to cynical disengage-ment without significant exhaustion, before things get worse.

The most common profile on the burnout spectrum is frustra-tion, which reflects a high score only on the ineffectiveness dimen-sion of the MBI (or, in fact, low on the personal accomplishment dimension, which is scored on a reverse scale). People in this cat-egory exhibit relatively mild negative experience with their jobs, compared to overextended, cynical, or burned-out workers. Still, frustrated workers' experience is less satisfying, compared to that of workers in the no-burnout profile. Leiter and Maslach call frustration a "somewhat less than neutral state."[17] Another study notes the "limited health effects" on workers fitting the frustrated profile.[18] Because frustration does not appear to be severely debilitating, it is easy to overlook. In fact, researchers often ignore frustration entirely in their study designs. The high-profile Mayo Clinic studies of burnout among US physicians do not measure personal accomplishment at all.[19] In Europe, an influential model of burnout uses a test that measures only exhaustion and disengagement from work; feelings of ineffectiveness are not part of the model.[20]

But ineffectiveness plays a crucial role in the experience of burnout and in burnout's place in society. Ineffectiveness is a crisis of spirit, an assault on self-esteem and meaning. It may be that, by itself, feeling ineffectual causes less harm than exhaustion or cynicism. People can roll along with low self-efficacy, going through the motions of work. About a quarter of American workers are doing just that, reporting *no* source of meaning at their jobs.[21] I want to pause for a moment with that statistic. One in four workers finds *nothing* meaningful in their work. No feeling of usefulness, no sense that they are helping society or exercising their talents, no aspiration toward personal goals. These dispirited workers are everywhere, but they seem to cluster in a few types of unglamorous jobs. A study by researchers working for the US Veterans Administration found the frustrated profile (which they called "unfulfilled") especially prevalent among administrative and trade staff in VA hospitals—the workers responsible for billing, ordering supplies, and maintaining the hospital's physical space.[22] In other words, frustrated hospital workers are disproportionately the ones who rarely confront trauma and illness, but who also rarely get to see cancer go into remission, help a woman give birth, or witness an amputee take his first steps on a new artificial limb.

Meaninglessness and frustration may not cause much damage by themselves, but they amplify the physical harm of exhaustion and the moral injury of cynicism. If you're worn out or hardened by your work, then feeling frustrated by it will make matters worse. For this reason, the VA study's authors maintain that the negative experience of burnout, and especially its chronic character, is driven mainly by the sense of ineffectiveness.[23] This contrasts with Maslach's long-standing view that burnout typically begins with exhaustion that the worker tries to deal with by putting people at a distance emotionally.[24] VA hospital workers exhibiting the frustrated profile were especially vocal about their dissatisfaction with promotions, recognition, and praise.[25] They truly are the overlooked.

Frustrated workers feel that their effort on the job is in vain. They cannot see the good they accomplish. The fruit of their labor may be abstract or ephemeral. They may have too little real work to do. They may be passed over for promotions, or there may be no possibility for promotion, or their supervisors may barely notice their effort and achievements. They may have what the anthropologist David Graeber calls "bullshit jobs," jobs that even the people who hold them suspect do not need to exist. Such workers may do little more than tick boxes or mediate between other mediators or project the image that their bosses are important.[26] The exhaustion-only view of burnout cannot appreciate how many of us are hardly doing anything all day and can feel our talents rusting over and gathering cobwebs. The violence that uselessness does to the person is often invisible. It doesn't look like stress. A frustrated worker may not look burned out because they were never lit to begin with. But if the burnout spectrum works like the depression spectrum of Jules Angst, then experiencing frustration may make it more likely that a worker will eventually exhibit exhaustion, cynicism, or full-on burnout. And if a core part of frustrated workers' problem is a lack of recognition, then recognizing them can head off significant problems down the line.

A sense of futility was the gateway to my burnout; it was the first symptom. It led me, during my first semester of full-time teaching, to lament that education was "an impossible lie." This does not mean ineffectiveness is always the first step to a more severe case of burnout. It surely is for many, but there are other pathways in. The prevalence of the frustrated profile may signal that burnout is a chronic illness that workers can learn to manage but that can flare up into acute episodes.[27]

I managed being frustrated, overextended, and cynical for years, without realizing that burnout was the problem. And I likely slipped off the burnout spectrum for long periods when my faith in education felt validated. I saw students' knowledge fall into place when they did in-class activities I designed. I felt proud of them while I watched them scribble in their blue exam booklets, occasionally shaking out their sore hands; they were working so hard, trying to prove to me that they had learned. It sometimes even felt like a privilege to read their papers. They were sharing their best ideas with me. In these moments, my ideals and reality had realigned. But only for a while.

.   .   .

We perhaps overlook uselessness in burnout research and the broader cultural conversation because it isn't socially acceptable to say you are ineffective at your job. Incompetent workers are losers, not heroes. Overextended workers, by contrast, exemplify a praiseworthy ideal. If you say you're exhausted from work, then you are saying you are a good worker, upholding the norms of the American work ethic. In fact, you're so devoted to work, you sacrifice yourself to it. Even depersonalization is more socially acceptable than ineffectiveness. The hard-boiled cynic who dispenses with niceties in order to accomplish a difficult task is also something of a hero, an archetype of police procedurals and hospital dramas on television.

Because there is often a social reward for claiming the overextended profile, I want to argue against equating it with burnout, and argue for ineffectiveness as a crucial dimension. The state of full-on burnout—afflicting the 5 or 10 percent of workers who score high on all three MBI dimensions—makes workers wonder if they can go on, not discover that, yes, they can. The temptation of this "hero" narrative underscores how burnout reflects the American virtue of rugged individualism and ceaseless hustle. *I worked hard until I couldn't, but then I conquered my limitations and learned to work harder!* One brazen example of this narrative was a 2017 subway ad for Fiverr, a virtual marketplace for small, often low-paid freelance gigs. The ad depicted a young woman who looked both harried and glamorous, staring straight out at the viewer over the text, "You eat a coffee for lunch. You follow through on your follow through. Sleep deprivation is your drug of choice. You might be a doer." Her far-off gaze perfectly captured the merger of ambition and exhaustion, her apparent focus on a distant goal indistinguishable from the burnout's thousand-yard stare.

We have been over-diagnosing ourselves with burnout as a means of self-praise for the entire history of burnout culture. Lance Morrow wrote in his skeptical 1981 essay on burnout, "The term perfectly captures an American habit of hyperbole and narcissism working in tandem: a hypochondria of the spirit. The idea contains a sneaking self-aggrandizement tied to an elusive self-exoneration."[28] Researchers Ayala Pines and Elliot Aronson spent the 1980s giving workshops on burnout. They report that "When participants realize that the most committed workers burn out most severely, it frees them to admit burnout without shame or embarrassment." Indeed, Pines and Aronson found that when they told workers in advance that idealists exhibit more signs of burnout, those workers scored higher on measures of burnout.[29] In other words, if burnout is heroic exhaustion, then ambitious workers aspire to attain it. Exhaustion is not really a negative in America's work culture; there is no taboo against being overextended. The taboo is admitting you can't do your job.

I will confess that, because I gave up my career following a long period of frustrated, cynical exhaustion, I raise an eyebrow when someone claims to be burned out but doesn't seem to suffer negative professional consequences. In my worst periods at work, my performance deteriorated—and so did my health. I felt that I had to quit or else risk severe personal damage. I was proud of my hustle, of heading up multiple faculty committees while teaching and publishing. I was glad to say yes when someone asked me to take on extra work, especially if it might earn me a reputation as someone who could get things done. Yes, I was a doer.

But all of that wasn't burnout. It was the *prelude* to burnout. I wasn't exhausted or cynical about my job on my first day back from sabbatical, when I arrived early to an 8:00 a.m. meeting and didn't go home until my night class ended. I was thrilled to be back, to have so many people depending on me to do a good job. Months later, when I was ranting on the phone to my wife about a scholar who I thought snubbed me at a conference reception—*that* was cynicism. Ignoring the papers I needed to grade and lumbering through class unprepared—*that* was ineffectiveness. Having to take a nap two hours after getting up most mornings—*that* was exhaustion.

The status and virtue that burnout signals make it an attractive self-diagnosis, one that can cover over severe problems carrying a stronger social stigma, like clinical depression. In fact, it may be that burnout is a form of depression. Herbert Freudenberger, the godfather of burnout, wrote in 1974 that a burned-out worker "looks, acts and seems depressed."[30] It's another of his off-the-cuff observations that later earned scientific backing. The psychologist Irvin Schonfeld finds strong correlations between depression symptoms and burnout scores; in fact, exhaustion correlates more strongly with depression than it does with the other two dimensions of burnout: cynicism and ineffectiveness.[31] In one study, Schonfeld and his coauthor found that 86 percent of American public-school teachers with burnout also met criteria for depression; of those without burnout, fewer than 1 percent also met depression criteria.[32] Both syndromes impair daily functioning, and both can feature social withdrawal and cynicism.[33] For these reasons, Schonfeld argues that it makes sense to treat burnout as depression, rather than as a separate condition. Doing so might help convince workers to seek the talk therapy or medication that could help them.[34]

Schonfeld's research is a challenge not just to other researchers but to our burnout-obsessed culture. If he is right, then the attention we give to burnout only distracts us from a more fundamental problem, one psychologists understand much better. While I obviously think it is worth paying attention to burnout, I also do not see equating burnout with depression as a problem for my view of burnout as a spectrum that comprises several profiles. If there are multiple ways of experiencing burnout—including the partial conditions of overextension, cynicism, and frustration—then you would not expect strong correlations among the three burnout dimensions. I agree with Schonfeld that, because true burnout is more than ordinary tiredness, you can't heal it with just time off.[35] It often takes significant changes to your job, including possibly quitting it, to recover from burnout. I also agree that people with severe burnout symptoms should get screened for depression. And while neither talk therapy nor antidepressants helped me much, they might help others who went through the same kind of job stress I did.

The research on the link between burnout and depression is encouraging. It takes work-related stress seriously and pushes back against expansive definitions of burnout that leave us unable to treat it. The gap between workers' ideals and the reality of their jobs can wreak havoc on their well-being and prevent them from flourishing. And we are all susceptible to being stretched across that gap. That's because, when it comes to work, our collective ideals and our reality have parted ways on a national and global scale.

4 *How Jobs Have Gotten Worse in the Age of Burnout*

Teaching was not the only aspect of my career as a theology professor where the reality of my job departed from my ideals for work. Teaching was at least a part of the job I could picture when I dreamed of academic life, entranced by my own college classes. I never pictured the amorphous set of tasks faculty just call "service": the committee work that (allegedly) has to get done, but that is nevertheless somewhat avoidable. During my time at the college, I served, at different times, on the curriculum committee, an ad hoc committee to reform the curriculum, the committee that ran a new pilot program within the curriculum, the curriculum assessment committee, a steering committee on accreditation, the college mission committee, a lecture committee, and an online education working group. Many of these committees also had subcommittees. In several instances, I was committee chair, which meant extra responsibilities without extra compensation. Plus, there was the ordinary work of my academic department. And on top of everything else, I was the director of a teaching development center. The committees were where my dream job felt most like a *job*.

Service work is vexing not only because there is so much of it, but because it involves pushing and pulling against university administration in a way that teaching and research don't. It's where you are most likely to be thwarted. It's also, quite literally, thankless. I was frustrated, even angry, when I met what seemed like arbitrary administrative roadblocks. I began to question if it mattered that I went above and beyond the strict requirements of the job. It seemed like I would get the same reward, regardless of whether I pushed myself to do more. I sometimes regret caring as much about the college as I did. I could have done so much less.

I took perverse consolation in the words of the German sociologist Max Weber, who more than a century ago habitually asked aspiring university professors, "Do you believe that you can bear to see one mediocrity after another promoted over your head, year after year, without becoming embittered and warped?" Academia, like many other career fields, is often unfair. It pretends to reward merit, but years of hard work can be easily undone by bad luck: a grant program ends, intellectual fashions change, a new dean prefers some other initiative to yours. "Needless to say," Weber says, when you ask a budding scholar about perseverance In the face of unfairness, "you always receive the same answer: of course, I live only for my 'vocation'—but I, at least, have found only a handful of people who have survived this process without injury to their personality."[1] I had been one of those eager young faculty who believed academia was fair, and if it wasn't, then my vocation would sustain me. It didn't. At least I wasn't alone in my injured personality; if Weber's report is true, then academics have been undergoing the same trials for more than a hundred years.

The long history of unfairness and unrecognized labor plays only one part in academic burnout. Over the past five decades, academic labor has also undergone changes that reflect the way work across many industries has become less rewarding and more psychologically injurious. Universities have much larger administrative staffs now than they did at the dawn of burnout culture in the 1970s. By one count, the number of administrators in the California State University system, the largest public university system in the United States, more than tripled between 1975 and 2008, while the number of full-time faculty grew by only a few percent.[2] Paradoxically, the growth of non-teaching staff has not lessened faculty workloads. If anything, faculty are responsible for *more* paperwork now, to satisfy the demands of the bloated administration. Particularly in the area of assessment—that is, not teaching itself, but evaluating the effectiveness of teaching—the administrative load has increased dramatically. The push to run universities "like businesses" has created more work that's detached from what most faculty got into academia to do.

While the administrative sector expands, the percentage of university instruction done by full-time, tenure-track faculty is shrinking. Increasingly, the typical university teacher is not a tweedy, tenured professor but a part-time or adjunct instructor hired semester by semester, making less than $3,500 per class, with no benefits and maybe not even an office.[3] In 2018, 40 percent of faculty were part-time adjuncts, and another 20 percent were graduate students, a second pool of cheap, temporary labor.[4] The fact that so many people with advanced degrees sign up for adjunct work—including me, during the past few years—testifies both to the power of the vocation Weber described and to the diminished state of professional work in the post-1970s era. As bad as the conditions of adjunct teaching are, it can seem like the best thing available, the best match for your skills and inclinations.

In every sector of the economy during the past several decades, the typical job has become more stressful and less rewarding. As a result, we have to stretch further than ever to connect our job to our ideals for work. Because this bad bargain is so prevalent, burning through employees can seem like a conscious human-resources strategy: recruit, burn out, lay off, repeat.

.   .   .

Most people work for a specific organization: a store, a hospital, a school, a company, a police department, and so on. The conditions in each workplace contribute greatly to whether a worker will burn out. Those conditions vary, and, of course, two workers can experience the same conditions differently. But the working conditions in any organization—think of them as the local "weather"—are shaped by the overall "climate" surrounding work, the big-picture trends in the economy and culture. Since the 1970s, that climate has turned against workers in the United States. In that period, an era often called either postindustrial (to emphasize the shift toward service work) or neoliberal (to emphasize the growing power of financial markets and the decline in organized labor), work has laid greater psychological burdens on us and become more precarious, while our ideals for it have risen. Even amid the historically-low unemployment of 2019, the ratio of good-quality to low-quality jobs in the US economy had fallen to its lowest level since researchers began tracking this data in 1990.[5] In short, for at least the past three decades, jobs have simply gotten worse.

A big reason work demands more and returns less is that business doctrines have shifted costs and risks from employers to workers. Aided by deregulation and other policy changes that are friendly to owners of capital, employers now see many workers as liabilities rather than assets. That is, according to post-1970s doctrine, each employee represents a significant cost in salary and benefits rather than a source of productivity. To maximize profits, then, a company should always try to find the smallest and cheapest possible staff, just as it might try to find lower-rent office space or less-expensive packaging.[6]

The liability model of employment has roots in the early temp industry of the 1950s, the sociologist Erin Hatton argues. Ads at the time depicted the "Kelly Girl" as a competent, even glamorous office worker for hire—who did not demand high wages because the work was her pastime. Her husband was assumed to be the breadwinner, so anything she made was just "pin money."[7] In the late 1960s and early 1970s, that critical era right before burnout came on the cultural scene, the temp industry expanded rapidly as firms promoted the idea that permanent employees were lazy and complacent. You had to pay full-timers even during slow periods. A temp, by contrast, just shows up when you need her, gets the job done, and leaves. What the employer doesn't see is how the temp's unstable, unpredictable work harms her financial and psychological state. Because she isn't an employee, those things are not the company's problem.

The liability model became increasingly attractive to employers in subsequent decades, and the temp became the ideal worker. If only they could all be temps! In the 1970s, businesses began removing employees from their payrolls, then hiring the same workers back on temporary contracts.[8] This made it easier to "right-size" the staff quickly and quietly as the business cycle turned. A mass layoff of full-time employees would surely attract negative attention. But the release of officially-temporary workers would go unnoticed.[9]

If you work for an organization of any size, then you know that this "lean and mean" approach to staffing leads companies now to contract out services that, several decades ago, they would have hired people to perform directly. In 2014, Apple, the most valuable company in the United States, directly employed only 63,000 people. The other 700,000 who made Apple's products, cleaned Apple's offices, and administered Apple's operations were subcontractors employed by other firms.[10] Colleges and universities don't only rely on temporary workers to teach; they also routinely contract out food service, maintenance, and other activities that, administrators say, fall outside the "core competency" of the institution. The university hires the lowest-bidding company to oversee this work, and the outside company, in turn, hires the cooks, counselors, and IT technicians to do the work, while that company also seeks its own profits.[11] By hiring a large periphery of contracted workers to orbit a small core of direct employees, a company can separate the messy costs of actual production from the more abstract activities, like branding and innovation, that supposedly create value. The company can then build its brand by insisting on the standards its contractors, franchisees, and vendors must adhere to, but avoid taking "any responsibility for the consequences of that control," the economist David Weil writes.[12] Weil calls this model the "fissured workplace."

The model is bad for workers on both sides of the fissure. It reduces compliance with labor laws, including those covering minimum wages and overtime pay; it makes work riskier to health and safety; and it shifts the rewards of productivity from labor to capital.[13] Contracted workers end up with lower wages and more precarious employment. For example, when universities closed down their dorms during the Covid-19 pandemic in 2020, they quickly laid off contracted food-service workers while keeping their direct employees on payroll.[14] In addition, outsourcing leads to significant confusion for workers caught between apparent employers. If you're a janitor at a hospital but your paycheck comes from a third-party firm, who is your actual boss? Who are you responsible to? And which organization's mission are you really helping to advance?

Core employees enjoy greater security, but fissuring piles pressure on them, too. Companies cut staff to eliminate slack and raise efficiency in their labor systems, but, as the business scholar Zeynep Ton shows, they lose their capacity to deal with contingencies like illness or simply a busier-than-expected day. Everyone has to work harder and, probably, less effectively, than they would if there were simply more available hands.[15]

The gig economy, headlined by ride-hailing service Uber, goes one step further, breaking down the worker's contract to the smallest possible unit: the single, isolated task. "Fissured" would be an understatement; the gig economy turns the workplace into gravel spread over a vast empty lot. The result is that employers hold basic labor rights in even greater contempt. Uber identifies itself as a technology company, not a transportation company, claiming that its drivers are not employees but consumers of its services, just like its passengers are. Uber and its competitor, Lyft, have argued publicly that driving isn't their core business activity, so drivers are peripheral contractors, not employees.[16] If drivers are contractors, then the companies can avoid paying minimum wages, benefits, or employment taxes—in other words, all of the "liabilities" of having an employee. Furthermore, as the investigative journalist Alex Rosenblat reports, Uber uses its purported status as a technology company as cover for unethical practices; lost payments to drivers are "glitches," and apparent price discrimination is the algorithm's fault.[17]

The rhetoric around contract work emphasizes autonomy and independence. Workers aren't stuck in a single job; they're entrepreneurs loyal only to themselves, hired guns who set their own terms. Temporary workers are "a company of one," thriving on risk and solely responsible for their own success (and failure). It's an outlook embraced by white- and blue-collar workers alike—especially men.[18] Once again, gig work takes the trend even further, portraying labor that's performed via micro-contract as the hip, self-reliant hustle of the millennial generation.[19] Despite this talk of independence, though, gig workers are typically subject to burdensome control and supervision of their work. Uber, for instance, monitors the amount of vibration in drivers' dashboard-mounted phones, giving drivers grades on their acceleration and braking during each ride.[20] And because wages for gig work tend to be low, workers have an incentive to keep going through every free hour. If they try to log out of the company's mobile app, the savvy algorithm will promise that a lucrative gig is just around the corner, a new contract just a swipe away.[21] Like addictive video games, the app entices you to accept one more ride, one more task. For a precarious worker, the hustle never ends.

· · ·

The shift of risk from capital to labor is only half the story of labor conditions since the 1970s. The other half is the shift from an economy dominated by manufacturing to one dominated by services. It was in human services—the intense interpersonal work of free-clinic volunteers, social workers, and poverty lawyers—that burnout first emerged as an occupational hazard.[22] And in the past several decades, more jobs in the United States and other rich countries resemble these high-burnout professions, putting people's emotions to work, potentially at all hours of the day.

The transition from a manufacturing economy to a service economy has been underway since World War II. In 1946, a third of all nonfarm employees in the United States made things for a living. In 1973, when labor power had peaked and burnout first gained psychologists' attention, manufacturing employed about a quarter of US workers. In 2000, it employed 13 percent, and as I write this, less than 9 percent of workers are in manufacturing.[23] Job losses have occurred in waves, usually following a recession. In the early 2000s and again in 2008–2009, a million manufacturing jobs disappeared *every year*.[24] Thanks to highly-skilled labor and efficient technologies, including automated production lines, US manufacturing is as productive as ever.[25] It just no longer relies on very many people to do the producing.

Instead of making things, American workers sell them. In 2018, retail salesperson was the single most common job in the United States, with cashier in third place, customer service representative in seventh, and waiter or waitress in eighth.[26] All of this selling demands a "customer service" mentality: a readiness to manage and respond to other people's desires. And when we aren't selling things, we are attending to each other's business, educational, or health needs. In all of this work, we talk, we listen, we make eye contact, we imagine and anticipate other people's mental states, we chide without offense, we reassure. Our personalities and emotions are now the chief means of production.

As a result, employers impose ever-more insidious discipline on workers' mental and emotional habits. Bosses can hire, evaluate, promote, and terminate them "on the basis of their attitudes, motivation, and behavior," in the words of political philosopher Kathi Weeks.[27] That means employees' emotions are *negotiable;* employers rent those emotions, shift by shift, and in doing so, alter them.

For example, female flight attendants found it hard, after their shifts ended, to turn off the smiling, accommodating persona their employer called their "biggest asset," according to Arlie Russell Hochschild's classic 1983 study of emotional labor, *The Managed Heart*.[28] As a result, the attendants became alienated from the feelings that were integral to their off-duty identities. When emotions matter to the bottom line, then aspects of workers' inner lives that run counter to corporate goals must be "corrected." Employees at a dotcom-era media consultancy who struggled with the job's psychic demands were invited to meet with the company's Morale Team, whose Orwellian mission was to help employees "fix how [they] feel."[29]

The postindustrial economy did not only see the manufacturing sector diminish as the service sector grew. It also transformed the blue-collar jobs that remained, so that they, too, now demand a white-collar service ethic. One change was the expansion of "professionalism," a norm that pulls everyone from police to truckers to nurses to professors in two directions at once, requiring a delicate emotional balancing act.[30] As Weeks puts it, "A professional invests his or her person in the job but does not 'take it personally' when dealing with difficult co-workers, clients, patients, students, passengers, or customers."[31] Being a professional means you are willing to give up your day off to pull an extra shift at a call center, but you maintain a polite demeanor when a caller berates you for a problem they created. This strange, self-contradictory psychological state—wherein you merge yourself with your job, but not too much—is a postindustrial innovation that controls workers by changing an aspect of their selfhood, just as the early industrial age created the time discipline that we now take for granted and that makes us anxious when a meeting starts two minutes late.

"Professionalism" puts new pressures on workers and exposes more of who they are to the logic and conditions of work.

Postindustrial business doctrines also got blue-collar workers to think more like the white-collar workers who employed them. In the participative management style pioneered by Toyota, a small team of workers built each entire car, offering higher-ups their suggestions for how to improve the process. Toyota's success prompted American industries to adopt this method in the 1980s and 1990s, imposing new mental disciplines on workers.[32] A key shift was getting them to leave behind the "hourly perspective" instilled in them through years of working in the industrial paradigm and to start thinking of themselves as "neophyte managers" who can, as the sociologist Vicki Smith writes, "step outside themselves and activate their human and cultural capital to improve quality, innovation, and efficiency."[33] At a lumber mill that made this change, one longtime worker explained the shift to Smith by saying that, in the old days, "we came in and we did our job and then went home and that was it. We weren't paid to think, we were there for our backs."[34] In other words, the workers could shield their minds from their work—a discipline of disengagement that was reinforced by strong, obvious, externally-imposed boundaries, including both a well-defined schedule and their union's contract with management.

For the most part, Smith reports, the millworkers embraced the change to a more participatory management style, where they had a say in how production was done. But in doing so, they accepted new, ambivalent burdens, and their responsibility at work migrated deeper into their minds. On the older industrial model and under their previous contract, the workers didn't have to make many judgment calls. They were not accountable for the financial health of the plant, the satisfaction of its customers, or the efficiency of its manufacturing process. With a weaker contract and under policies of participative management, workers gained more autonomy in some respects, but they felt pressure to "continually seek to brainstorm in the absence of concrete problems" and, with their main tasks becoming more abstract, to do a lot of what seemed like "busywork."[35] The new regime also placed more individual responsibility onto the workers to police the invisible and internal boundaries between their work and the rest of their lives.

No one can maintain those boundaries perfectly. And when your job capitalizes on your personality, you can barely separate work from the rest of your life at all. Disciplines acquired at work carry over into your family and civic life. The results of that carryover are mixed. For employees of a photocopying company Smith studied, learning self-management meant adapting to the intellectual, emotional, and imaginative demands of the fissured workplace; the workers constantly had to reconcile their direct employer's standards with the corporate culture and expectations of their client, a large law firm. These low-wage workers reported that the communications and conflict-resolution training they received—and which they greatly valued—translated into other areas of their lives, including their families. But the work also habituated them to the flexibility in role and schedule that corporations demand in the postindustrial era. Management kept shuttling them to different job sites, making it impossible to form working relationships with (or organize) their coworkers.[36] Because you cannot change out of your work mentality as easily as you can change out of your work uniform, the person your job wants you to be is the person you tend to become.

.   .   .

The big post-1970s workplace trends—the increasingly fissured and precarious nature of employment, the growth of job sectors that demand interpersonal labor, and work's colonization of blue-collar workers' inner lives—create the perfect conditions for burnout. Workers are more likely to exhibit burnout symptoms if they have to perform emotional labor like suppressing negative feelings and performing cheerful professionalism.[37] In addition, companies that constantly cut staff increase pressure on the workers who remain. The conditions of their work get worse and worse, departing ever more from what they hoped their work could accomplish for themselves and others. They strain to keep a grip on both their ideals and the day-to-day reality of their jobs, pushing them further down the burnout spectrum.

Just as our everyday experience is more directly affected by the weather than the climate, workers' risk of burnout depends primarily on their specific workplace. Of course, climate change affects the weather, making it more likely that a Dallas resident will feel a need to wear shorts and sandals on a Tuesday in November. But the conditions we react to—both meteorological and occupational—are local.

Gaps between working conditions and ideals typically appear in a few specific aspects of work. Christina Maslach and Michael Leiter identify six areas where workers most often experience "mismatches between people and their jobs": workload, control, reward, community, fairness, and values.[38] Such mismatches, in turn, make workers more likely to burn out. A key point is that burnout does not result only from overwork. Your workload might be manageable, but if no one ever recognizes it, or if you have no control over it, or if what you do conflicts with your personal values, you are still likely to land on the burnout spectrum. Likewise if you receive unfair treatment or the sense of community among your coworkers breaks down.

For Jessika Satori, an entrepreneur with a varied career spanning everything from costume design to information management, community was the linchpin of her job as a business professor at a college near Tacoma, Washington. Once the pin was removed, the wheels came off. Satori told me she began the job with a strong commitment to the students. And she had support within her department. Two other faculty members, both of them women, had a tradition of taking a walk two or three times a week together around a lake near the campus, rain or shine. When Satori arrived, they invited her to join them. Satori described a "ritual" of removing her high heels and putting on tennis shoes for the walk along the forested trail.

It took forty-five minutes to walk around the lake. That gave each of the women fifteen minutes to be the focus of the conversation. In the first five minutes, "you just vented," Satori said, whether the problem was with a student or the college's tenure committee. "You could use as much emotion or volume as you needed to." The other two would listen and then spend ten minutes offering suggestions, support, and mentoring. Satori's colleagues were both more senior than her, but she said they saw her as a peer with a valuable perspective to contribute. The walks "afforded us a way to practice what we preached about dealing with conflict or dealing with human relations," she said. "We were modeling that with each other."

After her first year, Satori was transferred to a different campus in the college system. She remained just as committed to her students, but she had lost her mentors and their ritual. She recalls thinking, "I'm just trying to do this tenure thing, and it's just not working." She lost the community that made the work possible. The entrepreneurial go-getter started having trouble getting out of bed. She quit after one semester on the new campus. Later, though, she brought that experience to her work as a life coach and spiritual director, helping people navigate transitions in their lives.

Maslach and Leiter argued in 1997 that conditions in each of the six crucial areas were getting worse, creating a "crisis" in work. They saw globalization, technology, the decline of unions, and the increasing role of finance in steering corporate decision-making as the foundation of this crisis.[39] Decades later, that crisis is still turning workplaces into burnout factories. In the post-1970s employment climate, conditions have eroded even further in the areas where workers most feel the tension between ideal and reality. The liability model of employment and the increased power of finance in the neoliberal era bear much of the blame for this trend.

Workloads are greater and more intense in many industries—especially in the United States, where working hours have remained high, even as they have diminished across wealthy countries.[40] Half of American workers report catching up on work in their free time; 10 percent say they do so every day.[41] Wages, meanwhile, have been flat in real terms since 1973, which means all that work leads to no greater material reward.[42] While some blue-collar workers have gained a measure of autonomy through participative management, that autonomy comes at the cost of a more intensive, personally invasive workload. And other manufacturing, retail, and transportation workers are increasingly subject to intrusive surveillance, severely limiting their autonomy on the job.[43] The fissured, precarious workplace undermines community and fairness, as each worker becomes an isolated contractor with little chance of recognition or promotion within the organization they serve.

Amazon, for example, keeps wages low and exercises control over its many temporary workers by holding out the prospect that if they work hard, they can become direct employees. But only 10 to 15 percent ever get the promotion.[44] Fissuring also increases "role ambiguity," a contributor to burnout that weakens employees' control over their work.[45] And the growing managerial perspective puts service workers' values at odds with the imperative to increase efficiency and shareholder value.

Even while work is expanding and intensifying, there is also evidence that it is becoming more trivial and pointless, forcing workers to spend time and energy on tasks that don't matter. Much of what people do at work is mere administrative "box-ticking," or else it's ancillary to companies' actual production, like the assessment of teaching I did as a college professor. Think of the millworkers Vicki Smith interviewed, creating work for themselves to demonstrate that they were effective self-managers. Such work is typical of the "bullshit jobs" David Graeber theorized. Bullshit jobs are a charade; they look like work but accomplish nothing of social value, and the people performing the labor often realize it. Graeber suspects "that at least half of all work being done in our society could be eliminated without making any real difference at all."[46] Pointless work is still work; it can wear you down as much as real work can. More than that, the very pointlessness of bullshit work puts the reality of it at odds with *any* ideal the worker may have brought to their job. They wanted to teach, or to serve the community, or to sell products people need. But they end up mired in administrivia. This insult is what makes bullshit work so conducive to burnout.

.   .   .

The problems of overwork, bullshit work, and managerialism coincide in a crucial profession where burnout is a serious problem: medicine. When doctors burn out, all of society suffers. The Covid-19 pandemic increased workloads for physicians dealing with major outbreaks, but it reduced the hours (and pay) of doctors who perform non-emergency procedures.[47] In more ordinary times, physicians tend to have long workweeks. Family practitioners in one Wisconsin health system worked, on average, 11.4 hours a day, according to a 2017 study.[48] Among US physicians as a whole, a 2019 study found that 38.9 percent reported working more than sixty hours per week, compared to just 6.2 percent of other workers who did so.[49] That same study found significantly higher rates of emotional exhaustion and depersonalization (or cynicism) among physicians, compared to the general working population. And there is evidence that intensive-care units with emotionally-exhausted staff have higher standard mortality ratios. In other words, when doctors and nurses are overextended, patients are more likely to die.[50]

Whenever I go to the doctor, I am impressed by the calm, friendly attentiveness of the people who care for me. They put up a good front. But the reality of medical work is often one of constant, conflicting challenges. As the physician Danielle Ofri describes it,

> You are at your daughter's recital and you get a call that your elderly patient's son needs to talk to you urgently. A colleague has a family emergency and the hospital needs you to work a double shift. Your patient's MRI isn't covered and the only option is for you to call the insurance company and argue it out. You're only allotted fifteen minutes for a visit, but your patient's medical needs require forty-five.[51]

On top of those difficulties, doctors spend a huge amount of their workdays on data entry, labor you hardly need a medical degree to perform. Physicians now spend nearly twice as much time per day on electronic health records and communication—documenting exams, reviewing lab results, ordering medications—as they do in face-to-face interaction with patients.[52] And physicians who spend more time working on electronic records are more likely to show signs of burnout.[53]

Because burnout arises from the gap between ideals and reality, it's no surprise that doctors who spend their days parked at a computer burn out so often. No aspiring practitioner writes about their passion for electronic health records in their med-school application essay. Sumner Abraham, an internal medicine physician in Mississippi, told me that when he supervised medical residents, he frequently saw these new doctors struggle with the gap. "They feel aimless, because it's not what they signed up for. They signed up for spending a lot of time with people, a stable income, and weekends off," he said. "Instead, they're making nine dollars an hour, working lots of nights and weekends, and sitting in front of a computer screen." They become exhausted and unhappy. Abraham said the exhaustion was not because of overwork, since the medical profession has cut back residents' long workweeks over the last two decades. Rather, the residents are exhausted because "they can't make sense of themselves," he said.

The increasingly corporate and bureaucratic character of medical practice intensifies the conflict doctors feel, because it pits caring for patients against minimizing costs. "The system is built for billing and not taking care of patients," Liselotte Dyrbye, a researcher at the Mayo Clinic, told the *Washington Post* in 2019.[54] Ofri likewise sees clinicians bridging the gap between their principles and their employers' demands by stretching their own time and energy. "If doctors and nurses clocked out when their paid hours were finished, the effect on patients would be calamitous," she writes. "Doctors and nurses know this, which is why they don't shirk. The system knows it, too, and takes advantage."[55]

And all the extra work might not even accomplish anything. The surgeon and author Atul Gawande observes that much medical labor consists of tests and treatments for over-diagnosed or ultimately harmless ailments, with no net health benefit. Worse, this extra "care" often brings unnecessary and damaging stress to the patient. Gawande cites a 2010 study that estimated that 30 percent of health-care spending is waste.[56] Another way to put this is to say 30 percent of all health-care *work* is pointless. Performing exams and procedures that patients don't need, when you aren't just stuck in front of a laptop, is a prescription for feeling useless, even as you work all day long.

It is easy to sympathize with doctors, nurses, and other clinical workers who devote themselves to caring for us. It is harder to sympathize with hospital and insurance administrators we speak to mostly when we have been overcharged. But those administrators—whose ranks grew about tenfold between 1970 and 2018—have ideals that their work thwarts, too.[57] In fact, Veterans Affairs hospital administrators were more likely to be on the burnout spectrum than the VA's physicians. (So were wage-grade employees in areas like food service and housekeeping.) As I mentioned in the previous chapter, the administrators were much more likely to exhibit the frustrated burnout profile, indicating a high sense of ineffectiveness, than their clinical colleagues.[58] They don't look like heroic life-savers, but they are caught in the same crummy corporate system, subject to the same burnout culture.

The changing climate of work in the postindustrial era fosters dismal "weather" conditions in our workplaces, but two people working in the same conditions will not necessarily both burn out, just as different people can have different experiences of the same rain shower. One may have brought an umbrella. Another may have allergies that flare up when it's wet out. And someone else may just love a rainy day. Though economic forces contributed a great deal to burnout culture, our psychological character does affect our likelihood of burning out. For instance, burnout correlates with the personality trait psychologists call neuroticism. That is, people whose moods fluctuate and who are prone to anxiety (like the author of this book) are more susceptible to burnout. And Type-A go-getters are especially prone to exhaustion.[59]

There are demographic patterns to burnout, but they are not all what you might expect. For example, you might think that, because stress seems to accumulate over time, older workers are more likely to be on the burnout spectrum than younger ones. When I was teaching full-time, I didn't think much about burnout, but I connected the term with aging; the burnouts were the fossils, faculty who had petrified over many decades, buried under thousands of exams and papers. But in fact, across industries, burnout is more prevalent among early-career workers. Younger physicians are more likely to have burnout symptoms than older ones.[60] And burnout is a likely factor in the high turnover rate among early-career teachers.[61] This is a longstanding phenomenon. Christina Maslach observed in 1982 that early-career social-service workers exhibited higher levels of burnout than their older colleagues.[62]

Given the role ideals play in burnout, it makes sense that younger workers would be especially susceptible to it. In your early years in a job, especially a job to which you bring a sense of calling, your ideals are likely to be at their highest. And then the reality of the work hits you, like it hit the medical residents Sumner Abraham talked about. If you experience something like they did, then every day is a struggle to hold onto ideal and reality, and you are pulled taut across the growing space between them. If you can't hang on, then you might quit and seek a line of work where you will find greater alignment between these two poles. The people who remain after the initial trial are the ones who, for whatever reason, managed to keep a firm grip. Maybe they had lower ideals to begin with. Or they are lucky enough to have slightly better conditions at work. Or they have a rare quality of resiliency. In any case, they are, in Maslach's words, "the survivors."[63]

Beyond one's resiliency or age, the pervasive injustices of American social life—racism, sexism, and homophobia among them—may also aggravate burnout. It stands to reason that people with marginalized identities would carry additional stress into their workplaces. Likewise, we would expect discrimination to exacerbate other pressures people face on the job. Some prominent studies do indeed show that women experience burnout at higher rates than men in the same profession. Among physicians, for instance, women have a 30 percent greater likelihood of exhibiting high levels of either exhaustion or cynicism.[64] A probable reason is that female doctors face more discrimination, abuse, and harassment from patients and colleagues than their male counterparts do. In one study, medical residents who reported undergoing such mistreatment were more than twice as likely to show symptoms of burnout, and women were much more likely than men to say they had been mistreated.[65] In addition, gender disparities in burnout may result from the "second shift" of childcare and household maintenance women workers must often take on at home.[66] The link between burnout and gender is not definitive, though. Many studies show no burnout disparity between men and women, and we cannot make good comparisons in professions that are dominated by a single gender.[67] Researchers have also found that women typically score higher than men on the Maslach Burnout Inventory's exhaustion component, while men score higher on depersonalization.[68] These differences lead some researchers to wonder if women appear to undergo burnout more often because the MBI is more sensitive at detecting exhaustion.[69]

Regardless of possible gender differences in burnout prevalence, women's experience with work is a leading indicator of how burnout has expanded throughout the workforce since the 1970s. Workplaces across the world have been "feminized" in recent decades, which means, in one sense, that many more women are working for pay outside the home. It also means that in the postindustrial era, more work resembles traditional "women's work"—the interpersonal and office jobs that come with a heavy burden of care and emotional labor. In an often-sexist society, that means more workers (men included) receive the diminished respect typical of those "female"-coded jobs. The economist Guy Standing sees this as an ironic outcome of "generations of efforts to integrate women into regular wage labor as equals." Women gained much greater opportunity in the workplace, but a major reason was that men began to exhibit "the type of employment and labor force participation patterns associated with women."[70] That is, all workers experience conditions similar to those that women faced in the mid-twentieth century temp sector. The paradigmatic temp was a young, eager

"Kelly Girl" who (allegedly) didn't need a living wage or even want more permanent employment. The liability model of employment and the fissured workplace, which together bear so much responsibility for the climate of postindustrial work, ultimately rely on a gendered view of labor: men, as breadwinners, deserve stable, well-paid jobs with opportunities for advancement, while women, whose paid labor is no more than a bonus for the family income, do not. There is also a racial component to this view, as black women in the United States traditionally had high rates of employment, often bringing home much-needed wages as domestic workers in white households.[71] Once temporary female labor became a norm in managers' eyes, male labor became a pricy liability, and companies began cutting permanent jobs and contracting out everything else, feminizing the status of many male workers just as more women were entering the workforce. In the words of the journalist Bryce Covert, "We're all women workers now, and we're all suffering for it."[72]

The story of burnout and race is equally complex. Inadequate rewards for work contribute to burnout, and black and Hispanic workers in the United States make significantly less money than white and Asian American ones do.[73] The racial wage gap also intersects with the gender wage gap, so that black women, on average, make less than equally-qualified members of any other demographic group.[74] In addition, as the poetry professor Tiana Clark writes in her essay on black burnout, workers of color can feel that their every action gets added scrutiny. "Setting boundaries while black can cost you your job or your life," Clark writes. "If I don't answer an email or attend a department meeting at my university, I might suffer different consequences than my white, male millennial counterparts."[75] Racial disparities that add stress in the broader society appear at work in subtle and insidious ways, particularly when they intersect with gender disparities, according to Clark. She has to manage not only herself, but the emotions and reactions of the white people around her, all while she tries to demonstrate an indefatigable competence not expected of others.

Addressing the role of race in burnout takes us to the limits of current research, however, and clear answers are hard to come by. Very few studies consider the relationship between burnout and race. The ones that do consider it have produced inconsistent findings and show no greater prevalence or intensity of burnout among black workers, compared with white workers in the United States.[76] These studies suggest that working conditions and personal coping methods play a bigger role than race in burnout. In one study, black mental-illness case managers exhibited less emotional exhaustion and depersonalization than their white peers; in another, black childcare workers had higher scores on depersonalization than white ones did.[77] The study of childcare workers, though, found that coping strategies were more strongly correlated with all three burnout dimensions than race was. Workers of any race who used an avoidant strategy for dealing with stress—like denial or disengagement—were the most likely to burn out.[78] Researchers have made similar findings in blue-collar workplaces. A study of bus drivers and train operators in San Francisco's Muni transit system, relying on data from the 1990s, found no statistical correlation between burnout and race within its racially diverse workforce.[79] The researchers instead found that drivers had higher burnout scores if they had also reported on-the-job problems—anything from unfair treatment to trouble with passengers to getting into an accident—or ergonomic problems like an uncomfortable seat or vibration on the vehicle.[80]

Psychologists and other researchers need to focus more on the question of burnout and race, including its intersection with other identity categories. Throughout US history and up to the present day, workers of color have disproportionately held undervalued jobs and have often been locked out of labor protections that would improve their working conditions.[81] It's hard to imagine that this history and present reality have *no* effect on burnout. At the same time, we need to bear in mind that burnout is not the same thing as oppression, nor is it simply an index of how bad your job is. It's an experience of conditions that depart significantly from ideals about work, ideals that are themselves implicated in societal injustice. Until we have a deeper pool of research on this topic, commenters can only offer informed speculation about why the existing literature does not show a significant link between burnout and race. It may be that the long experience of discrimination has led workers from some racial groups, on average, to expect less from work than others. The political scientist Davin Phoenix writes, "For many African Americans, the image of people working long hours and barely scraping by while an elite class thrives off their effort represents not a departure from a satisfactory norm to which they feel entitled. On the contrary, this image represents the *norm* itself."[82] Because burnout is partly a matter of expectations, such tempered hopes may mitigate the specific risk of burnout while workers suffer other forms of injustice.

It is also possible that burnout surveys falsely assume that people of different races experience or report burnout symptoms the same way. That possibility reflects an explanation for lower reported rates of depression and anxiety among African Americans, compared with white Americans.[83] It could be that white people exhibit higher rates of mental illness because the ways researchers measure mental illness are biased toward the ways white people express themselves. Along the same lines, people of different cultural backgrounds may experience stress differently; after all, stress is itself a cultural phenomenon as well as a biological one. So we have to consider the possibility that researchers wrote surveys like the Maslach Burnout Inventory in a way that make them more likely to discover white people's burnout. As Tiana Clark claims, black burnout may be different; our measures of burnout may need to change, so we can better see it.

. . .

Looking again at the six areas of their jobs where people most often experience the strain that causes burnout, I see language that's familiar from my years of studying and teaching ethics. Workload and reward represent what you put into work and what you get in return. The relation between them is a question of justice, of getting what you deserve. Fairness is also about justice. Autonomy is indispensable to moral responsibility and action. Community is the human context for our ethical actions and the source of our moral norms. And values inform all aspects of our moral lives.

Justice, autonomy, community, values: these are the basic components of ethics. And when they are damaged or absent in a workplace, employees are likely to feel drawn across a widening gap between their ideals and the reality of their jobs. They're more likely to become exhausted and cynical and lose their sense of accomplishment. This means burnout is fundamentally a failure of how we treat each other; it's a failure of ethics, the norms of action within our culture. People burn out because, in our organizations, we do not afford them the conditions they desire or deserve.

And while burned-out workers are victims of this moral failure, they also compound it when they are unable to perform their best. I could not be the teacher my students deserved. Worn-out and despondent doctors cannot provide the best possible care to their patients. Anyone whose burnout leads to cynicism is likely treating coworkers and clients as less than full persons. Workers themselves are not the only ones unjustly harmed by low-quality jobs.

Still, better conditions do not always mean less risk of burnout. Think again about physicians. They enjoy high salaries and great public respect, yet they still score significantly higher on burnout measures than the general population. It's true that medical work has become more time-intensive in recent decades, but the problem is not that doctors work in objectively poor conditions. The problem is that those conditions do not align with their ideals. Danielle Ofri points to her colleagues' dedication to patient care, their willingness to "do the right thing for their patients, even at a high personal cost," as the ideal that animates all work in the hospital. And in an era of increasingly corporate management of health care, "It is this very ethic that is being exploited every day to keep the enterprise afloat."[84]

Working conditions are only one side of the gap we stretch across that leads us to burn out. On the other side are our ideals. They, too, are a matter of ethics, since ideals are what motivate us to seek the good life through our work. Because these ideals are broadly shared, they are also an aspect of our culture. And during the five decades in which working conditions have gotten worse, our ideals for work have only risen higher.

5   *Work Saints and Work Martyrs*

The Problem with Our Ideals

The rich are irrational when it comes to work. Out of everyone in our society, they have the least need to earn more money, but they work the most. Billionaire tech-industry titans brag about their hundred-hour workweeks, even though *their* labor isn't what boosts their companies' stock prices and enriches them further. Americans with advanced degrees have the highest average earning power but typically work more and spend less time on leisure than people with less formal education. The children of rich parents are twice as likely to have summer jobs as poor kids are. And many older American professionals with plenty of money saved for retirement keep showing up at the office.[1]

Meanwhile, the miseries of having too little work are not just material but psychological. For white working-class men, being without a steady job means falling short of the standard of honorable manhood. As a result, depression, addiction, and suicide are now worryingly common among white men without college educations.[2] And even though teaching played a leading role in my burnout, I felt so aimless without it that, less than two years after quitting my full-time academic job, I became a part-time adjunct instructor making just a few thousand dollars per course, a fraction of what I had made before.

All of this is evidence that we don't only work for the money. Many people—volunteers, parents, and starving artists among them—don't get paid at all for their labor. Even workers who aren't rich, who really do need every cent of their paycheck, often say there's more than money at stake. They're doing their jobs for love, or service, or to contribute to a collective effort. They work not just for a material good, but for an ideal.

The worsening labor conditions I surveyed in the last chapter, including more emotional intensity and less security than work featured in the mid-twentieth century, only tell half the story of why we live in a burnout culture. Our shared ideals about work tell the other half. Some of these ideals predate the industrial era, but they have grown higher in recent decades. As a result, the gap between our ideals for work and the reality of our jobs is greater now than it was in the past. That's why burnout is characteristic of our age, even though work is physically much safer than it was during the industrial era. Textile mill workers in Manchester, England, or Lowell, Massachusetts two centuries ago worked for longer hours than the typical British or American worker today, and they did so in dangerous conditions.[3] They were not more burned-out than we are now, however, because they did not believe their work was the path to self-actualization. That isn't to say they weren't exhausted. But they did not have the twenty-first century disorder we call burnout, because they did not have twenty-first century ideas about work.

The ideal that motivates Americans to work to the point of exhaustion today is the promise that if you work hard, you will live a good life: not just a life of material comfort, but a life of social dignity, moral character, and spiritual purpose. We work because we hope it will help us flourish in every sense. I mentioned in the introduction how I wanted to be a professor because my own college professors seemed to be living the good life. They were respected, they seemed to be people of good judgment, and their work had the clear and noble purpose of gaining knowledge and passing it on to others. I knew virtually nothing of their lives outside the classroom, or the private demons they battled. Two of my mentors were eventually denied tenure and had to find new jobs. A third died of a heart attack a few years after taking on a major administrative role. I made no connection between their misfortune and my own career prospects. How could I? I was blinded by my trust in the American promise: if I got the right kind of job, then success and happiness would surely follow.

This promise, however, is mostly false. It's what the philosopher Plato called a "noble lie," a myth that justifies the fundamental arrangement of society.[4] Plato taught that if people don't believe the lie, then society will fall into chaos. Our particular noble lie gets us to believe in the value of hard work. We labor for our bosses' profit but convince ourselves we're attaining the highest good. If burnout is the experience of stretching between two stilts that are falling away from each other—our ideals for work and the reality of our jobs—then we come into our jobs already holding one of them: our ideals. We hope the job will deliver on its promise, but that very hope gets us into the conditions that will eventually burn us out. Hope gets us to put in the extra hours, take on the extra project, and live with the lack of a raise or the recognition we need. Ironically, believing in the ideal of a good life earned through hard work is the biggest obstacle to attaining what it promises.

Hard work is arguably what American society values most. In a Pew Research Center poll conducted in 2014 that asked people about their personalities, 80 percent of respondents described themselves as "hardworking." No other trait drew such a strong positive response, not even "sympathetic" or "accepting of others." Only 3 percent said they were lazy, and a statistically insignificant number identified strongly as lazy.[5] These numbers say more about what we value than what we're actually like. That is, we all know that more than a few of us are genuinely lazy. Think about your coworkers. How many of them are slackers? And how many of them would say they're anything but? Americans do work hard, by and large, but we aren't *all* laboring diligently all day, straining over our reports and sweating through meetings with clients. Rather, we Americans say we're hardworking because we know we're supposed to think of ourselves that way. It's how we esteem ourselves and others. The value we place on hard work doesn't lead everyone actually to work hard, but it does lead many people to work harder than their bodies and minds can bear. It makes our labor profitable. It also creates millions of burnouts.

. . .

The noble lie about work as the source of dignity, character, and purpose has grown during its four-hundred-year history in America. The goods it promises have multiplied and become more abstract, to the point where, now, we expect something as lofty as *fulfillment* from our jobs. The only good that work promised at first was much more concrete and crucial: survival. In fact, the noble lie began as less a promise than a threat. Soon after Captain John Smith took command of the diseased and dying Jamestown settlement in 1608, he issued a decree that would become the foundation of the American work ideal: "He that gathereth not every day as much as I do, the next day shall be set beyond the river, and be banished from the Fort as a drone, until he amend his conditions or starve."[6]

Smith's pronouncement took away any middle ground between workers and worthless people, or the deserving and the undeserving, or members of society and rightful outcasts. American political leaders still make this distinction when they set society's "makers" against its "takers." The same dichotomy is built into the ideal of "full employment," which the political left and right valorize equally.[7] It's the basis for arguments that people should have to work if they're going to receive social-welfare benefits, and it grounds proposals for a universal job guarantee.[8]

Smith's threat, borrowed from Paul's second letter to the Thessalonians—"Anyone unwilling to work should not eat"[9]—is a counterpart to the promise that having a job is the sole pathway to dignity. Dignity, as the sociologist Allison Pugh defines it, is "our capacity to stand as fully recognized participants in our social world."[10] Dignity is social citizenship. In America today, if you have a job, then others will acknowledge you as someone who contributes to society and thus deserves a say in how it operates. Think about the passerby who shouts "Get a job!" at people protesting social injustice. It's as if the First Amendment right to free speech only applies to people who work, as if paid employment was the sole ticket to complain about society or to claim its benefits. Of course, hard work was historically the path to dignity only for white men. White women worked in the home for centuries before they won property and voting rights. Millions of African American women and men labored in slavery, and then still were denied social citizenship after they could legally earn a wage. The promise is noble: through work, anyone can earn the right to count in American society. Yet racism and sexism make it often a lie.

The second promise of work is that it builds character. This claim is a staple of parental wisdom. By mowing lawns, babysitting, or taking fast-food orders, the story goes, shiftless children become upright adults. The idea behind it is that any action we perform over and over changes us. We develop habits, and our collected habits, good and bad, make up our character. "We are what we repeatedly do," Will Durant wrote, summarizing Aristotle's moral philosophy. "Excellence, then, is not an act, but a habit."[11] In this view, the good life is about developing virtues like courage and temperance. If a teenager can just put her phone away long enough to apply for minimum-wage work, then by showing up and performing her job duties, she'll learn punctuality, responsibility, and grit—all essential traits for leading a moral life. This second component of the work ideal, a step beyond simple dignity, became prominent in the 1820s United States, when factory owners simultaneously imposed stricter work discipline and fretted about their employees' whiskey consumption, which they linked to a host of moral failings. So the bosses banned drinking on the job.[12] The virtue of temperance, they believed, would make better workers, and work, in turn, would make better men.

Work's third and highest promise is that it is a pathway to purpose. The great prophet of purposeful work is Apple cofounder Steve Jobs, who said in a 1985 interview that his company needed to grow fast, but not because of "the dollar goal, which is meaningless to us." Apple, he explained, was aiming higher: "At Apple, people are putting in 18-hour days. We attract a different type of person. . . . Someone who really wants to get in a little over his head and make a little dent in the universe. . . . I think we have that opportunity now. And no, we don't know where it will lead. We just know there's something much bigger than any of us here."[13] Of course, Apple eventually far surpassed the modest market value goal Jobs set for it in 1985. In 2011, shortly before his death, it became the most valuable publicly traded company in the world. But that's "meaningless."

Jobs's secular language of self-transcendence resonates with ancient and modern arguments that justify hard work on spiritual grounds. The noble lie of Plato's *Republic* was that the gods had implanted metals in the souls of the people, ordaining each one to a social position from which they must not deviate.[14] The Bible's first pages are filled with language that lends significance to human work. God creates human beings to tend the garden. When they disobey him, he divides labor between the sexes and condemns them to a life of difficult toil. And in the Protestant Reformation, John Calvin and Martin Luther developed the modern concept of vocation to explain how one's work as a farmer or merchant was implicated in God's providential design for human society.[15] Work, according to this theology, would not save your soul, but it would carry out a divine command. Today, the language of "purpose" signals that work does not just satisfy the mundane need for a paycheck or health insurance. It means that work is about, vaguely, more.

Work's transformation into a spiritual enterprise—the site of our aspirations to transcend ourselves, to encounter a higher reality, to be fulfilled—is the highest step in the work ideal, but any worker in the present-day economy supposedly can attain it. That is a significant change from the industrial-age vision of work; it was only when people started doing more abstract and human-service work that a job became, for most workers, a path to transcendence. In the 1960s and 70s, feminists made the right to pursue meaning a major pillar in their arguments for women's greater access to paid labor. Betty Friedan writes in her landmark 1963 book, *The Feminine Mystique,* that her era's "identity crisis—for women, and increasingly, for men" stemmed from the wealth and abundance of postwar society. Technology had solved the problem of material productivity, and so work had to become a way to attain something immaterial. "[T]he human significance of work," she writes, is "not merely as the means of biological survival, but as the giver of self and the transcender of self, as the creator of human identity and human evolution."[16]

Today, the language of self-fulfillment even appears in rhetoric around low-pay, low-status work. "Vocation" remains a common catchall term for work in Christian circles, sacralizing every position in the business hierarchy. And "love" supposedly gives purpose to labor across industries.[17] The Wegmans grocery store chain has used the phrase "Do What You Love" in ads inviting applications for work stocking shelves and ringing up groceries. To be fair, Wegmans is consistently rated as one of America's best companies to work for.[18] Still, when work is love, or a means to salvation, why should workers care about the conditions in which they do it? To work for an ideal is its own reward.

. . .

According to the American work ethos, dignity, character, and purpose are all available to workers if only they *engage* with their jobs. Employee engagement is also supposedly good for the bottom line. If profit is the Holy Grail of American business, then engaged employees are Sir Galahad—tireless, devoted, and pure of heart. Gallup, which surveys workers on engagement, describes them in heroic, even saintly terms:

> Engaged employees are the best colleagues. They cooperate to build an organization, institution, or agency, and they are behind everything good that happens there. These employees are involved in, enthusiastic about, and committed to their work. They know the scope of their jobs and look for new and better ways to achieve outcomes. They are 100% psychologically committed to their work. And, they are the only people in an organization who create new customers.[19]

One hundred percent psychologically committed to their work. Who is like that? If we believe Gallup, about a third of US workers are.[20] Most of us are not customer-creating maniacs, a fact that leads business commenters to report these figures with brows furrowed, lamenting that "only" a third of workers are enthusiastic about their jobs, that 15 percent or so are actively disengaged, and that most are "unengaged" and just don't care either way.[21] To managers and consultants who accept Gallup's findings, the two-thirds of workers who are not engaged are a serious problem. One business writer claims that disengaged employees cost employers an additional 34 percent of their salary through absenteeism and lost productivity.[22] Another describes them as "silent killers."[23] Gallup warns that unproductive, complacent workers might even be lurking, unnoticed, in upper management. The actively disengaged will even destroy others' time and accomplishments. "Whatever the engaged do," Gallup asserts, "the actively disengaged try to undo."[24] In short, they are villains, bent on undermining our heroes' mission.

Such rhetoric is not just laughably absurd; it's also inhumane. The fact is, American workers are more engaged than those in every other rich country, by Gallup's own measure. Their level of engagement may indeed approach the human limit. Or their high reported rate of engagement may be nothing more than a sign that American workers know they are supposed to say they are engaged at work, just as they know they are supposed to tell pollsters they're hardworking. In Norway, the engagement rate is half the level it is in the United States, and yet Norwegians are among the richest and happiest populations on earth. Syrians are among the poorest, but civil war, and not their country's 0 percent employee engagement rate in 2013, is largely to blame.[25]

As I learned firsthand, engagement with work can ruin your life. In the wrong conditions—which is to say, in the typical conditions of American workplaces—culturally-enforced enthusiasm for work causes burnout. That's why I do not call the absence of burnout symptoms "engaged," as Christina Maslach does. A worker who is unengaged with work is not necessarily on the burnout spectrum. She might simply have found a way to keep her ideals for work in line with the reality of her job, possibly by keeping her expectations for work relatively low. If she is only 80 percent psychologically committed to the job but is nevertheless reasonably competent, then what's the problem? The exhaustion that burned-out workers feel, their inability to face another day at work, or in my case, to grade another paper or prepare for class, results from having already committed too much to the job. It comes from workers making their work personal and coming up against the fact that their employers' priorities are impersonal.

To be sure, engagement with work really does fulfill some people. Some of my friends who are doctors, editors, and even professors work hard, love their jobs, and flourish. Some professions, such as surgery, seem to promote flourishing more than others. Although all physicians are prone to burnout, surgeons receive not only some of the highest salaries of any workers but also high job satisfaction and high levels of meaning.[26] Surgeons do important and difficult work and can point to people whose lives they saved. When they step back and think about what they do, surgeons *ought* to feel good about their work.

Engagement is not about stepping back, though. It's about immersion. In the minute acts of performing a procedure, surgeons do work that lends itself to the experience of "flow," the loss of self-consciousness in an activity that is challenging but that offers regular, progressive feedback and rewards. As psychologist Mihaly Csikszentmihalyi describes them, people in flow states shut out the world and their own bodily needs, forgoing food and sleep as they do something that seems good for its own sake. It's a state of engagement that computer game designers try to foster, because it makes the game hard to quit. "Just one more turn" or "one more level" often leads to finding oneself unblinking at 3:00 a.m., with a half-eaten bag of Doritos close at hand.

In a state of flow, you cannot tell the surgeon from the surgery. Although games are meant to induce flow, Csikszentmihalyi thinks it occurs most readily at work, which has "built-in goals, feedback, rules, and challenges, all of which encourage one to become involved in one's work, to concentrate and lose oneself in it."[27] Exemplary workers he studied—among them a farmer, a welder, and a cook—became "lost in the interaction so that their selves could emerge stronger afterward. Thus transformed, work becomes enjoyable, and as the result of a personal investment of psychic energy, it feels as if it were freely chosen, as well."[28]

Csikszentmihalyi thinks flow is the key to happiness. As he and his coauthor Jeanne Nakamura put it, "Viewed through the experiential lens of flow, *a good life is one that is characterized by complete absorption in what one does.*"[29] I know what flow feels like. I felt it sometimes while working on this book. Figuring out how to improve a sentence, and recognizing that I've actually made it better, and then doing the same to the next sentence, and the next— that's what Csikszentmihalyi's talking about. An honest and challenging classroom conversation among people committed to learning: same thing.

The ideal of flow is tantalizingly universal; you don't have to be a surgeon or professor to attain it. Csikszentmihalyi points to a welder named Joe Kramer as an example of the "autotelic" personality— that is, someone who readily gets into a flow state at work, which then becomes an end in itself. Though Joe only had a fourth-grade education, he could fix anything in the railroad-car plant where he worked. Joe personally identified with broken equipment— he empathized with it—in order to repair it. Because Joe made the tasks of his job into an autotelic experience, his life was "more enjoyable than that of people who resign themselves to life within the constraints of the barren reality they feel they cannot alter," Csikszentmihalyi claims.[30] All his coworkers agreed that Joe was irreplaceable. Despite his rare talent, Joe refused promotions. His boss claimed the plant would top the industry if he just had a few more guys like Joe.[31]

The promise of greater productivity without greater cost: *that's* why engagement and flow are such appealing concepts to management in the postindustrial age. Employees are a liability, according to current business doctrine. Hiring another one is risky. So why not see if you can get a little more effort out of the ones you already have? And why not convince them, through surveys and workshops and airport-bookstore bestsellers, that if they commit themselves totally to their jobs, they will be happy? More than that, they will, like Joe Kramer, be numbered among the blessed, the communion of work saints.

. . .

It is hard for any worker to know for sure if they have the value Joe had to his employer. In the neoliberal era, good workers can be let go with little warning, if management's favor turns against them. (Hence the need to make yourself into a "company of one," dependent on no single employer.) The system that gives esteem to engaged employees also creates anxiety that employees try to quell through working more intensively. Even workers with lifetime job security, like tenured college professors, absorb the anxiety of America's insecure labor environment and find reasons to fret over their status. We keep going back to work for validation of our worth, but the cure is also poison. To calm our anxiety, we work too much without adequate reward, without autonomy, without fairness, without human connections, and in conflict with our values. We reach to hold onto our ideals while we're stuck in these conditions. We become exhausted, cynical, and ineffective. We work in pursuit of the good life, but paradoxically, our jobs make us even worse off.

Anxiety is built into capitalism. That's a key premise in Max Weber's 1905 book, *The Protestant Ethic and the Spirit of Capitalism*, which still perfectly captures the mindset that sustains our work ethic today. Weber shows how European Protestants created a mode of thinking about money, work, and dignity that we now cannot escape. The fact that European and North American societies are more secular now is irrelevant. Protestant ways of thinking are still with us; even atheists exhibit them. Without meaning to, our Protestant forebears built, for themselves and for us, an intellectual "iron cage."[32]

Weber saw capitalism as "a monstrous cosmos."[33] He meant it as a compliment. In his view, capitalism is an all-encompassing economic and moral system, one of humanity's most marvelous constructions. We who live in the system can rarely see it. We take its norms for granted, like the air we breathe. And yet capitalism "determines, with overwhelming coercion, the style of life *not only* of those directly involved in business but of every individual who is born into this mechanism."[34] Everything you do, from going to the "right" preschool to laboring in a productive career to receiving medical care on your deathbed, you do because somewhere, someone thinks they can make money from it. Regardless of how you participate in the capitalist cosmos, it imposes a choice on you: adopt its ethic, or accept poverty and scorn.

As an academic, Weber was not involved in industrial commerce. But he was nevertheless as caught in the iron cage as any businessman. Prior to writing *The Protestant Ethic,* he spent five years dealing with nervous exhaustion: neurasthenia. He went through several cycles of intense teaching and research, followed by physical and mental collapse, treatments, and leaves of absence to restore him. Then he would go back to work, and inevitably his condition would deteriorate, leading him to shed his responsibilities and seek treatment again. His wife Marianne later wrote that during this time he was "a chained titan whom evil, envious gods were plaguing."[35] He was irritable and depressed and felt useless; any work, even reading a student's paper, became an unbearable burden.[36] He ultimately took a two-year leave of absence from his university, after which he resigned and became an adjunct professor, loosely attached to academia, at age thirty-nine.[37] I'm no Weber, but I take personal encouragement from his story. His professional collapse was not the last word. After he quit his job, he undertook his most influential work.

The Protestant ethic is basically a psychological trick that believers play on themselves to cope with religious anxiety. The ethic, as Weber argues, derives from the theology of John Calvin, the sixteenth century Christian reformer noted for his doctrine of predestination. Predestination means God chooses, or "elects," some people for salvation, with the rest destined for eternal death. God does this both unconditionally and outside of the ordinary passage of time. He doesn't change his mind about someone's ultimate fate, because God is perfect, and to change would imply imperfection. Only God knows who has been chosen for salvation and who hasn't, but humans understandably want to find out. Good works, in Calvinist theology, cannot *earn* you salvation—it's impossible to do anything to deserve God's favor— but they can be *signs* of election. That is, God's elect will perform good works as an outgrowth of their blessed status. So if you are curious about your election, examine your actions. Are they saintly? Or sinful?

To find out, a Calvinist should think about whether his or her actions contribute to a prosperous society. God cares about the world he created (a belief known as providence), but instead of directly intervening in world affairs, God ordains people to different "callings" to carry out his will for humanity. Human workers are God's hands, and so, as Weber puts it, "labor in the service of this social usefulness furthers the divine glory and is willed by God."[38] To gain assurance of your election, then, you need to know you are being productive, enriching yourself and your community through labor in your calling.

Secular, twenty-first-century residents of wealthy countries don't worry much about whether we're God's elect. But we're still trapped in the Calvinist cage. We are anxious to demonstrate to potential employers, and to ourselves, that we are talented, are autotelic personalities, are work saints. Like divine election, this type of status is an abstract condition that we cannot assign to ourselves, but we hope others will recognize we have it and thereby keep us employed.[39] When our status anxiety wells up, we reach back into our culture's religious heritage for a balm: hard, disciplined work. For example, Tristen Lee, a millennial-generation British public-relations worker, tells a too-familiar story of how long hours, lack of sleep, no real time off, and excessive rent keep her in the grind. "I throw my absolute heart and soul into" work, she writes. "I am so obsessed with reaching some notable level of success and hitting my financial targets, that I've forgotten how to actually enjoy life." She echoes Anne Helen Petersen's self-diagnosis of "errand fatigue": "even menial, low-reward tasks like going to the bank or returning clothes start to feel impossible."[40]

Lee says she feels like she has "something to prove—but to who?" To herself, Weber would say. Lee's experience is the twenty-first-century echo of sixteenth-century Calvinist theology. She has internalized the all-seeing judgment of a society that values her only insofar as she works, so she feels a need to assure herself of her worth. But there can never be enough assurance; in the present-day work ideology, your accomplishments matter less than your constant effort toward the *next* accomplishment.

"What is the end result?" Lee asks. "When does the constant agonising stop? At what point do we reach satisfaction in life and think 'f*** yeah, I'm really proud of what I've achieved and how far I've come'?"[41] Well, never. That's what it means to be in an iron cage.

. . .

Four decades after Weber published *The Protestant Ethic and the Spirit of Capitalism,* his homeland, destroyed by war, began a natural experiment in political economy, as it attempted to rebuild itself as two separate countries under rival economic systems. But in the eyes of the German philosopher Josef Pieper, capitalism and communism shared a common moral failure. They both created a condition he called "total work."[42] Pieper feared that if Europeans did not resist it, total work would take over the new culture of the continent. "There is no doubt of one thing," he wrote in his 1948 book *Leisure, the Basis of Culture.* "[T]he world of the 'worker' is taking shape with dynamic force—with such a velocity that, rightly or wrongly, one is tempted to speak of demonic force in history."[43]

The demon turns human values upside-down. It makes it so we no longer work in order to live, but rather live in order to work. It convinces us that work is our highest activity, that the only value is *use* value, the kind accountants track in their ledgers. The demon gets us to think of ourselves as functionaries, beings who define themselves solely by the actions they perform on the job. Possessed by the demon, we devalue anything that doesn't have an obvious use, from poetry to worship. "Is there a sphere of human activity, one might even say of human existence," Pieper asks, "that does not need to be justified by inclusion in a five-year plan and its technical organization? Is there such a thing, or not?"[44] The demon makes us answer no, and as a result, we rob ourselves of our full humanity.

The demon lives in twenty-first-century society, too. You can tell by our language. We have no words for praiseworthy activity that isn't labor. We call parenthood "the hardest job in the world."[45] We think of education almost entirely in terms of work. A friend of mine reports receiving a letter from his first-grader's school that stated, "It is important that we start on time. We are training our children for the work force."[46] Another friend tells me that her kindergartner's teachers lead the kids in a call-and-response chant every day at lunchtime: "Hard work . . . pays off!" The top reason college students give for pursuing a degree is "to be able to get a better job."[47] We say marriage is hard work. Even death is a labor. Steve Jobs's sister said in a eulogy that in his final hours, Jobs's breathing "became severe, deliberate, purposeful. . . . This is what I learned: he was working at this, too. Death didn't happen to Steve, he achieved it."[48]

With every aspect of life transformed into work, we who live in the total work society are suspicious of anything that comes easily. We believe we have to earn everything through toil—not just money, but insight and pleasure. Even, in the case of Steve Jobs, death. In Pieper's words, the person who values only work "refuses to have anything as a gift."[49] Unproductive time is a waste. We justify time off as "self-care," which sounds like resistance to total work but which we often frame as a way to stay strong enough to carry a heavy workload. As Pieper writes, "A break in one's work, whether of an hour, a day or a week, is still part of the world of work. It is a link in the chain of utilitarian functions."[50] The "fun" workplaces of stereotypical tech startups, with their game rooms and napping pods, are not really designed for leisure. They're designed to keep you at work forever.

This relentless commitment to our jobs doesn't only add to our workload. The habits we form at work also narrow the range of human abilities we can exercise, undermining the moral growth work allegedly fosters. Adam Smith observed that labor in eighteenth-century factories really did turn people into functionaries. In the first pages of his book *The Wealth of Nations* he marvels at the productivity of a pin factory where each of the workers on the line performed just one action over and over, all day long.[51] But Smith also recognizes that those actions, repeated long enough, become character, often bad character:

> The man whose whole life is spent in performing a few simple operations . . . has no occasion to exert his understanding. . . . He naturally loses, therefore, the habit of such exertion, and generally becomes as stupid and ignorant as it is possible for a human creature to become. . . . His dexterity at his own particular trade seems, in this manner, to be acquired at the expense of his intellectual, social, and martial virtues.[52]

Things aren't so different for the "knowledge worker" of today. Prestigious consulting and finance companies expect their young employees to put in long hours.[53] At first, they can manage to work effectively on an eighty-hour-a-week schedule. But after a few years, their bodies and minds begin to suffer, according to Alexandra Michel, a scholar of business culture. "Technical skill, the ability to do math, remains unaffected," Michel says. "But creativity, judgment, ethical sensitivity, those decline."[54]

Michel's research highlights how burnout is a moral problem; when we pursue the wrong ideals in the wrong conditions at work, we damage human capacities like empathy that we need in our ethical lives. Pieper believed that as our abilities narrowed, so did the range of our desires. The functionary, he writes, "is naturally inclined to find complete satisfaction in his 'service' and thereby achieves the illusion of a life fulfilled, which he acknowledges and willingly accepts."[55] Total work occupies not only our time but our psyches, too. We have no way to understand ourselves, and no way to express our humanity, except through our jobs. Even before we burn out, we lose much of our identity and our ability to live a good life.

· · ·

One of the most zealous proponents of the Protestant ethic—and thus of American work ideals—was the educator Booker T. Washington. His life and teaching exhibit the opportunities and perils that face anyone who embraces that ethic, including ourselves. Born into slavery in 1856, Washington developed a single-minded focus on industrial education and hard work that led him to found the Tuskegee Institute, an industrial school in Alabama for black students, and become an internationally-known figure by the turn of the twentieth century. Like a Silicon Valley CEO would today, Washington preached the secular gospel of work everywhere he went, arguing that only diligent, skilled labor would enable the victims of racial injustice to improve their condition. He also practiced what he preached; his personal example demonstrated the tragic way anxiety fuels our total work mentality to the point of self-abnegation.

The heart of Washington's philosophy was a "law" he expresses repeatedly in his 1901 book *Up from Slavery:* "there is something in human nature which always makes an individual recognize and reward merit, no matter under what colour of skin merit is found."[56] According to this law, you earn merit through hard work that serves a community's material needs. Ultimately, your good work can make you indispensable, like Joe Kramer in his rail-car plant.[57] After all, no rational employer would fire a valuable employee, right? Because the fruits of skilled labor do not have a race, Washington believed that learning a trade was the best way blacks could become full citizens of the post-Reconstruction South. So he set up a brickyard and a wagon-making shop on Tuskegee's campus, which were operated by his students, who then sold the finished products to their neighbors. Racial tensions abated, Washington claimed, through fair commerce between Tuskegee's black artisans and their white clients. In these exchanges, the school made money, its white neighbors got good bricks and wagons, and the students earned work's ultimate prize: self-reliance through doing "something which the world wants done."[58]

But there is a contradiction in Washington's ideal of self-reliance. If your reward comes from doing something others want done, then you aren't self-reliant at all. You depend on the whimsical tastes of the market. When they shift, your livelihood can collapse. Your dignity, your confidence in your own worth, is in another person's hands. It isn't enough to do good work. You also have to attend to the nagging worry: Will they like it? And when you perform interpersonal labor like most of us do in the postindustrial age, then your product is yourself, and your worry becomes: Will they like *me*?

Washington worried constantly, especially in Tuskegee's early years. Ostensibly, he was anxious about money, but keeping the school financially solvent meant much more. "I knew that if we failed it would injure the whole race," he writes. "I knew that the presumption was against us." He struggled to sleep at night. The stress felt like "a burden which pressed down on us . . . at the rate of a thousand pounds to the square inch."[59] So Washington traveled constantly to raise money from Boston Brahmins and wealthy industrialists, both to attain his goals for the school and to quell his own fears. His effort mirrored Weber's theory of religious anxiety fueling a drive to work. Only Washington wasn't worried about his soul so much as the success of a school that, to him, symbolized African Americans as a people.

Appropriately enough, Max and Marianne Weber missed meeting Washington when they visited Tuskegee in 1904. He was out fundraising.[60] On these trips, Washington never relinquished control over Tuskegee's operations. He demanded micromanagerial updates, sent via telegraph, on every detail of the school's activity, down to how the food in the cafeteria was prepared.[61] His effort paid off. Every check from a Northern philanthropist "partially lifted a burden that had been pressing down upon me."[62] Partially— because you can never create a large enough university endowment, or have enough profits, or add enough lines to your resume, just as a Calvinist can never give God enough glory. The American work ethic demands you prove yourself through labor, but you never prove yourself once and for all. You have to do it all again the next day.

The unceasing demand that you demonstrate your worth through work helps create the total work society, which, combined with the disappointing conditions of postindustrial-era jobs, becomes burnout culture. To keep going, you tell yourself you're indispensable. This is another bar in the work ethic's iron cage. In Washington's case, his benefactors saw he was working too hard, so they conspired to send him on a long European vacation. He tried to convince them he couldn't go, because "Each day the school seemed to depend upon me more largely for its daily expenses. . . . [T]he school could not live financially while I was absent."[63]

This attitude is common today even among the vast majority of American workers who are not running an entire organization like Washington was. Before the Covid-19 pandemic, American workers only took about half their paid vacation time every year, and even when they were on vacation, about two-thirds of them worked. In the first months of the pandemic, they took even less paid time off.[64] When asked why in a survey, many cited the same reasons as Washington over a century earlier; a third said they work while they're on vacation because "they fear getting behind," roughly another third claimed there was no one else to do their work, and more than a fifth "are completely dedicated to their company."[65] Personal finance blogger Sarah Berger speculates that millennial-generation workers leave most of their vacation time unused because they "feel like they have something to prove and want to dispel these negative stereotypes that have labeled them as entitled or lazy."[66] It's worth asking to whom they are trying to prove this invisible characteristic: their bosses, or themselves? Whether workers' sense of indispensability stems from ego or job insecurity, though, the person trapped in this iron cage is actually afraid the school, store, or company *can* function without them. Walking away is the truest test of whether the firm can get by in their absence. If they never take vacation, they never have to find out.

Eventually, Washington "was compelled to surrender" to the vacation his benefactors offered. "Every avenue of escape had been closed," he writes.[67] He slept fifteen hours a day on the steamer to Antwerp, Belgium. The ten-day voyage was the first time in years he had been out of telegraph contact with Tuskegee. I wonder how he managed without knowing the menu at the school's dining hall.

Despite being cut off from electronic communication—a trial we need never endure—Washington quickly found ways to work. While he was still aboard the ship, he gave a speech at the request of some other passengers (that is, potential donors). When he got to Europe, he met with dignitaries, gave more speeches, and talked about industrial education as the pathway to interracial peace. In Holland, he toured dairy farms, "with a view to utilizing the information in our work at Tuskegee."[68] Thrown into an uncomfortable situation away from his familiar domain, Washington managed to adapt. He beat back any doubts about his value or purpose with the hard assurance of work.

If the doctrine of employee engagement holds up an ideal of work sainthood, then the total work regime creates an ideal of the work martyr, who maximizes productivity without regard for the self. The work martyr resembles Pieper's functionary, whose chief virtue is a willingness to suffer.[69] This was Washington's ideal, too. He believed that the best worker "loses himself," even "completely obliterates himself" in the work.[70] The words sound like those of an addict, but Washington connects them to biblical terms for the self-sacrifice of Jesus Christ. Of Dr. Hollis Frissell, the white principal of the Hampton Institute in Virginia, Washington writes that his "constant effort" was to make himself 'of no reputation' for the sake of the cause."[71] The words "of no reputation" come from Philippians 2:7 in the King James Version of the bible. In a modern translation of that passage, Paul says Jesus "emptied himself, taking the form of a slave. . . . [H]e humbled himself and became obedient to the point of death—even death on a cross."[72] That is Washington's model for African American workers.

Washington's ideal of work martyrdom sits just below the thin veneer of present-day work sainthood as embodied by the autotelic welder Joe Kramer. To be like Joe, you need to commit yourself totally to your work. Lose yourself in it. Stay up all night. Forget to eat. These imperatives are inhuman. When workers break down and can't "engage" anymore, they are simultaneously revered—they gave it their all, they did what it took—and reviled. Who can the boss more easily justify terminating than the burnout? As a final act of martyrdom, they might even quit.

I'm critical of Washington, but I can't condemn him. Like so many Americans, I believe much the same as he did. I wish his law of merit, the conviction that hard work will always earn its proper reward, were true. The idea itself is noble. Tragically, though, Washington taught it to students whose society was never going to honor that promise. The gap between his ideals and the reality his students faced in the Jim Crow South was enormous, and he taught them to throw themselves into it. He threw himself in, too. On some level, he knew the law of merit was a lie. In Sunday-night lectures to students, not in the best-selling books he wrote for Northern whites, he admitted that there would be struggle, that the reward might never come.[73] The violent oppression black people experienced in Washington's world far exceeds the injustice American workers typically encounter today. But the promise—dignity earned through labor—is the same. For the sake of that hollow promise, we enter the gap, and we keep stretching ourselves across it.

· · ·

This book began with my desire to understand what had happened that made me so miserable and ineffective after getting my dream job and then tenure. That desire has led me to investigate the contested cultural understanding of burnout, the history of burnout's appearance in the 1970s, reams of psychological research, the diminished state of work in the United States and other rich countries today, and finally the ethical and spiritual ideals for work that keep pulling further and further away from those conditions.

I believed the ideals, the noble lies about work as a site of meaning and purpose. So I identified with my role and kept anxiously trying to prove I was indispensable to the college's mission. I believed I gave the college more—better teaching, more research, superior leadership—for the same salary as my colleagues. The pride I felt in being such a productive, engaged employee turned into anger at the unfairness of the situation: *I'm giving the college so much more than that guy is, but we're getting paid the same amount!* Then I kept working to prove that the college and its students underestimated me, until I could barely work at all. My ideal image of a good professor both motivated my work and fostered my burnout, because it was at odds with the reality of the job. I wanted to be a work saint and became a work martyr, though a resentful one. In short, I was a typical worker in our burnout culture. The very thing our culture says will make us flourish—our work—keeps us from doing so.

Now that we can identify this paradoxical problem, we need to figure out how to break through it. The post-pandemic period is our best chance in half a century to change the culture of work. To do so, we first need a new set of ideals, based on a recognition of every person's human dignity, regardless of whether they work.

II *Counterculture*

6 *We Can Have It All*

A New Vision of the Good Life

Before I became a professor, I was a parking lot attendant. I had just finished my PhD program and couldn't land an academic job. But I knew a few guys who worked at a lot across the street from the university, and they introduced me to their boss. Before long I was collecting money in a small, weathered booth behind a pizza place. Every day, I sat in the driver's seats of the Volvos and Beamers of the professors I desperately wanted to be like, and yet the work I did felt as distant from theirs as possible.

I loved it. The work was easy, even fun. My boss cared about his employees and treated us well; he knew the job was not our whole lives. My coworkers were bright undergrads and grad students, several of whom were covered in tattoos, rode fixed-gear bicycles, and played obscure hardcore punk rock in the booth. A few were in bands themselves. I was older and un-inked, drove a bright blue Honda Civic, and read Kierkegaard. They called me the Pope, because as a religious studies PhD, I was the closest thing to a spiritual authority they knew. During the year I worked at The Corner Parking Lot, I fell in love with a woman who was also in a liminal stage of her career, and she brought me coffee and pastries to help me through my night shifts. She's now my wife.

The contrast between my happiness in a low-status job and my misery in a tenured academic position points toward a way to end burnout culture. I expected being a college professor would fulfill me not just as a worker but as a human being. I expected it to be my complete identity, my vocation. Few jobs could ever live up to those expectations, though I had certainly absorbed the notion that the right academic job could. Of course, it didn't live up to them, and I labored for years before the disappointment and futility became so much to bear that I quit.

By contrast, I had no lofty ideal of work as a parking lot attendant. I thought of it as just an undemanding way to make rent money. I didn't expect to "engage" with the job. There is no real possibility of experiencing "flow" if you're a parking lot attendant. There is no progressive challenge to collecting money in a booth. No one gets better at it over time. The only people who give you feedback are irate drivers trying to escape their fees. When I worked that job, I never sank so far into the zone that I forgot to eat; in fact, I spent much of my time in the booth, and much of my conversation with my coworkers, deciding what to order for lunch. (Usually pizza.) The job did nothing to foster the absorption in a task that supposedly makes work productive and the worker fulfilled. It was perfect.

I am convinced that my *lack* of engagement with work was the paradoxical reason I was so happy during my year as a parking lot attendant. The job resisted any effort to make it morally or spiritually meaningful. It did not promise dignity, growth in character, or a sense of purpose. It never held out the possibility of the good life. Because I couldn't find fulfillment through my job, I had to look for it elsewhere. And I found it: in writing, in friendships, in love.

My job at the parking lot did more than just stay out of the way of my flourishing as a person. My ideals for the work were low, but its conditions were pretty good. The pay was decent. My fellow attendants quickly became friends. Our boss trusted us with his business, and we trusted each other. We all adhered to an unwritten rule that if you were near the lot, you would swing by the booth to see if the attendant on duty needed a break or a coffee or just someone to talk to. There were occasional conflicts with customers over how long their parking validation lasted or how much they owed us for leaving their cars overnight, but there were many more friendly conversations with regular customers that continued, in thirty-second increments through open car windows, for months. A documentary about the lot, *The Parking Lot Movie,* emphasizes the conflicts and the potential for burnout, but my experience was generally better than what director Meghan Eckman depicts on screen.[1]

I am just one worker; I want to be careful not to overdraw any conclusions about *work itself* from experience that may be peculiar to me. But my experience as both a professor and a parking lot attendant does fit the model of burnout my research has led me to, namely, that the cultural ideals we bring to our jobs have a major effect on how burnout affects us.

So many workers are at risk for burnout because the degraded reality of our jobs since the 1970s coincides with a too-lofty ideal of work. The gap between our ideals and our experience at work is too great for us to bear. That means, if we want to halt the burnout epidemic, we need to close the gap, both by improving working conditions and lowering our ideals. In chapters 7 and 8, I will introduce you to people who labor in more humane conditions. But because our burnout culture results as much from our ideas as from the concrete facts of our jobs, we will need different ethical and spiritual expectations for work as much as we will need better pay, schedules, and support. In fact, we will need a new set of ideals to guide us as we construct those conditions.

The Protestant ethic that we carried into the postindustrial era helped create the vast wealth of the countries that are today most concerned about burnout. But it also valorized a destructive ideal of working to the point of martyrdom. To overcome burnout, we have to get rid of that ideal and create a new shared vision of how work fits into a life well lived. That vision will replace the work ethic's old, discredited promise. It will make dignity universal, not contingent on paid labor. It will put compassion for self and others ahead of productivity. And it will affirm that we find our highest purpose in leisure, not work. We will realize this vision in community and preserve it through common disciplines that keep work in its place. The vision, assembled from new and old ideas alike, will be the basis of a new culture, one that leaves burnout behind.

We have to form this vision soon, because automation and artificial intelligence are poised to unsettle human labor in the coming decades. Once humans are only worth employing in limited roles, we won't burn out, but the system of meaning we have built on work will stop making sense.

. . .

To build a new model of the good life, we need to dig a foundation deeper than the noble lies that make us work to assure ourselves of our value. The first point to challenge, then, is the basic promise that work is the source of dignity. Dignity is a tricky word. Everyone agrees that the dignity of work is worth defending, but as with burnout itself, there is no agreement about what the dignity of work means. Sociologically, it means the right to have a voice, or to count, in your society.[2] Dignity can also mean something beyond that: the ability not just to count but to hold your head up high, to earn others' esteem. In the United States, politicians on both right and left invoke the dignity of work to justify labor and public welfare policies. There's good reason for them to do so; the concept resonates with a citizenry that thinks of itself as hardworking. But beneath the good feeling Americans get when they hear the phrase "the dignity of work," the policies these officials propose run in opposite directions. Appeals to the dignity of work often justify the inhumane working conditions that contribute to burnout.

Conservative politicians and writers in the United States talk about the dignity of work when arguing for looser labor regulations and reduced social welfare protections for people who do not work. Because there is dignity in work, they say, they want to eliminate artificial barriers to employment like minimum wage laws.[3] When, in 2019, the Trump administration tightened rules that require adults who receive public food assistance to have jobs, Secretary of Agriculture Sonny Perdue, whose department oversaw the program, claimed that stricter work requirements would "restore the dignity of work to a sizable segment of our population."[4] More liberal politicians have made similar arguments. President Bill Clinton, in signing a welfare reform bill in 1996, stated that unconditional public aid "exil[ed]" recipients "from the world of work." Work, Clinton continued, "gives structure, meaning and dignity to most of our lives."[5] It's certainly true that workers feel a measure of pride in having a job and providing for themselves and their families. But Perdue's and Clinton's approach also depresses wages and undercuts workers' ability to demand better conditions. It is as if dignity were reward enough.

This pro-market view of the dignity of work isolates workers as individuals and then puts pressure on them to keep earning their dignity, because their dignity is not assured in advance. This view also encourages derision for anyone who cannot find work, or who cannot work at all due to age, illness, or disability. It puts additional pressure on workers who cannot rely on their identity as white or male or native-born for social esteem. And as we saw in the case of Booker T. Washington in chapter 5, people become anxious when their dignity is perpetually in question. They'll do anything to hang onto a job not only because it's their economic lifeline, but because their social standing is at stake. In a society that views work as the means to prove their value, they're going to work harder, exposing themselves to the physical and psychological risks of labor, including burnout. All of this benefits bosses and owners of capital—at least, it benefits them right up until workers' ability to do their jobs degrades and their productivity declines. Even then, so long as there are replacement workers available, the cost of churning and burning through employees eager to prove their dignity is relatively small.

Pro-labor politicians in the United States, most of them Democrats, take a different approach to the dignity of work. For them, dignity is not something people attain through their jobs, but something jobs attain when they meet workers' needs. That means the dignity of work is less a permanent state than a political goal worth fighting for. Under this view, the labor people perform *ought* to be dignified with decent wages and protections for workers. For example, Ohio Senator Sherrod Brown based an entire slate of policy proposals, from a higher minimum wage to paid sick leave to education funding, on the idea of the dignity of work. "Dignity of work means hard work should pay off for everyone, no matter who you are or what kind of work you do," reads the website for Brown's

2019 Dignity of Work Tour. "When work has dignity, everyone can afford health care and housing. . . . When work has dignity, our country has a strong middle class."[6]

The call for work, and not the worker, to gain dignity is a first step toward closing the gap that causes burnout. It takes the pressure off workers to prove themselves and to hold their ideals and conditions in alignment, even as standard postindustrial business practices try to drive them apart. Employers, with the right push from government, have the power to dignify the work people do; that means they bear the responsibility for closing the gap from the working-conditions side. The culture as a whole, then, needs to push from the other, the side of ideals.

. . .

Senator Brown's approach to the dignity of work is rooted in the basic promise of the American work ideology, namely, that material and moral rewards come to those who work. His stated aim is to make good on that promise. But his language that work ought to have dignity commensurate to the worker also reflects a view of labor that Catholic popes have espoused in their social teaching for 130 years. I want to turn to the popes for guidance on labor and dignity because they do not take the industrial-age, capitalist ethos as an unquestioned norm. As a result, their thinking runs obliquely to ours. In fact, papal writing on labor is much more radical and favorable to workers than you might assume. Besides, if a new vision of work is going to take hold in our culture, then it will have to appeal to religious people. And in the United States, a majority of the population is Christian. However, religious sources are not the only ones that should justify our ideals for work. If they are going to have wide appeal, we will need to justify them on multiple grounds. That's what I will do in this chapter.

In 1891, Pope Leo XIII published a document titled *Rerum Novarum,* on the relationship between capital and labor. It was a landmark, the first papal teaching that directly addressed modern social injustice. Its argument reveals a Church clearly spooked by Marxism; Leo makes an extended case for private property and scolds socialists for promoting a "false teaching" and exploiting "the poor man's envy of the rich."[7] Nevertheless, Leo frequently takes labor's side against the capitalist class. Employers' first duty, he writes, is "to respect in every man his dignity as a person ennobled by Christian character."[8] As a consequence of that dignity, workers have a "natural right" to a living wage.[9] That means, regardless of the type of work they do, anyone who works rightly deserves a wage sufficient to support a family. Furthermore, Leo argues that hours of work and rest should "depend on the nature of the work, on circumstances of time and place, and *on the health and strength of the workman.*"[10] He cites miners in particular as laborers who deserve shorter workdays because of how physically difficult and dangerous their jobs are. Leo's point is that the dignity of the *person*—not the dignity of work—is the highest principle when it comes to labor, and bosses owe it to their employees to provide conditions commensurate to that dignity, even if it means giving infirm workers fewer hours. Still, there is no excuse for paying someone less than a living wage, regardless of his or her ability to work a full day.

A workplace organized around Leo's principles is nearly unimaginable to twenty-first-century Americans. It would be one where employers took the flourishing of their workers as seriously as they take their profits. Because people have different needs and capacities, they would have to be treated differently at work. A nurse whose chronic back pain makes it impossible for her to stand for her entire shift would receive lighter duty or shorter hours, all while earning a full-time, living-wage salary. Most Americans cannot tolerate thinking of justice in terms of people having their particular needs met, or their true value honored. As things are now, people resent teachers who go on strike.[11] *Don't they already get paid all year for doing just ten months of work? Must be nice!* Few see teachers' success in negotiating a better contract and think, *Maybe I should join a union, too.* These objections bubble up from the deep individualism in which Americans' ideas about work are steeped—an individualism fed by Calvinist theology. To the American mind, it's up to you to find and keep the work that demonstrates your value. "No one owes you anything" is the mantra of people who believe in this degraded notion of justice.

Leo and subsequent popes have aimed to set labor justice on a higher foundation. Ninety years after *Rerum Novarum,* John Paul II, another pope worried about Communism but committed to the rights of workers, wrote another document on work, *Laborem Exercens,* in which he affirmed that work only has dignity because human beings do. "[T]he basis for determining the value of human work," John Paul writes, "is not primarily the kind of work being done but the fact that the one who is doing it is a person."[12] That is, work doesn't dignify us; we dignify work. For John Paul, that is because the person is a creature made in the image of God. In a pluralistic society, we would not have to ground our commitment to the inherent worth of each person theologically, as John Paul does. A secular human-rights argument would also do the trick. The economist Gene Sperling puts forward such an argument in his book *Economic Dignity.* Sperling argues, following the philosopher

Immanuel Kant, that people deserve economic dignity because they are never just the means to some economic end but are always "ends in themselves."[13]

Regardless of the metaphysical basis for claims to dignity, though, we can only break the anxiety that fuels the Protestant ethic by affirming the dignity of each person, whether they work for pay or not. Doing so will lower the stakes of work considerably. Assured of our value in society, we will no longer feel so much pressure to prove it on the job. The ordinary slights we experience in interpersonal work—from nitpicking bosses, plagiarizing students, or drivers unwilling to pay for the privilege of parking their cars—won't seem like personal affronts. They won't smother our self-worth or stoke our cynicism.

Working in the parking lot trained the attendants to think of our dignity as distinct from our job. In the documentary about the lot attendants complain that university alumni and parents of new graduates offer them unsolicited advice about how a college degree could help them get out of their dead-end job. One attendant says that alumni condescendingly tell him, "Good luck with your *life*" when they meet him at the booth. He imagines telling them, "You don't know what my life's about. Just because you see me at my job doesn't mean you know what my life's about."[14] What these drivers couldn't know was that the attendants often did have degrees. Or they were supporting families. Or they were musicians and artists. Not that any of that should make a difference to the dignity they had before they ever went to work. But their job didn't define them. They found engagement and meaning somewhere other than in the booth.

The notion of dignity as inherent to the person will also equip us to argue for working conditions that measure up to that dignity:

a workload adapted to the worker's ability, wages and job stability that sustain their families, trust in their ability to make decisions, and fair treatment on account of the fact that each worker is equally valuable. Ethically better work will cascade from that single source and extinguish burnout.

· · ·

To me, the most compelling secular vision of human dignity in the face of dehumanizing work belongs to Henry David Thoreau. Thoreau did not think it was possible to live an authentic life under industrial-age conditions. So he escaped them. It's true that his retreat into Walden Woods did not remove him from society altogether. His cabin was a brisk twenty-minute walk from the guesthouse his mother operated in central Concord. In *Walden's* first sentence, Thoreau boasts that he lived "a mile from any neighbor," but in fact the woods were thick with human inhabitants: laborers, travelers, outcasts, and gawkers at the local celebrity who made a spectacle of deliberate living.[15] And, as he makes clear, Thoreau counted the birds and woodchucks as neighbors, too. But the "experiment" he documents in his 1854 book forcefully challenged the industrial-age wisdom about work that would later coalesce into the Protestant ethic of Booker T. Washington and ourselves.

Some readers today fault Thoreau for boasting of his independence while relying on the labor of women. Most notoriously, he stands accused of having his mother and sisters do his laundry.[16] For what it's worth, Thoreau was devoted to his family and welcome company at home. As his biographer Laura Dassow Walls writes, "how hurt Cynthia would have been had her own son refused her famously generous table!"[17] Meanwhile, Henry, like his mother, was a committed anti-slavery activist. Cynthia's home was a station on the Underground Railroad, and Henry helped many former slaves escape to safety in Canada.[18] He was also the first public figure to defend John Brown's unpopular and failed attempt to arm a slave rebellion in 1859, giving a speech in Concord that was reprinted in newspapers nationwide.[19] It's easy to poke fun at Thoreau's alleged hypocrisy, but it would be foolish to deprive ourselves of his moral vision on account of it.

I did not become a Thoreau fan in the stereotypical way. I did not pick up *Walden* as a teenager longing for freedom from my parents' and teachers' constraints. I read *Walden* for the first time in my mid-thirties, after my earliest frustrations with my teaching job but before I realized I was on the way to burnout. When I finally read it, I was surprised by how much the book was about work. When Thoreau looks to his fellow New Englanders, he sees that work has forced them into absurd postures and ossified their bodies and minds. He takes pity on poor laborers who diminish themselves to get work, then diminish themselves further on the job, often in an ironic pursuit of living larger in the future. Their days are so consumed by the "superfluously coarse labors of life that its finest fruits cannot be plucked by them. Their fingers, from excessive toil, are too clumsy and tremble too much for that."[20]

Thoreau lived decades too early to be concerned with neurasthenia, never mind burnout, but he recognized that the frantic American work ethic was both self-defeating and morally harmful. When the self expands and contracts repeatedly to fit the demands of work, it ultimately cracks. "[T]he laboring man has not leisure for a true integrity day by day," he writes. "He has no time to be any thing but a machine."[21] Like Adam Smith, who in the previous century fretted over what repetitive stress did to factory workers' senses and sensibilities, Thoreau believed the main problem with industrial work was its power to impose habits on workers. To him, work sets people into routines that, over time, define them and close off possibilities for growth. And then workers become the living dead. Farmers are "ploughed into the soil for compost."[22] The teamster lives only to feed his horses and scoop their manure.[23] The Irish laborers who lay ties beneath the railroad become what they build: "The rails are laid on them, and they are covered with sand, and the cars run smoothly over them."[24] According to this theory of alienated labor, you are under great pressure to identify with your job, which then dehumanizes you. We feel that pressure still. Even a good job threatens to turn you into a machine. Just ask the doctors trying to examine a patient and make a diagnosis in fifteen minutes while typing on a laptop keyboard all the while.

Thoreau wanted better for workers. As long as people sold their lives cheap in labor, he thought, it was obscene for preachers or poets to speak of "a divinity in man."[25] To enable people to live up to their actual divinity, they would have to break the negative habits work imposes. And the way to do that is with a more positive self-discipline. Thoreau aimed to be a living model of this new asceticism. Going to the woods was his experiment to show what a flourishing human life could look like, once he stripped away all deadening labor and built up new habits.

So Thoreau relentlessly economized, ridding himself of all unnecessary possessions (he boasts of chucking away three pieces of limestone that would need frequent dusting), building his cabin himself, and finding the easiest way to "earn ten or twelve dollars by some honest and agreeable method."[26] He settles on cultivating beans as a cash crop, a chore that nets him nearly nine dollars on only six weeks of work all year. As a bonus, the work of hoeing beans carries Thoreau into a state of aesthetic joy and psychic rapture: "When my hoe tinkled against the stones, that music echoed to the woods and the sky, and was an accompaniment to my labor which yielded an instant and immeasurable crop. It was no longer beans that I hoed, nor I that hoed beans."[27] He enters a state reminiscent of flow, but, contrary to what today's gurus of engagement profess, it doesn't inspire him to work longer or invest himself more in the task. It's a pleasure, but one that's delimited by what he needs to earn. Any work, even good work, will turn bad if you do it too much. Had Thoreau kept up his "amusement" in the bean field, he jokes, it "might have become a dissipation."[28]

· · ·

We have all read the standard advice on business and wellness websites for how to prevent or heal your burnout. Get more sleep. Learn to say no. Organize your tasks by urgency and importance. Meditate. These are all basically superstitions: individual, symbolic actions that are disconnected from burnout's real causes. Our workplaces and cultural ideals contribute more to our burnout than our personal organization methods do. Still, individuals are not powerless in the face of burnout. We do have a role to play in aligning our ideals with our reality at work. And Thoreau, the individualist who preached self-reliance, can help us identify it.

Thoreau occasionally sounds like a twenty-first-century life hacker, the kind who touts his two-hour workweek that nevertheless earns him enough money to retire by age seventeen. This may be why he rubs some readers the wrong way. *He* has let go of his earnest worker-bee hangups, while *you* are still leading a life of quiet desperation. He sounds unfairly judgy in telling a laboring family that they would have more money and better health, not to mention a cleaner conscience, if they gave up coffee and switched to a vegan diet.[29] If anything can redeem Thoreau's smugness, though, it's his sincere belief that we are all capable of much more than the blinkered concerns our work imposes on us. It's a radical belief in the ideals of American independence; each of us can determine the course of our own life, because each of us has unlimited potential. Thoreau sees this potential in the humblest of workers, like a belly-laughing Canadian wood-chopper whose self-possession makes Thoreau think "that there might be men of genius in the lowest grades of life . . . who are as bottomless even as Walden Pond was thought to be, though they may be dark and muddy."[30]

My favorite parable from *Walden* expresses this optimism about what can happen when people turn from work and free their latent abilities. Thoreau introduces John Farmer, who, "after a hard day's work . . . sat down to recreate his intellectual man."[31] Already, the man's condition resonates with any exhausted worker today who tries to reassemble their complete self after a full day as the functionary for someone else's ends. There is a wonderful ambiguity in Thoreau's word "recreate." Is it rē-create or rĕc-reate? The man may need to do both. As he sits, his mind is on his work, but after a while, the sound of flute music intrudes on his thought. He tries to ignore it, but it keeps recapturing his attention. I love this hint of transcendence in ordinary life, this idea that beauty will not allow you to ignore it. The music "came home to his ears out of a different sphere from that he worked in, and suggested work for certain faculties which slumbered in him." Soon, the music carries John Farmer beyond his immediate surroundings.

A voice said to him,—Why do you stay here and live this mean moiling life, when a glorious existence is possible for you? Those same stars twinkle over other fields than these.—But how to come out of this condition and actually migrate thither? All that he could think of was to practise some new austerity, to let his mind descend into his body and redeem it, and treat himself with ever increasing respect.[32]

Those three actions that occur to John Farmer are not, in fact, separate things. You undertake the austerity, cutting your consumption and labor, in part because you already realize you are meant for greater things than your work allows. You have already heard the music and the voice, and you are ready to undertake a moral and spiritual program that will make you whole again. You are better than your burnout, and you can do something about it. Begin by honoring the dignity you already have.

Thoreau limited his ordinary labor so he would be free to "follow the bent of my genius, which is a very crooked one, every moment."[33] This genius is a spiritual reality, a personal *genius loci*, that is simultaneously each person's alone and also connected to nature and higher human ideals. Your genius calls you toward self-transcendence, "to a higher life than we fell asleep from." The problem is that it competes with the "mechanical nudgings" of the factory's clock and whistle—or the phone notifications—that call us to sell ourselves short.[34]

Limiting his work for the sake of his genius doesn't just buy Thoreau more time; it changes his relationship with time altogether. Ordinary work consumes your few days on earth, while pursuing your genius allows you to pass beyond time and into eternity. Thoreau boasts of spending whole mornings in his doorway, "rapt in a revery," luxuriating in time that would have been wasted had he tried to hoe beans. These hours "were not time subtracted from my life, but so much over and above my usual allowance."[35] They were not earned; they were gifts.

It is even possible to escape time altogether while working, so long as the work is attuned to your genius. A final parable in *Walden* concerns "an artist in the city of Kouroo who was disposed to strive after perfection" by carving a wooden staff. "As he made no compromise with Time, Time kept out of his way," Thoreau writes of the artist. "His singleness of purpose and resolution, and his elevated piety, endowed him, without his knowledge, with perennial youth." As he works, his friends grow old and die. Kingdoms fall and are forgotten. Even the stars move on. But the artist makes something truly new, "a new system in making a staff, a world with full and fair proportions." As he finishes, he realizes that "the former lapse of time had been an illusion, and that no more time had elapsed than is required for a single scintillation from the brain of Brahma to fall on and inflame the tinder of a mortal brain."[36]

We don't normally experience work time in quite this way. The artist of Kouroo's instantaneous entry into eternity again calls to mind the flow state theorized by Mihaly Csikszentmihalyi. It's a reversal of the restless time of total work, in which it is imperative to make every moment profitable. In the total work regime, we do not have whole days but rather "twenty-four potentially monetizable hours that are sometimes not even restricted to our time zones or our sleep cycles," in the words of the artist and writer Jenny Odell.[37] When I was a burned-out college professor, my brain was hyper-aware of the passage of time. It always seemed like I was behind. *It's nine p.m. and I don't have a lesson plan for tomorrow morning,* I would think, as I stared at a book and drank another beer. *Now it's ten, and I'm no closer to being ready for class.* To escape time anxiety and to escape total work may be the same thing.

Like Pope Leo XIII's proposal of a living wage for all laborers, Thoreau's vision of pursuing your genius seems hopelessly idealistic to people who believe their working hours, not to mention their thoughts and desires during that time, belong to their bosses. It is hard to picture a C-suite executive issuing a memo that employees can feel free to miss a morning's work for the sake of contemplation. But we can imagine that realizing Thoreau's principles would cut off many proximate causes of burnout. Too much work and too little autonomy contribute to burnout; Thoreau's program limits work in order to foster self-determination. Thoreau's individualistic streak means he undervalues community. But he wants to create conditions in which people who recognize their own dignity can follow their genius and thus perform a higher labor: to harmonize themselves with their supreme sense of value.

. . .

To end burnout culture, we have to improve working conditions while we reduce our social, moral, and spiritual expectations from work. But there is a case to be made that improving some conditions of work—increasing wages, giving workers more control over their schedules, instituting a more collaborative management style—would open the door to even greater dominance of work over our lives. If work is well-paid, comfortable, and even enjoyable, then why not do it all the time? Improving conditions can therefore end up raising both workloads and ideals.

If ideals and conditions are like a pair of stilts that always threaten to fall away from each other, pulling the person who holds them in opposite directions, then better but more intense work might not actually alleviate burnout. It might bring conditions into closer alignment with ideals, but on a much higher set of stilts, on which even slight wobbles can turn catastrophic—as with physicians' well-paid but stressful labor in corporate health-care systems. This is not an argument against making work better, but rather an argument that improving workers' comfort and compensation might not be enough to prevent burnout if doing so also makes work more demanding.

To ward off greater labor intensity, then, we should call for *less* work even as we call for *better conditions* of work. That is exactly what political philosopher Kathi Weeks does in her 2011 book, *The Problem with Work,* in which she attempts to loosen work's hold over our morals and imagination. Weeks writes from a Marxist feminist perspective, but she is critical of the dominant strains in both Marxist and feminist thought that endorse work as the key to broader political liberation. In her view, the feminist push for gender equality, in a context where work is a chief source of social prestige, only increased women's workloads.[38]

It is certainly true that women now work for pay more than they did in the middle of the twentieth century, before the dawn of burnout culture. The percentage of American women in the workforce increased dramatically between 1950 and 2000.[39] Women in numerous wealthy countries have, over the same period, spent an increasing amount of time per day on childcare; across these countries, university-educated women spend more time with their kids than their less-educated peers. The time men spend on childcare has also increased significantly, though it remains less than the time women spend.[40] Women and girls who grew up in the postindustrial era heard over and over that they could "have it all":

children, career, community, friendships. But having it all, especially when motherhood is itself seen as a job, means subjecting your entire life to the cruel logic of total work.[41] The problem with work, as Weeks views it, is similar to the problem Thoreau identifies. More work means more exposure to your job's power to form and deform you. Work "generates not just income and capital, but disciplined individuals, governable subjects, worthy citizens, and responsible family members," Weeks writes.[42] This was Max Weber's point, too, when he called capitalism a "monstrous cosmos" that, "with overwhelming coercion," turns us into the industrious moneymakers it needs us to be.[43]

Weeks wants feminism to liberate women by means other than work; she wants it to espouse "a vision of the work society not perfected but overcome."[44] She admits she does not know what that society will look like, but that's part of the point. We need more time away from our jobs "to forge alternatives to the present ideals and conditions of work and family life."[45] In short, less work is necessary if we are going to break the constraints of patriarchy and heterosexism, because work helps perpetuate them. Mainstream feminists argue today that reducing work hours will make it possible for men and women alike to spend more time raising children. To Weeks, that is just a call to reduce one form of labor for the sake of another. She wants us to think bigger, arguing that a shorter workweek would liberate people "to imagine, experiment with, and participate in the relationships of intimacy and sociality that we choose."[46] What could our lives look like if we stopped trying to justify parenting in terms of work? What if we stopped organizing our time according to productivity and (other people's) profit? What modes of being would that make possible? If self-determination is the political goal, then work must be limited so that people can shape themselves within communities according to how they imagine the good life.

The very different perspectives of papal teaching, transcendentalism, and Marxist feminism all converge on a handful of points in opposition to the industrial work ethic that forms the intellectual and moral background of burnout culture. Leo, Thoreau, and Weeks all point toward a model of flourishing in which work plays only a supporting role. The diverse ways they approach principles for a post-work-ethic society—the dignity of the person, shorter hours, living wages, and self-determination—suggest a possibility for broad social agreement on a replacement for the work ethic that has dominated industrial societies for more than two centuries. Despite their different perspectives, these thinkers all agree that waged labor gets in the way of a life well lived. In some cases, they have diametrically opposite reasons for limiting work. Leo XIII wanted to reduce working hours and institute a living wage in order to shore up the patriarchal family he saw as central to human flourishing. He hoped better wages would fulfill the "most sacred law of nature that a father should provide food and all necessaries for those whom he has begotten."[47] Weeks calls for similar policies—a standard thirty-hour workweek and universal basic income—but aims them at opening up possibilities *beyond* patriarchy.[48]

Weeks sounds surprisingly like Thoreau when she writes, in the final pages of *The Problem with Work*, "a life is what each of us needs to get; one cannot get a life if its terms are only dictated from the outside." But she parts ways with the more individualistic Thoreau in the next sentence: "That said, getting a life is also necessarily a collective endeavor; one cannot get something as big as a life on one's own."[49] It will have to happen within a community that can honor its members' dignity and embody new, collectively-imagined terms for living.

. . .

I have watched *The Parking Lot Movie* many times. Even if I hadn't worked at The Corner Parking Lot or appeared briefly in the film, I like to think I'd be drawn to the wisdom the attendants share concerning work. One quote from Scott Meiggs, who worked at the lot years before I did, always puzzled me. Meiggs reflects on the parking lot as a place of transition for its employees. Most of us had bigger dreams for ourselves, and the parking lot was a good place to plot them out. But dreams don't always materialize. Meiggs says in his punk-inflected drawl, "And whatever we do, it doesn't seem to amount to nearly the sort of potential that we seemed to have held in the parking lot. In the parking lot, we were dynamos, whirlwinds. We were rulers. We had complete autonomy. We had it all in a world that had nothing to offer us."[50] It's a stirring monologue. Its images connect me to the self-esteem I built during the year I worked there, after years of ego-crushing graduate school. But I never quite got what Meiggs was saying in his last sentence. It always seemed like it was meant to be profound, but on closer examination, it didn't make sense. How did we have it all? And didn't the world have something to offer us? It just seemed incoherent to me.

After I burned out and quit the job I dreamed of while I worked in the lot, I started to understand. While you're still unproven, you can think you're capable of anything. You can have it all in your mind, in potential. You could be a great artist or musician or scholar or whatever else—potentially. Once you actually set out to become that, however, you risk not measuring up. Except for maybe Beyoncé or Tom Brady, everyone knows what it's like to have it all in your mind but encounter lower ceilings in reality. It isn't that different from the gap that leads us to burnout. In fact, burnout can surely result from the stubborn insistence that we can still have it all with a little more effort. We usually associate potential with youth; it's what employers look for in workers they will eventually push too hard, or not support, and then be disappointed by. Still, it's legitimate, maybe even necessary, to hang onto those high hopes. Even in middle age and beyond, it's good to imagine that we will do great things in the future, that our best days are ahead of us. Without that, we have no basis for self-development. So we need to dream of our potential. We need, in Thoreau's terms, to keep listening for the music from the different sphere, the vision of the higher life.

As I thought more about burnout and potential, I realized there may be a more radical notion of it in Scott Meiggs's oracular claim that "We had it all in a world that had nothing to offer us." Perhaps potential isn't something to fulfill in "real life" at all. Potential could just be that feeling of "complete autonomy," but detached from a felt need to translate that autonomy into the world beyond, and certainly not into some profit-making enterprise. I am now convinced that Meiggs is talking "about the joy of boundlessness, as a present experience," in the interpretation of the writer who goes by the moniker Alonzo Subverbo, in a blog post about the film. He continues:

> It is not about anticipating being dynamos, whirlwinds, rulers, but being those things at the time. Potential is not something that realizes its value at some point in the future, but presently. . . . This is

very far from the potential solemnly discussed by educators and employers. It is lighting out for the territory, Walt Whitman, rock 'n roll. It is The Corner Parking Lot.[51]

What does Kathi Weeks want but a radical reimagining of what it could mean to "have it all"? At Walden Pond, what did Thoreau have—in a world that ignored his first book and offered only degrading labor—other than it all? "[M]y greatest skill," he writes, "has been to want but little."[52] He hoped austerity, along with an unfettered imagination, might liberate him to follow his genius and redeem himself. That's how you can have it all. But it is never your sole possession. Alonzo Subverbo calls attention to "we" and "us" in Scott Meiggs's pronouncement.[53] *We* can have it all. Our potential is held in common. It belongs to everyone, all at once.

To prevent and heal our burnout, we need to lower our ideals for work, but we don't need to lower our ideals altogether. If anything, we need *higher* ideals for ourselves: universal dignity, infinite potential, having it all, refusing the nothing that the world, as presently constituted, has to offer. It would be a daring move to build a life, even a community, around those ideals. But some people are trying. Let's find out how they do it.

7 *How Benedictines Tame the Demons of Work*

In a remote canyon in northern New Mexico in the mid-1990s, Benedictine monks of the Monastery of Christ in the Desert spent their mornings at a dozen Gateway computers in a room with a dirt floor, creating the internet. A crucifix hung on the wall right above a whiteboard where they sketched out webpages. The monks were doing a digital-age version of work that Benedictines have done for more than a thousand years. They were scribes.

The monks gave their web-design service the cringeworthy dotcom-era name scriptorium@christdesert and targeted the vast Catholic market of parishes and dioceses; they even hoped to land a contract with the Vatican. The scriptorium produced pages that approximated the look of medieval illuminated manuscripts (and must have taken forever to upload on the single, primitive cell-phone that served as their modem). Because their product was electronic, the monks' remote location was no obstacle to the work, though their phone bill ran to over a thousand dollars a month.[1] The project aimed to profit both the bottom line and the HTML scribes' spiritual lives. "What we're doing now is more creative, and that's good for the monks," Abbot Philip Lawrence, who led Christ in the Desert from 1976 until his retirement in 2018, told a reporter at the time. "If you're doing something that's creative, it brings out a whole different aspect of the soul."[2]

The scriptorium was a hit. It got a boost from national news stories and soon had an abundance of orders—including one from the Holy See. In 1996, Brother Mary-Aquinas Woodworth, a systems analyst in his secular life, predicted it would quadruple the monastery's revenue.[3] At one point, traffic to the monks' website was so great, it caused the whole state's internet service to crash.[4] Brother Mary-Aquinas pitched the idea of a Catholic internet provider to the US bishops, naming AOL, then a ubiquitous provider of dial-up service, as "the model, the competitor."[5] (The bishops passed on his proposal.) As the scriptorium's reputation grew, he began hatching plans to open an office in Santa Fe but was willing to look to bigger cities—including New York and Los Angeles—if he couldn't get the space he needed in New Mexico. He dreamed of hiring up to two hundred people.[6]

But then, in 1998, the scriptorium closed up shop. Monks can't pull eighteen-hour shifts to fill orders. They can't respond to clients' emails while they're praying, studying, or eating together— the non-negotiable activities that make up most of their day. Abbot Philip told me in an email that the project ended because he couldn't justify the labor the scriptorium demanded. It took a long time to train monks for the work, but he couldn't fully capitalize on their skills, because soon after a monk would begin designing web pages, the abbot would need to send him off for theological study. In her history of the monastery, *Brothers of the Desert,* Mari Graña writes, "There were so many orders for design services that what at first seemed the perfect answer for work that would not interfere with the contemplative life, soon began to take over that life."[7]

It goes without saying that no company in the world beyond the canyon would call an end to an enterprise with as much promise as scriptorium@christdesert. If its staff couldn't keep up with orders, it would hire more workers. Possessed by the spirit of capitalism, it would encourage people to work overtime. But the monks couldn't do that, not without thwarting the reason they joined the monastery in the first place. So they quit.

. . .

I sought out the monks of Christ in the Desert hoping to find a model of work in the United States that was as far from burnout culture as possible. I wanted to dig beneath our industrial-age assumptions about labor until I struck medieval bedrock. I knew that work has been essential to Benedictine life for 1,500 years. *Ora et labora*, "prayer and work," is a motto for the Roman Catholic monks and sisters who live their lives according to the sixth-century Rule of St. Benedict. But I also knew that the Rule makes prayer the top priority in a monastery. I learned via their website that the monks of Christ in the Desert worked six mornings a week, from 9:00 a.m. until just after noon. I wanted to know what it was like to live in a community that works only a few hours a day, one that would give up a project with as much potential as the digital scriptorium.

So I went to the desert. I rented a car in Santa Fe one autumn and rumbled down the thirteen miles of pitted gravel road that parallels each curve of the Rio Chama from the highway to the monastery, which sits at the base of an ochre mesa dotted with piñon trees. Across the broad canyon and under a cloudless sky, bright yellow cottonwood leaves shimmered in the wind. I had never been in such a beautiful place.

Still, I had misgivings, a lurking uncertainty about what I'd have to confront there. To prepare for the trip, I read some sayings of the Desert Fathers—the earliest Christian monks, who left the maddening bustle of third-century cities to live in the Egyptian wilderness. They spoke often of demons, including the "noonday demon" of acedia, the unproductive restlessness that drew them away from prayer. St. Antony, the fourth-century hermit, said that if you go to the desert but don't renounce all the things of this world, the demons will tear at your soul in the same way wild dogs would tear at a man who walked through town wearing meat on his otherwise naked body.[8] What demons, I wondered, would visit me in the silent, starlit canyon? On the second day of my visit, I told a brother who was about my age and who wore glasses and a black knitted skullcap that the Desert Fathers had me worried. I hoped he would reassure me, tell me they were just exaggerating. No such luck. "There are many demons," he replied, without a hint of irony. "That's why we're here."

Over several days of working and praying with the monks, I realized that the ceaseless, obsessive American work ethic was one of those demons, certainly the one that haunted me, and most of the people I knew. We are a society almost totally under its power. It inflates our ideals for work even as our working conditions decline. We assess people's value by their jobs and demean anyone who can't work. We forego vacation time, anxious to prove we're indispensable. Josef Pieper called total work a "demonic force in history."[9] That demon is driving burnout culture.

These monks battle the demon, too. Abbot Philip observes in his weekly newsletter that "spiritual life is spiritual combat." Every so often, he writes, the temptations of mundane existence arise—including "conflicts with others, too much time on the internet, making my work in the community more important than taking the time to pray, and so on." He admits that "At times it seems it would be much easier just to abandon the whole effort" of contemplative life.[10] Abbot Philip's remarks remind me of the gospel story of Jesus being tempted by Satan in the desert. Satan offers Jesus real goods: bread, property, authority.[11] The work ethic offers real goods, too, from increased pay and productivity to the esteem of others. But the tempter's offer always comes at a cost. For monks, the benefits of work compete with their spiritual ideals and relationship to God. In secular life, they can entail subjection to bosses, physical and emotional erosion, and the eternal sense that there's more work to do. To win the work ethic's prizes, you necessarily risk burnout. An additional temptation is the false belief that it can't happen to you.

Abbot Philip and his brother monks manage to tame the demon of this work ethic, though, by limiting their labor while they pursue higher goods. We who live in what monks simply call "the world" need to learn their strategies. I don't think we all have to join monasteries to live the good life. But the monastic principles of constraining work and subordinating it to moral and spiritual well-being might help us keep our demons at bay, align our labor with our human dignity, and end the culture of burnout.

. . .

It's 3:30 on a cold Monday morning, the third day of my visit, and the monastery's steady-clanging bell has me up. I pull on my boots and coat, grab a flashlight, and trudge a quarter-mile up the canyon from the low-slung adobe guesthouse to the chapel. I enter and take a seat in the corner that's reserved for guests. The bell rings again just before four, this time more urgently, and thirty-some monks, all yawning and sniffling and wearing either trim black cassocks or broader-cut habits, file into the two sets of choir stalls facing each other across the altar.

We open our spiral-bound breviaries and begin the first session, or "office," of the Liturgy of the Hours, the seven periods of communal prayer that punctuate the monastic day. The monks and guests recite the psalms in Gregorian chant for about seventy-five minutes. We break for fifteen minutes, then come back for another hour. Guests mumble along while they puzzle out the medieval musical notation. No one, not even the monks, projects their voice, creating a soft conformity of sound.

At one point, a brother stands at a lectern and reads the usual Monday-morning passage from Paul's second letter to the Thessalonians: "If anyone was unwilling to work, neither should that one eat."[12] It's a stark admonition to begin the week. The brother finishes reading and returns to his stall. We continue to chant, then have Mass. When Mass ends, at around seven in the morning, the monks file out two by two. They bow deeply to the altar in the center of the chapel, then genuflect before the tabernacle that contains the eucharistic host, bow to each other, and exit, hoods up.

The bell clangs again at 8:45, and the monks are back in the chapel dressed in short, hooded tunics over jeans—their workwear. The youngest, in their early twenties, wear track pants and sneakers. At this office, they pray that they'll remember the sacrifice of Christ, who hung on the cross for three hours—hours they'll spend cooking and cleaning, tending their garden and their flock of sheep, minding the gift shop, sorting through the immigration paperwork of the many brothers who have joined the community from abroad, and making products whose sale will help keep the monastery afloat: beer, soap, wooden rosaries, leather belts, greeting cards.

Work ceases for the day with a 12:40 p.m. bell. That's it; the monks have upheld their end of Paul's bargain. They clean up, pray another brief office, and then eat their main meal in silence while one monk reads to them from a book on the history of Catholicism in the United States. They spend the afternoon at rest or in silent prayer, eat a light meal, and have a brief communal meeting in the evening. The final office of the day, entirely in Latin, concludes by 8:00 in the evening with a ritual of sprinkling the community with holy water. Thus begins the Great Silence, when the monks return to their cells and may not speak. They won't go back to work until the next morning.

I asked Fr. Simeon, a monk who spoke with a confidence cultivated through the years he spent as a defense attorney, what you do when the 12:40 bell rings but you feel that your work is undone.

"You get over it," he replied.

.   .   .

Getting over it is a spiritual discipline we rarely practice in secular life. But it's one thing that makes the deeply humane approach to work at the monastery possible. The Benedictines who live in the canyon keep strict watch over their time and attention. Doing so keeps their desires in order. But it also keeps labor within limits. They get over work so they can get on with something much more important to them.

The subordination of work to prayer reflects Josef Pieper's contention that the way to break through total work is with leisure. And to Pieper, the highest form of leisure is worship. "Celebration of God in worship cannot be done unless it is done for its own sake," he writes. "That most sublime form of affirmation of the world as a whole is the fountainhead of leisure."[13] Worship is not useful for anything else. It is antithetical to our tendency to value only "productive" activity. The Jewish theologian Abraham Joshua Heschel echoes this notion in his 1951 book, *The Sabbath*. To his eyes, a weekly day of rest is incommensurate with "technical civilization" and the conquest of nature through work. "The Sabbath is not for the sake of the weekdays; the weekdays are for the sake of the Sabbath," Heschel writes. "It is not an interlude but the climax of living."[14] The primacy of leisure translates into secular contexts, too. The political philosopher Julie L. Rose argues that free time is a human right, a resource that's essential to the self-determination liberal societies promise their citizens. Because you can't pursue many civic, recreational, or family activities unless others have the same time off you do, laws that forbid most work one day a week can rightly have a place in a pluralistic society.[15] But no matter how we justify it, the point is to allow some higher good to place a hard limit on work. *Something* must be sacred, so that work can be profane.

It's hard to uphold such limits on our own, so we need communities to help us get over our work and to enforce the boundaries around it. St. Benedict writes that "nothing is to be preferred to the Work of God," by which he means the Liturgy of the Hours.[16] Monks who show up late are supposed to "do penance by public satisfaction."[17] On two or three occasions during my visit to Christ in the Desert, a monk arrived at the chapel after an office had already begun. Each time, he walked directly to the altar at the center of the chapel and knelt on the concrete floor, head bowed, until a superior signaled with a knock that he could rise and take his place in his choir stall. The penance lasted for just a few seconds, but it was a clear reproach for making something—a brief conversation, a final check of his work, a trip to the bathroom—more important than the Work of God.

In work and prayer alike, monks typically take their time. *Un travail de bénédictin*—literally, a Benedictine labor—is a French expression for the sort of project someone can only accomplish over a long time through patient, modest, steady effort. It's the kind of thing that can't be rushed: illuminating an entire Bible, writing a thousand-year history, recording the position of stars at each hour of the night for a whole year. It's work that doesn't look good in a quarterly earnings report. It doesn't maximize billable hours. It doesn't get overtime pay. But it's a way to work without the anxiety that drives us to put in long, intense hours and uproot our lives every few years in pursuit of "better" jobs. One elderly, stooped monk with bright eyes behind his glasses told me over homemade cookies and instant coffee after Sunday Mass that he was cataloging all the books in the monastery's library, a task he had been assigned fourteen years earlier. He started the work and kept going, day after day, book after book. He wasn't even close to finished.

Benedictines sometimes say they aim to unite prayer and work, turning *ora et labora* into a single activity. And in some ways, their prayer itself looks like a kind of work, with early hours and a rigid schedule. But monastic prayer is much more unlike secular work than like it. There are no salaries, no promotions, and no productivity quotas. It never hangs over the monks' heads, unfinished. They can't put off the day's offices and vow to pray twice as hard tomorrow. They can't use prayer to prove their worth in others' eyes. They don't get anxious that robots will replace them. In the Middle Ages, monks were early adopters of water mills, to improve their agricultural labor and make more time for prayer.[18] The monks at Christ in the Desert rely on solar power and satellite communication. Benedictines care about efficiency. Just not when it comes to their prayers. In fifteen centuries, they've made no effort to streamline them.

In fact, the monks at Christ in the Desert go out of their way to resist efficiency in the Work of God, reciting prayers much more slowly than people do in ordinary Catholic parishes. During the first few offices I attended, I grew impatient with the pace, another demon needling me. The monks sing the Psalms antiphonally, with choirs in opposite corners of the chapel alternating verses. The pause between verses extended too long for me. We were wasting precious milliseconds. The monks could pray faster, but they don't want to. They don't have something better to do.

.   .   .

On Monday morning, after prayers, I reported for work to the office of the monk who deals with guests—the guestmaster—but there was nothing for any of us to do. So, led by the demon of our work ethic, we found things to do. Someone noticed the windows in the monastery's reception area were dirty and wondered if there was Windex to clean them. Others dusted the windowsills and picked up stray bits of trash in a courtyard. A tall guy, fiftyish, said he wanted to clear a gravel path that was becoming overgrown with weeds. I wanted to be useful, too, so I went with him. After an hour of uprooting tumbleweeds and marking the edges of the path with rocks, we admired our work.

I headed back to the guesthouse and encountered two middle-aged women who were straightening up the kitchen. I got a drink of water and left them to it. Meanwhile, young brothers wearing blue nitrile gloves were ducking into and out of bathrooms and empty guest rooms, preparing for new arrivals. One wore a discreet pair of earbuds. When they finished their work, they leaned back in chairs outside a guest room and chatted in Vietnamese. They were taking a load off, like any manual workers. They headed back toward the cloister even before the bell rang.

Fr. Simeon told me that, in mentoring novice monks from all over the world, he gets to see many different cultures' work ethics. Americans are the most obsessive about work, he said. But he finds that, regardless of their nationality, younger monks need time to adapt to the monastic schedule and the priority of prayer. Young brothers are often anxious about their labor, he said. They struggle to get over the fact that they can leave it at the end of the work period and pick it up again the next day. They want to prove themselves, because they haven't yet learned what it means to live a life of prayer for the world, a world they've renounced. "You're giving your life away and not seeing any results," Fr. Simeon said. "So *of course* you want to work."

. . .

Monks may not be driven by a desire for measurable results, but they do need to support themselves. They have to engage with the world; that's where the money is, after all. The guesthouse is a major source of the monastery's income. (It closed when the pandemic began.) The monks rely on donations, too. They have tried many ventures in recent decades to find the right balance between profitability and the integrity of their calling. They opened a thrift store and a gift shop in Santa Fe that each lasted a few years. They also attempted beekeeping but never produced enough honey to sell at a profit. They signed a record deal with Sony Masterworks to produce CDs of their chants and hosted a reality TV show for the Learning Channel, on which five men—including one obligatory loose cannon—lived like monks for forty days.

The scriptorium was the most ambitious project; its potential seemed revolutionary. At the head of it was Brother Mary-Aquinas, a monk with rare technical ability and an expansive vision. He said in 1998 that there needed to be "a new kind of spirituality" for monks doing work in information technology. "It's extremely demanding, it takes a lot of concentration. It often takes you eight to ten hours to get your mind around a problem," he said. "It doesn't fit easily into the monastic schedule." He drew a contrast between the agrarian roots of Benedictine labor and information-age models: "The modern sense of work is, in a way, a much more perfect vision."[19]

St. Benedict himself acknowledged that the monastic community would include members with marketable skills. If it's going to survive, it ought to. But he had a stern warning for his monks. An artisan who "becomes puffed up by his skillfulness in his craft, and feels he is conferring something on the monastery" should be ordered to cease his work until he's able to do it with humility.[20] This rule makes no sense to secular eyes. Out in the world, talent is considered a rare commodity. Firms compete for workers with expertise—whether they're coders or surgeons or goalkeepers—and then try to get them to work as many hours as possible. That's how corporations believe they'll make the most money. In the monastery, though, expertise can get in the way of the community's health and impede the expert's spiritual development. If a skilled artisan invests himself in his craft, he'll develop his talent and become more productive. But this investment carries the risk of pride, the fundamental human sin. If the monk isn't vigilant, or if his brothers aren't vigilant on his behalf, the pleasure he takes in the craft might overtake the purpose for which the craft is done.

Abbot Philip wrote in an email to me that "one of the challenges, even now, is to develop artisans and artists whose first identity is to be a monk." A talented weaver and a furniture maker each left the monastery to pursue their crafts in the world. "The challenge for us is the formation of a monk," Abbot Philip continued. "And sometimes the other activities have become more important and we lose the monk while producing a great artist."

Brother Mary-Aquinas left the monastery, too, in 1998, the same year the scriptorium closed. According to the current website for NextScribe, a scriptorium spinoff he started, he returned to secular life after "his Archbishop judged that his new vocation in the field of Computer Supported Spiritual Development . . . was no longer that of a hermit monk."[21]

.   .   .

Henry David Thoreau thought asceticism could free us from our endless, desperate, and desolate toil. Figure out what is truly indispensable, pitch the rest, and work for only as long as it takes to stock your pantry with what you absolutely need. Then you can strive for higher things. Thoreau had confidence in his neighbors' ability to carry out this way of life, but he thought they would each have to do it alone. Social conventions can add to your burdens, and besides, your task is to follow *your own* genius. No one else can lead you to it.

The political philosopher Kathi Weeks takes the opposite approach to getting over the work ethic. To her, the post-work society is, by its very nature, a communal endeavor. But she is suspicious of asceticism as the means to attain it. In her view, desiring less in order to work less is just a mirror image of the work ethic's rule, articulated at least since St. Paul, that your desires must be only in proportion to your labor.[22] To get past the work ethic, Weeks thinks, we should demand more and more in exchange for less and less work.

Even if we prefer Weeks's admittedly utopian vision, we have to live, for now, in a system where work is most people's sole means of satisfying their material needs and desires. How should we work, and what should we desire, in the time between now and the era of post-work abundance? Benedictines show that, when you're trying to decenter work in your life, there is no opposition between community and asceticism. In fact, *only* a community that has pledged to honor your human dignity can make bearable the asceticism it takes to forge a life beyond total work and burnout. The community not only provides for your needs, from the day you join it until the day you die, but it also sets limits on your work.

One pair of early burnout researchers posited that "ideological communities" like Catholic religious orders and Montessori schools exhibit low levels of burnout because the shared ideology gives structure and meaning to ordinary tasks, equalizes relationships between members, and reduces the conflict and ambiguity that cause stress to workers.[23] But as I have seen, the Benedictines' vocation is not a superpower that enables them to stretch across the gap between the ideal and reality of work without suffering burnout. Rather, what keeps ideal and reality aligned is the specific form of life their shared vocation inspires. Benedictine communities are already built around practices that keep the most common institutional "mismatches" that foster burnout at bay: overwork, lack of recognition or autonomy, unfairness, breakdown of community, and conflict of values. The whole point of a monastery is to live together; community is protected above all else. Benedictines' commitment to the Rule keeps their values in harmony. It's true that Catholic religious give up a great deal of their autonomy—they take a vow of obedience, after all—but they don't necessarily give up more than office workers would. And they set limits on work. At Christ in the Desert, the monks rotate their work assignments, as St. Benedict instructs.[24] Monks get lighter duty as they age. Prayer time keeps the work period in check. They are striving to be holy, but they don't have to be work saints.

I drove back down the gravel road away from Christ in the Desert feeling exhilarated. It was thrilling to realize that the way I lived, with my usual work, sleep, eating, and time-wasting routines, was not the only way. I did not fundamentally change my life after my visit. But I realized that change was possible. Every one of the brothers had lived in the world, just as I do, and then made the radical choice to retreat far away from it, to live as close to the letter of St. Benedict's Rule as possible, and to give his life to contemplation. Few of us can live like the monks do. Crucially, because Benedictines do not have children to support, they are free from the duties of parenting. (They do care for aged and infirm members of their community.) Still, their lives suggest that alternative ideals exist—ideals for ourselves that are so high, we can't afford to let work interfere—even if we could never realize them on a large scale. So I looked for Benedictines who are more engaged with the world, whose way of life embodied these same values but might be more approachable to secular people. I found them on the prairie of central Minnesota.

· · ·

Sr. Cecelia Prokosch, a member of St. Benedict's Monastery in the town of St. Joseph, Minnesota, told me that when she entered the order in the late 1950s, the running joke was that the sisters lived a life of *ora et labora et labora et labora*. In those days, she managed the food service for the entire monastery and the adjacent College of St. Benedict, a women's college. "It was all work, and I hardly ever made it to prayer," she told me as we sat across the table in a spotless kitchen in the monastery. "I pretty well lived in my office." Sr. Cecelia slept in a college dorm at the time, and she would miss morning prayer so she could make it to work by 7:30 or 8:00 a.m., then continue working until well into the night. She kept this schedule for fourteen years, and for part of the time she was also teaching classes and studying for an MBA. "It just wore me out," she said. "But I was young and energetic then."

When I met Sr. Cecelia, her job for the past fifteen years had been as the monastery's hospitality coordinator, the person I emailed to set up interviews with members of the community. Her lighter schedule meant she could focus more on the contemplative side of monastic life: the Liturgy of the Hours, *lectio divina* (prayer focused on scripture), and meditation. She hardly ever misses communal prayer now.

Central Minnesota is Benedictine country. In the middle of the twentieth century, four hundred monks and over a thousand sisters belonged to the two great monasteries of the region, the women at St. Benedict's Monastery and the men at St. John's Abbey in Collegeville, five miles of cornfields away. The sisters staffed more than fifty schools across the state, while the monks served as parish priests and ran an array of ventures, including a university, a high school, a publishing house, a radio station, and the woodworking shop that turned out the bed I slept in during the week I visited Collegeville.

Benedictines came to central Minnesota in the nineteenth century to teach and evangelize German immigrants settling in the region. It was a labor-intensive mission, one that demanded the monks and sisters make compromises with St. Benedict. Although the monasteries' population is now a fraction of what it once was, and only a handful of members are currently teaching or serving in parishes, there is still work to do in the community. Sisters have sought to promote cultural and religious understanding between the descendants of those German immigrants and more recent arrivals from Somalia.[25] Their spirit of active engagement with the world remains.

And so the sisters and monks still make compromises. They gather three times a day for communal prayer instead of seven. They don't take every meal in silence. Benedict makes no provision for singing "Happy Birthday," but that's what the sisters did for someone who was turning eighty on the day I visited their monastery's dining room for lunch. A monk at St. John's told me there was no public penance in his community for being late to prayer, just the occasional reminder from the abbot to arrive on time. The sisters' and monks' whole adult lives have been a constant negotiation between the Benedictine Rule's ideals of monastic life and the reality of their work. None of them has to undertake that negotiation alone. The monasteries represent a whole culture that enables each of its members to find balance.

One of the chief compromises the monks and sisters make is with communal prayer. Benedict is strict on this point, saying they should prefer nothing to the Liturgy of the Hours.[26] That rule is the reason behind Fr. Simeon's imperative that monks "get over it" when the work period ends. But all the Benedictines I spoke with in Minnesota said their daily labor had, at some point in their careers, kept them from making it to every single office. "You have to adjust," said Sr. Lucinda Mareck, who has straight white hair and speaks with intensity. During her six decades in the order, she had worked in a high school, a retreat center, and a campus ministry; served as postulant director, director of vocations, and house coordinator in her community; done grief and divorce counseling for the Archdiocese of St. Paul and Minneapolis; and essentially ran a Catholic parish as its Pastoral Associate. For many of these years, it simply wasn't possible to get to noon prayer with the community. After fifty years in the "fast lane" of active ministry, Sr. Lucinda became a baker, realizing a longtime dream. She no longer works nights or weekends. Like Sr. Cecelia, she rarely misses an office these days.

· · ·

The Abbey Church at St. John's offers a striking visual metaphor for the monastery as a place of labor in community. One entire wall of the massive, brutalist structure—one of modernist architect Marcel Breuer's signature works—is floor-to-ceiling stained-glass windows, shaped like honeycomb. The church is a beehive, where the monks gather before going to work and where they return at midday and evening.

One place the monks have gone to work for as long as they have been in Collegeville is St. John's University, built on land surrounding the monastery. In the middle of the twentieth century, most of the faculty were members of the Benedictine community. Now, only about ten are. I met one of the youngest monks in the community, theology professor Fr. Nickolas Becker, in his office in the Quadrangle, a vast Victorian building that housed the community for a century. He is a big man, and on the summer afternoon when we spoke, he wore a crisp white Oxford button-down shirt and navy-blue pants. On his tidy desk sat an iPhone, a biblical commentary, and a Pomodoro clock—one of those tomato-shaped timers people use to stay focused on work for twenty-five minutes at a time.

Fr. Nickolas admitted he finds it challenging to hold a demanding job and participate fully in the life of his community. The challenge, as he told me, is that he is drawn to contemplative life, but he finds himself in an active role. It's a conflict between an ideal and the reality of his position; if he can't resolve that tension, he will risk burnout. Not only does he teach a full schedule of moral theology classes, but he lives with sophomores in a dorm. To get everything done, he employs productivity techniques from sources like Stephen Covey's *Seven Habits of Highly Effective People.* "I'm intentional about being disciplined and scheduled," he said: something that struck me as true for a monk almost by definition. Even so, he hasn't used the Pomodoro in a while.

Fr. Nickolas described the workload of his first semester of teaching as like "being hit by a Mack truck." Once exams were graded for the semester, he visited a Trappist monastery in Iowa for a retreat. He admires the more contemplative Trappist order, saying they have a "healthier" approach to work. While there, he gained a new appreciation for private prayer and spiritual reading. Now, an hour or two of that—he called it "my own vigil"—is one of the "non-negotiables" of his life during the academic year, along with communal prayer where possible, daily Mass, and a meal with the community. "I'm not going to let the job crush me, and I'm not going to give up on a vision of monastic life," he said.

I asked each of the Benedictines I met in Minnesota if burnout was part of their vocabulary for describing the stress of work, prayer, and community life. Nearly all paused for an uncharacteristically long time before answering. And despite the intensity of their work, all said no, burnout wasn't a problem in their communities. Only one said he had experienced burnout, but that was before coming to St. John's. The monks and sisters didn't espouse the ethic of work martyrdom that is so common in secular service jobs, either, despite the prominence of sacrificial love in Christian theology.

The one monk who said he had burned out did so early in his monastic career. Fr. Luke Mancuso, an English professor whose bald head and glasses lend him a passing resemblance to the French theorist Michel Foucault, said that before he joined St. John's Abbey, he belonged to a monastery in his home state of Louisiana. After his ordination as a priest in 1983, he served as a hospital chaplain, earning a salary the small community needed. For three years, he was on call six days a week. Monks pray at set times each day; the abbey bell functions as a clock for all within earshot. But as a chaplain, Fr. Luke faced an "implicit threat of constant intrusion." The call to work could come at any time. He had to keep a constant vigil.

As we sat in his office—the walls covered with movie posters and portraits of Walt Whitman, the English shoegaze band Slowdive playing on his computer—Fr. Luke described a classic case of burnout, using language of exhaustion, disengagement, and ineffectiveness. The hospital work was "depleting," he said. It just didn't fit who he was. At the time, he wanted to be like the

Trappist monk and writer Thomas Merton, who combined scholarship and political activism with personal wit and a sense of solidarity with people on the social margins. The tension between this desire and Fr. Luke's actual daily work "broke" him, he said. He stayed in the chaplain job as long as he did, though, out of a sense of duty to the community. He called duty one of "the demons I've had to struggle with" in his life as a monk. The demon kept him from realizing something was wrong with his work until it was too late.

Fr. Luke transferred to St. John's, then went to graduate school, got a PhD, and joined the university's faculty. He remains busy—"I have the opposite of acedia," he said—but he is no longer on call. He does not always make it to evening communal prayer after a long day of teaching, but he practices frequent solitary prayer. The two or three hours he spends alone in his cell in the evening energize him.

. . .

One area where the Benedictines make no compromise is in the dignity of their brothers and sisters. Each has a right to belong, regardless of the work they do. Both communities in Minnesota are aging, and their members express an acute awareness of the need for some of them to be earning salaries. The monks at St. John's know that some bring in more money than others. Yet, as Benedict's rule concerning artisans states, the ones who make more must "practice their craft *with all humility*" (emphasis added).[27] Fr. Luke, for instance, knows he is among the Abbey's top earners, but, he said, "You cannot judge the dignity or worth of this particular monk by the amount or quality of the labor they produce. . . . We have to think of them as having infinite worth." I heard words like these again and again from Benedictines I interviewed. Even when a monk loses his job, he has to have dignity in the community, Fr. Luke added. "We have to live with that person and support them as they reinvent themselves."

When it comes to belonging, the contrast could not be greater between the monastery and the fissured secular workplace, where "core" employees have dignity while temps and contract workers are invisible and replaceable. As Fr. Luke noted, he enjoys perpetual vows and tenure, as opposed to the precarity and expendability that prevails in the mainstream economy. The difference is a matter of promises. In the post-industrial, neoliberal era of minimal job security, a "one-way honor system" exists between employers and employees, the sociologist Allison Pugh argues. That is, workers maintain high levels of devotion to their work, even as they know their employers will not reciprocate.[28] It's a system engineered to cause burnout: you have high expectations for your job performance but no guarantee that your conditions will meet those ideals or that you will even get to keep your job.

The Benedictine system is based on vows made before God. Benedictines pledge "stability of life," binding themselves to a specific community in perpetuity, and only rarely can they transfer their vows as Fr. Luke did. According to the Benedictine Rule, the abbot or abbess is supposed to provide everything the professed members of the monastery need so the "vice of private ownership may be completely uprooted."[29] This commitment makes it possible for Fr. Nickolas to have high ideals for what it means to be a monk, including two hours of private prayer a day. He knows not everything depends on him being a professor. Even if he doesn't get tenure at the university, he will still have a home. He will be assigned another job. "But," he adds, "I also have no money and no wife and family." He is wedded to the community.

The nearest secular analogy to the Benedictine model of perpetual support for all community members is little more than a dream as I write this. Proposals for universal basic income would constitute a society-wide promise to care for people whether they work or not. That baseline income would lower the stakes of any job and make it easier to leave bad jobs or to work simply for the love of an activity that does not pay well. Combine that security with a stronger emphasis on the dignity of each person—which is itself a solid justification for a basic income—and we would go a long way toward eliminating the anxiety about money and status that drives us to work to the point of burnout.

. . .

The hive at St. John's Abbey is quieter now than it was fifty years ago, when monks buzzed around the region, educating, building, and ministering to rural communities. Its members' median age is over seventy, and like their sisters at St. Benedict's Monastery, they are becoming a more contemplative community as they age. Still, Benedictines never really retire, one of them told me. They just get another job, like Sr. Cecelia becoming hospitality coordinator or Sr. Lucinda becoming a baker. I have been arguing that by limiting their work, Benedictines make it more humane, and the fact that several I met were still active in their eighties may seem like the *lack* of a limit. But I think it paradoxically reflects how the brothers and sisters continue to have dignity throughout their lives. Because their work does not exhaust them—in both senses of the term—they can keep contributing to the community until they die. The work older Benedictines do is adapted to their capabilities and determined in consultation with their superiors, as the Rule requires.[30] Their labor also reflects Pope Leo XIII's call for work schedules "adapted to the health and strength of the workman."[31] Even the most infirm members of the Benedictine monasteries in Minnesota have something to do: to pray for the concerns people bring to the community. One sister, who was eighty-eight at the time I met her, was responsible for coordinating the prayer requests that come to the monastery through its website, often on behalf of patients at the Mayo Clinic in southern Minnesota. She writes back to the people who make the requests, to understand better what is needed, then delivers the requests to sisters who live at a nearby retirement and assisted-living convent. The community still depends on them, too.

I met a ninety-year old monk who was minding the gift shop at St. John's Abbey. When I entered the shop, he handed me a slip of paper with a quote from St. John Henry Newman on it: "May He support us all the day long, till the shades lengthen, and the evening comes, and the busy world is hushed, and the fever of life is over, and our work is done! Then in His mercy may He give us safe lodging, and a holy rest, and peace at the last!"[32] Newman's words struck me as appropriate for meditating on retirement. The monk radiated good cheer, swapping stories with customers, including a married couple who had met while they were students at the colleges. Another monk, Fr. Rene McGraw, who had just retired from teaching philosophy at age eighty-four when I met him, was awaiting his new assignment from the Abbot. He said he was ready to do whatever was assigned, "whether it's cleaning urinals or sweeping floors."

Americans aren't good at retirement, partly because they have built so much of their identity, community, and sense of purpose around work, even though that work causes so many to burn out. They desperately look forward to retirement, yet they don't know what to do with themselves once their careers end. Since 2000, the percentage of working Americans over sixty-five rose steadily, even as the overall rate of adult labor force participation declined.[33] About 40 percent of those older workers had previously retired, then went back to work.[34] Henry David Thoreau mocked people who occupy "the best part of one's life earning money in order to enjoy a questionable liberty during the least valuable part of it."[35] Many Americans can't even do that.

The prospect of retirement does make some Benedictines nervous. Sr. Jeanne Marie Lust, for instance, a biology professor, has been a member of the community since she graduated from the College of St. Benedict in 1973. She loves her work, and she loves playing golf in the summers. When we spoke, Sr. Jeanne wore an Oxford shirt, untucked, over her T-shirt and capris. She has short white hair and glasses, with barely a line on her face. Once she retires, she doesn't know what she'll do next. "I can't see any jobs around here that I really want to have," she said. Sr. Jeanne sees herself as "not the holy type," so spiritual direction, something that older members of the community often do, doesn't appeal to her. Perhaps she could learn how to grow hydroponic vegetables for the community, she said.

Statistically speaking, it is likely that Sr. Jeanne will be as happy in retirement as Sr. Cecelia or Sr. Lucinda or the monk in the gift shop. One study found that German Benedictine sisters expressed significantly higher life satisfaction than the general population of

German women, both married and unmarried. In fact, while the typical German experiences a dip in satisfaction in midlife, the Benedictine women did not. They kept getting happier as they aged.[36]

. . .

I suspect that living out a belief in each other's dignity—and thereby keeping work in perspective while meeting each other's human needs—has something to do with the monks' and sisters' happiness. Regardless of our religious commitments, we need to acknowledge this dignity, in others and ourselves, if we're going to keep our desire for productivity from turning demonic. A quarterly profit goal isn't worth as much as the person who labors, at the cost of her health, to meet it. No reputation for customer satisfaction is worth as much as the person who fills orders and endures complaints. Your pride in a job well done, or your anxiety, or your burnout in service to your employer: none of those is worth as much as your dignity as a person.

I recall the way the monks at Christ in the Desert leave their choir stalls at the end of every prayer office. Each one bows to the altar, then to his brother opposite him. They repeat this action seven times a day. Compared with a culture that demands you labor constantly to prove your value, it might be the most radical thing the monks do.

8 *Varieties of Anti-Burnout Experience*

One afternoon while I was in Collegeville, Minnesota, I dropped by the pottery studio of Richard Bresnahan. The door was open, and I poked around for several minutes, admiring shelf after shelf of unglazed red and gray pitchers and cups, before Bresnahan, who was throwing clay for a shallow bowl, even noticed I was there. His apprentices were across the road, making early preparations for firing their massive lakeside kiln in a few months' time: pressure-washing shelves, splitting logs. They fire the kiln only once every two years, filling it with nearly 15,000 objects packed in tight formation and burning through twenty-two cords of wood.[1]

But every day at three o'clock, work stops so the potters and anyone else who wanders in can sit around the studio's three-foot square *irori* table. There is a burner in the middle of the table and an iron kettle suspended above it. An apprentice monitored the temperature of the water by eyeing its bubbles as she made pot after pot of green tea. We sipped the tea, shot the breeze, and passed around a bowl of the sweetest cherry tomatoes I have ever eaten, which one of the apprentices grew in his garden. When a potter from North Dakota dropped by unexpectedly with her husband, we shuffled our chairs to make room for them.

The table is a small monument to the principle that a flourishing human life needs community and regular leisure to set limits on our work and give people the opportunity to honor each other's dignity. It represents a more humane work ideal than most of us aspire to today.

We need a radical break with burnout culture. In my effort to understand what that break would be like, I feel drawn to the cultural fringes, to people whose lives appear unusual or "unsuccessful" by our current standards. Those standards are part of a culture that has to change. We can't eradicate burnout without also ending the culture of total work. We can't keep working the same way we have for the past fifty years and expect the results suddenly to improve. It's why the overwhelming majority of our discourse about burnout, which I talked about back in chapter 1, is so shallow and timid. We say we don't want to burn out, but we also don't want to give up the system of meaning—not to mention the system of profit-making—we have built around the work that causes our burnout.

The best examples of a good life that's built around something other than work are going to seem difficult. Still, people are giving them a shot. They are creating better workplaces. They are investing themselves in hobbies after work. And they are taking on art projects when disability prevents them from working for pay. Across these examples, we need to see what community structures and personal disciplines help people find dignity, moral value, and purpose outside of work. How do their ideals interact with the reality of their jobs? In other words, what are the characteristics of the anti-burnout counterculture?

·   ·   ·

On a rainy spring morning several months after my trip to Minnesota, I visited the monthly staff meeting of CitySquare, a Dallas nonprofit that does direct anti-poverty work through housing, food, and health programs. CitySquare's Chief People Officer at the time, Jarie Bradley, who invited me, said the meeting would feel like a party. It was held at an unassuming brick Baptist church adjacent to a highway in South Dallas. Inside, coffee, juice, and breakfast tacos sat on a table in a hallway. Gospel music played on the PA system in the sanctuary, which had blue walls, blue carpeting, and blue upholstery on the stackable metal chairs. The employees gathered there—CitySquare has about 160 altogether—were mostly women; among the racially diverse group, about half were African American.

Bradley, who was wearing an orange CitySquare T-shirt under a jacket and whose hair was dyed a deep burgundy, milled about the room as people trickled in, hugging everyone she saw. She began the meeting with an introduction of three women just hired to work in the housing department: "Let's give it up for our new poverty fighters!" We applauded.

Next on the agenda was "You Better Recognize," an open forum to acknowledge someone else's work. This seemed like the party aspect of the meeting. Bradley handed the mic off to one poverty fighter after another who wanted to praise a coworker. *You better recognize* the Food Programs Staff. *You better recognize* the Neighbor Support Services team, who had just gone through a successful program audit. Two dozen people stood up. "You better recognize these folks!" someone said, and everyone applauded again.

It became a cascade of appreciation. *You better recognize* Miss Andrea, who reserved space for a meeting. *You better recognize* everyone who helped a family find housing and school when they showed up during a board meeting. *You better recognize* "the special forces of the Outreach Team." *You better recognize* the guys who renovated a room for the program audit.

The mic came back to Bradley, who thanked everyone for exhibiting "the CitySquare way" throughout the audit. Not only did the organization receive a positive review, but once the municipal auditor finished her work, she immediately applied for a job there.

I got interested in CitySquare after meeting Bradley at a conference. She talked about her employer's work and the compassion that motivates it. CitySquare seemed like the answer to an important question: How can an ordinary workplace put human dignity at the center of its culture and, in doing so, defeat burnout?

Poverty fighters risk burnout all the time. "We know this work is hard as hell, and we know we have to take care of each other in the midst of taking care of the community," Bradley told me over coffee and a BLT in a strip-mall sandwich shop. CitySquare's commitment to appreciation, so evident in the "You Better Recognize" segment of the staff meeting, addresses one common workplace deficit that leads to frustration and burnout. More concretely, Bradley said CitySquare had increased its employee assistance program from three counseling sessions per year to six, with both part-time and full-time employees eligible. These policies reflect a recognition that stress and burnout are the reality in human-service work. As CitySquare President John Siburt told me in an interview, "There's not a sense of shame around burnout" in his organization. "It's understood that that's a normal human response to caring this deeply and this intensely about so many people." CitySquare has also increased the paid time off it offers in recent years; counting paid holidays and a two-week end-of-year break, employees get up to forty-two days off per year. That's forty-two days more than US federal law requires. Former employees told me their supervisors encouraged them to take all the time off they were entitled to.

More than time off, compassionately managing people's roles within the organization helps keep burnout in check, according to Bradley. This often means telling "hard truths to people, but all in love and all in wanting people to thrive and be in a space that's best for them." When someone's work is "not ideal," Bradley said, she asks their supervisor to recall the person's best qualities. What made them worth hiring in the first place? And what would the supervisor want done for them if they were in the employee's situation? The outcome of these conversations might be that the employee gets some time off or an internal transfer. Bradley mentioned one worker, a supervisor of case managers, who became tired of managing people. When she started managing grants instead, she thrived. Another employee's performance improved dramatically after some time off, some coaching, and a new role. Sometimes, if a long-tenured employee cannot find an alternative assignment, they aren't simply fired; CitySquare may offer them a few months' extra flexibility with their duties so they can figure out their goals and find a job outside the organization.

Several months before I met Bradley, she herself experienced burnout and needed a change in her role to continue to flourish at CitySquare. After ten years in the organization, she was doing the equivalent of two jobs: running both human resources and the community job development program. She loved the work, because it advanced a mission she believed in. She loved that it was "all-consuming." But that was also the problem. She worked all the time, without breaks, without asking for help. She would tell herself, "'You can go a little more. You can keep pushing.' Then I realized, you can't." Her blood pressure began spiking. After consulting with CitySquare leaders, she gave herself permission to admit she was tired, and she took a month off. When she returned, she focused solely on her HR job.

In her time at CitySquare, Bradley approached human resources management not as the process of setting rules and getting people to comply with them, but as a series of encounters with others. "Relationships mitigate risk," she said. Putting relationships first also means the boundaries around human resources work are always blurry. "Who says I can't cry with an employee or pray with an employee if that's what they want to do?" Bradley asked. CitySquare has religious roots as an organization. For most of its history, it was called Central Dallas Ministries and was affiliated with a church. Its former longtime president and current CEO emeritus, Larry James, is a minister. The staff meeting I visited concluded with a prayer. The welcoming of faith is part of a desire not to have people "compartmentalize" any aspect of themselves when they come to work, Bradley said. "We try to invite all the things that make us human," she told me. Former case manager Marley Malenfant said he experienced the religious identity of CitySquare as open to whatever employees brought to it. He described the environment as "come-as-you-are."

Former employees told me they appreciated how their supervisors often took an interest in their lives outside of work. Liz Curfman, the social worker I mentioned in chapter 3 who struggled with cynicism, said that when she worked at CitySquare, the director of her department presented her with a housewarming basket when she and her husband bought their first home. CitySquare's leaders wanted to see her thrive in all respects, she said. Malenfant said his team's Monday afternoon meetings always included a roundtable discussion of not just their cases for the week, but also what was happening in their lives, both good and bad. He told me his supervisors really listened in these moments. "I give them props for that," he said. "It's therapeutic in a lot of ways." The approach seems to work. CitySquare's turnover rate, about 12 percent at the time I spoke to Bradley, is low by industry standards.

. . .

At the CitySquare staff meeting, after "You Better Recognize," John Siburt got up to speak. Siburt, a big guy who was wearing a beige sport coat that morning, told story after story about Larry James. His upbringing in rural Texas. His relationships with the people he aimed to serve. His role as a second father to Siburt. Siburt choked up talking about how James once postponed a business trip Siburt was supposed to take, so Siburt could coach his own son's Little League baseball team in a tournament. Each CitySquare employee, he said, needed to focus on how they treat each other. The model was James. "His love for people lives in me," Siburt said, "and it lives in you."

But then I thought I detected a slight tone of hectoring when Siburt defended evaluating employees' "positivity" on their performance reviews. I wondered if some workers had complained about it. Siburt emphasized that positivity is essential to CitySquare's culture. "If you show negativity to your coworkers," he said, "we're screwed, and [James's] mission will die with him." (Siburt later told me he spoke about positivity because it's a core value of the organization, and the stress of their work can "erode [it], if we're not intentional.") He concluded by telling the employees that he wanted them to know "how much appreciated you are and how loved you are. It's a pleasure to show you grace with your warts and dysfunction and all."

"He cries at every meeting," one employee told me afterward. When Bradley received the mic back from Siburt, she wiped tears away, too.

I saw Siburt's talk as an attempt to resolve a deep conflict in any organization built upon the ideals of an inspiring leader. James is an example of what Max Weber called charismatic leadership: authority that flows from people's relationship to a single compelling figure, rather than from bureaucratic rules and procedures.[2] James writes in his book *House Rules* that a leader must not tolerate "people who do not and cannot love and respect everyone who moves in and out of the world of your organization. Friendship is so basic to our enterprise. Without it, we most certainly fail."[3] He also encourages leaders to embrace "chaos" to foster a vital community.[4] So long as people buy into a charismatic leader's authority, an organization can thrive.

Former longtime CitySquare employees told me their relationships with James and with each other made the emotionally intense work sustainable. Billy Lane, the former senior pastor of a church associated with Central Dallas Ministries as well as the organization's associate director from 1997 to 2005, said his work "didn't feel like work. It felt like *life*." Lane said James would convene weekly "huddles," when the staff or volunteers could not only "nurture each other" but vent their feelings about the work. It was a time to "exhale" and even call out each other, including James, for problems they were causing.

When Lane described the mutual trust he experienced at CitySquare, I thought of Christina Maslach and Michael Leiter's list of six critical areas where workers feel the strain of burnout. Lane's workload sounded heavy, but it was supported by a strong sense of community and shared values, enacted through rituals like the huddles. Such a community is harder to sustain in a larger and necessarily more bureaucratic organization. There is no better example of bureaucratic authority than an employee evaluation procedure, which John Siburt addressed at the staff meeting. To my eyes, Siburt was trying to connect that procedure to James's charisma. His answer to the implicit question of why employees should trust the system was that it shows whether the poverty fighters are still in touch with the mission of the beloved figure who established its culture, even when he is no longer closely involved in day-to-day operations.

Billy Lane's wife, Janet Morrison-Lane, worked at CitySquare for seventeen years because, from the moment during her job interview when James dropped her off at the food pantry with no instructions, he gave her something crucial to working without burnout: autonomy. Like Siburt, she said she views James as a father figure. Morrison-Lane was one of the first people James hired after he took over Central Dallas Ministries in 1994. She headed up the organization's education programs. For a while, she and James were the only full-time employees. In subsequent years, she said, the agencies that fund nonprofits began demanding more accountability metrics. In response, CitySquare grew, and, in her view, its culture changed. "Larry's hiring somebody who's hiring somebody who's hiring somebody," she said, referring to the larger, less intimate organization. It became harder to maintain community and connect everyone to the core values.

There is some debate among scholars over whether charismatic leadership benefits workers or burdens them.[5] A charismatic leader is inspiring, but being constantly inspired can also exhaust you, especially if the organization uses inspiration to cover over poor working conditions. In general, the evidence favors seeing charismatic leadership as preventing burnout.[6] One study found that workers, on average, experience less burnout if they have a supervisor who exhibits a charismatic or "transformational" leadership style—but only if the workers have moderate to high "openness to experience," a personality trait associated with imagination, emotional sensitivity, and curiosity.[7] The point is, charismatic leadership like I saw at CitySquare can help forestall burnout, but not for everyone.

Morrison-Lane told me the bureaucracy and all the staff meetings drained her. Because she knew CitySquare so well, she said, people assigned her more and more tasks. "But there was no promotion," she added, "and you still need your metrics." In addition, a coworker was murdered, as were two kids she worked with. On top of that, an educational program she led ended, and her focus shifted to homelessness, an issue outside her professional strengths. She pulled back emotionally from work, treating it more like a nine-to-five job. Morrison-Lane said James respected her autonomy even as her dissatisfaction with her new role and the attendant paperwork grew. "He had to have known it wasn't a good fit, but he didn't say, 'You're gone,'" she said. "He let me figure it out." Morrison-Lane left CitySquare in 2012 for a nonprofit that focuses on youth education in Vickery Meadow, a Dallas neighborhood with a large refugee population. She is one of just four employees.

Every model of authority carries risks. Bureaucracy can frustrate idealists. You go to work expecting to fight poverty, or to teach, or to heal, and you end up filling out forms. Bureaucracy has depersonalization—the cynicism that's typical of burnout—built in. Charismatic leadership, by contrast, is inherently unstable. How do you maintain a system of authority focused on a revered leader, once that leader is no longer around?[8] Charisma-centered organizations also depend on human feeling, which is often inconsistent. To manage a 160-employee organization with love is like a plate-spinning act; it requires constant emotional maintenance. Finally, the relationship-based culture of CitySquare depends on hiring people whose values already align with the organization's. "We realize we are not everybody's cup of tea," Jarie Bradley said. "We say we have a little crazy going on at CitySquare, but it's the right kind of crazy."

I'm impressed by the way CitySquare puts workers' humanity at the heart of its operations, even as it has necessarily become more bureaucratic. I wish I'd had someone like Bradley keeping an eye on my work, checking in on my well-being, when I was sliding onto the burnout spectrum. I could have used the kind of recognition CitySquare features in its staff meetings. But I also wonder if the emotional intensity the Lanes found there would have been too much for me. They thrived where someone who values detachment would wilt. Above all, I wonder if a humane bureaucracy could lower the stakes of work, so that a mission-driven workplace doesn't have to depend on love and the force of personality to keep it going.

. . .

In the 2006 documentary *Darkon,* about a live-action role-playing game club, several players say they get little meaning from their jobs in retail or manufacturing. But they spend hours during the week plotting their next adventure, creating elaborate medieval costumes, or learning to speak Elvish. Then, on weekends, they get to be heroes, with dignity and autonomy within a group of equals. As one player, Beckie Thurmond, says, "I go to work, my boss is in control. I go to Darkon, I'm in control."[9]

To disrupt burnout culture, we need to put a priority on employees' dignity, as CitySquare does. We also need to put a priority on leisure: to work, once again, for the weekend. But we need to keep in mind that leisure in Josef Pieper's sense is not just a "break" that allows you to come back to work refreshed. "The point and the justification of leisure are not that the functionary should function faultlessly and without a breakdown," Pieper writes, "but that the functionary should continue to be a man."[10] Done right, our hobbies can not only help us keep work in perspective; they can also keep us whole.

One worker who makes his hobby a priority is Paul McKay. He's a cyclist. When he was preparing for two-hundred-mile gravel-road races, he slept on the couch every other Friday night, so he wouldn't awaken his wife or their three children when he got up at midnight to train. Then he would mount his bike and ride seventy miles to Oklahoma City from his home in Stillwater to meet up with a friend at 4:00 a.m. The two of them would ride for another twelve or fourteen hours, going 160 miles round trip. Exhausted, McKay would then meet his family for dinner and get a ride back home with them.

Those night rides sound grueling, but to McKay, they were peak experiences, even meditative. "Who gets to be on a two-lane highway in the middle of the night, feeling excellent, and the moon is shining down, and you see your silhouette on the pavement?" he asked me during our phone conversation. If you found a way to feel like that, wouldn't you build your whole life around it?

McKay told me work never defined him. For years, he worked the night shift at a tire manufacturer because the schedule allowed him to ride for two hours in the afternoon before work. No one else was home, so he figured he wasn't missed. "Riding was where my heart and soul was, where some people's jobs are," he said. The endorphins from his afternoon rides helped him get through a difficult, dangerous job. He saw coworkers die in accidents at the plant. He lost a finger. "Cycling gave me an out," he said, a way to be more than his job title. "It gave me that self-worth and something to look forward to."

Other hobbyists I spoke to likewise resist merging who they are with what they do. For Ken Jurney, cars matter more than his job as a mechanic for a major airline. When I mentioned burnout to him, he immediately recalled street racing as a teenager in the 1970s: "We used to do a lot of burnouts alright!" His first car was a Chevy Nova. He later bought a 1964 Corvette with combat pay from his time in the Marine Corps, and he spent years restoring it. Then he bought a rare 1969 Nova and rebuilt its engine. He knows these vehicles in minute detail. When we spoke, he rattled off the firing order of the pistons on his Corvette in his classic Baltimore accent.

Jurney works seven twelve-hour shifts in a row, followed by seven days off. He said he doesn't have to work that hard, because he knows the airplanes so well and works on a team he can trust. He has the kind of job he can forget about on his days off; the planes don't follow him home. When we spoke, he was getting the cars ready for winter storage. Otherwise, he puts some time into a coin collection, and every month or so, he goes to "plink a few hundred rounds off" at the rifle range to keep up the skills he learned as a Marine. His hobbies are also about community. When I first met Jurney, at a Corvette show in Carlisle, Pennsylvania, he was moving from booth to booth, chatting with vendors he had gotten to know over coming to many shows. He wonders about people his age who work all the time and don't have hobbies: "What are you going to do when you retire and you have nothing?"

While my academic career was falling apart, I started playing beer-league ice hockey on Sunday nights. I also took a yearlong drawing class. These activities gave me something to look forward to, placed me in new communities. They took my mind away from my misery two nights a week. But they didn't save me from burnout. By the time I started them, it may have been too late.

Hobbies by themselves are not the pathway to the good life. They're meant to keep us from being obsessed with work, but they can become unhealthy obsessions, too. About two years before Paul McKay and I spoke, he said, he realized that he really was missed while he was riding. He wasn't fully present for his children while they grew up. "When you're working and you're riding and you have kids, it's all a blur," McKay said. "You think, 'Everything's going like it's supposed to.' You don't realize there's a kid out there thinking, 'Dad's riding. Don't get in the way.'" Working nights "blinded" him to what he was missing with his family, including mundane things like dinner and bedtime. He now sees that having his kids at home "is a fleeting moment in time. It's like a treasure. It's like this gift that's leaving you, and you want to wrap yourself around it. You can always get back on the bike" later, when the kids are on their own. McKay works days now, at a company that makes flooring. The work is safer, and he said he doesn't face any stress at it. He rides when he can, but no more than fifty miles at a time.

·   ·   ·

"I measure my weeks in hours," Erica Mena told me. Mena, who identifies as nonbinary, is a Puerto Rican artist and poet in their late thirties who lives in a small village in Finland. "Two hours a day over seven days gives me fourteen hours of time a week in which I can do anything," they said. "That includes cooking, that includes walking, that includes making art."

Mena suffers from chronic fatigue syndrome, which limits the amount of time they can be active. In addition, Mena told me, they've been diagnosed with borderline personality disorder and aphantasia, a condition that makes it impossible to create mental images. Every morning, after reading for an hour, feeding the cat, and having breakfast, Mena makes a self-assessment: "How do I feel? Do I feel like I have the energy to go for a walk? Do I feel like I have the energy to go to the studio?" If it can be a work day, then Mena goes to their home studio—a desk sitting a few feet away from their bed—or to their letterpress studio across town. They put on a playlist of songs that will run for an hour and then get to work. That might involve making paper, or cutting bookboard, or setting type, or mixing ink, or gluing or sewing together the parts of the book. They told me about one recent project, a book about Hurricane Maria called *Gringo Death Coloring Book,* which is a collaboration with two other Puerto Rican artists. Mena set a copy of the book on the floor to show me on our video call; once it's opened up and sitting upright, it's shaped like a star.

"I get really caught up in the work," Mena said. "And it takes on this sort of meditative quality for me, so it's easy for me to lose track of that and to stop listening to my body and to get lost in the rhythm of the work." That's what the playlist is for. When the music stops, Mena stops. Then they check to see if they feel they can continue. If they don't have the energy, then they take care of other errands or rest. It's a matter of self-compassion. The day I spoke with Mena was not a work day. "Some days all I can do is survive, and that's OK," Mena said. "That's still valuable."

Mena's work habits remind me of the monks at the Monastery of Christ in the Desert in New Mexico. Like the monks, Mena's schedule is strictly limited; in Mena's case, the reason is not communal prayer but health. The end of the playlist functions like Mena's chapel bell, calling them to stop their work, even good work, because something else is at stake. It's another ritual that sets a limit on labor.

CitySquare shows what an organization could look like if it aims to care for the full humanity of its employees. Hobbyists like Paul McKay and Ken Jurney show how it's possible to subordinate your job to other activities. The experience of artists like Mena—people of working age whose impairments keep them from working for pay—points the way to more inclusive models for finding dignity, freedom, and a sense of meaning. Art is an exemplary activity, because, like paid work, it produces something, but it is also an endeavor people undertake for non-commercial reasons. Artistic creation additionally depends on communities of other artists and on individual disciplines to support it. Artists like Mena who have disabilities, then, can get many of the moral goods we associate with employment through other means.

Mena did not always work in hour-a-day chunks. For more than a decade, they were an ambitious academic, adding lines to their CV and pursuing a tenure-track job while mentoring students and running a literary journal and a small publishing company. What appealed to Mena was the apparent freedom of academic labor. It was a lot of work, but it was not nine-to-five work. And much of it was work they would have done anyway.

Mena was teaching at Brown University in October 2016 when they got sick with what they thought was a cold. They ended up bedridden until the following April. The next fall, after regaining some physical capacity and learning to manage their condition, they began teaching full-time. But even with the help of their then-partner and an assistant, Mena could not keep up with the work. They eventually went to a psychiatric emergency room and an outpatient mental-health treatment program.[11] A year later, Mena left for Finland.

"I had approached freedom as the result of hard work," Mena said. But after getting sick and starting to read in the field of disability studies, they realized that conception of freedom was false. Without an ordinary job, Mena supports themselves with savings from their previous career, plus some freelance writing and editing and selling art. I ask Mena if they feel freer now that they live in Finland, a country often hailed as a happy and functional social democracy. "I feel freer now that I'm out of *capitalism*, insofar as I am removed from a lot of society by being disabled," they replied. The writer Johanna Hedva similarly connects disability to capitalism, describing sickness as "a capitalist construct." In Hedva's words, "The 'well' person is the person well enough to go to work. The 'sick' person is the one who can't." As a result, capitalist societies view illness as an aberration, not a normal part of being human.[12] To be chronically ill, then, is to be in permanent violation of the norm, to be ineligible for social respect.

Mena, though, says getting out of capitalism and the American culture of total work has helped them live in greater alignment with their ethical ideals. "I'm so much a better person," they said. Mena refers to disability as offering them a "gift" of presence with their body and feelings, of being "just inescapably present with them." As a result of this shift, Mena doesn't feel guilty on mornings when they have energy but take a walk in the forest instead of going to the studio.

Walking is an almost inherently non-productive use of time. It's contemplative; it creates nothing of monetary value; it's leisure. Mena walks slowly through the trees and carries a bag for objects they pick up along the way: animal bones, leaves, pieces of birch bark. These pieces will become part of a new project. Mena checks their energy every so often, and sometimes they can go a little further. But any time or distance they can manage is enough.

. . .

My friend Patricia Nordeen's story about work and disability is similar to Erica Mena's. Like Mena, Patricia was drawn to academia by the flexible schedule it offered for her to do what she most loved to do: read, think, and write. She was on an upward professional trajectory, with a PhD in political philosophy from Yale and a teaching job at the University of Chicago, but in her mid-thirties had to leave her career altogether.

Patricia's impairments mainly stem from Ehlers-Danlos Syndrome, a rare genetic condition that weakens the body's ability to produce collagen. As Patricia points out, collagen is in everything: joints, skin, corneas. Without strong collagen to bind them together, the body's pieces go out of place. Patricia's joints dislocate frequently. She has a metal plate in her skull, and all the vertebrae from the top of her neck to her shoulder blades have been surgically fused to prevent pinched nerves. She lost three years to daily spells of paralysis on her left side. She also has many allergies, including to opioids, which means she is in pain much of the time. Like Mena, she spends a lot of time in bed.

But where Mena's challenge is to find freedom beyond the work ethic, Patricia's is to find identity without the academic institutions that ratified her self-understanding for most of her adult life. She now lives with her widowed mother in the Michigan city where she went to college. Her most significant memories of the place are not of parties but of the building where she first read the Scottish philosopher David Hume.

The language of disability frustrates her. "'Disabled'—all of these words are really identity-sucking," she said. "It's just such a gigantic word, to cover every profession, everything. You're *disabled*." Patricia sees the old-fashioned term "invalid" in the same way: "*in*-valid." It reinforces the idea that, without work to focus your identity, you're no one.

Patricia eagerly accepted my request for a video interview; she said it was a rare opportunity to contribute to scholarship. The core activities that once defined her intellectual life are all but impossible now. "It's hard for me think very well. I get a thought and it's like, just as I start to hold it and express it, I get a pain blip, and it interrupts," she said, using her finger to draw a line in the air in front of her face. The pain erases thought. Even if she could physically write a book—for instance, on how to be a patient, drawing from her vast experience dealing with specialists—she couldn't publish it, she said, because of the limits the Social Security Administration places on how much money someone who receives disability benefits can earn.

Patricia has built her post-academic identity around art. She was a longtime knitter but had never drawn anything. Then a friend got her to join an online art group, where she received encouraging feedback on her first efforts. Learning technical rules like proportion became a problem to solve, a puzzle. She found an art journaling group on Instagram and began posting her art on social media without much worry about whether it was "good" enough. By engaging with posts by other amateur artists, she found a community.

"We are 'social' or 'political' beings, depending on how you translate Aristotle," Patricia said. Sharing her art "keeps me from being lonely. Just the act of hitting send on something I have painted or drawn, it definitely gives me a sense of validation, like I'm part of society." When I spoke with her in April 2020, Patricia and a friend she had met through Instagram were in the middle of a project they called "pandemic pen pals." They pledged to fill one sketchbook page a day for one hundred days, post the images online, and then send each other the completed books. For one day, Patricia made a collage of cancelled stamps and photos of two Victorian-era women, meant to represent her and her pen pal, making funny faces. The following day, she painted a picture of a magnolia tree in bloom and wrote a brief story about the first time she saw one after moving to Virginia for a postdoctoral position. The project "is really about reassuring each other, but also reassuring ourselves," she said. "It's all about recognition."

The project also imposes a self-chosen discipline on Patricia, similar to monastic prayer or Richard Bresnahan's tea break. "You have to show up" when you've promised someone you would make her a drawing a day, she said. For most people Patricia's age, work imposes that accountability and gives moral structure to our interpersonal lives. But it does so at the cost of exposure to the conditions that, when they depart from your ideals, lead to burnout. If we, on a societal level, remove work from the center of our lives, we will still need moral structures—schedules, goals, accountability— to aid in self-development.

Patricia pointed to her forty-five sketchbooks as evidence that she's getting better. "That's satisfying for somebody that likes to learn," she said. Patricia would like to set up a home studio, a place beyond her bed where she can begin painting canvases. She said she is pessimistic about her prospects for getting physically better. Her doctors tell her a treatment for Ehlers-Danlos Syndrome may emerge, but it will take a few years. In the meantime, she keeps filling the sketchbooks. "As long as I can stay curious, have some discipline, be compassionate, and be grateful," she said, "I can get through this. So far."

· · ·

All the people I encountered who are, intentionally or not, living out a post-burnout ethos—the Benedictines, CitySquare, the hobbyists, the artists with disabilities—share the conviction that someone's dignity has nothing to do with their labor. There are many paths to that conviction. Pope Leo XIII arrived there through the biblical notion that all humans are made in the image and likeness of God. Erica Mena gets there by thinking about their cat. "I love my cat more than any living creature in the entire world," they said, "and he does shit for work. Literally. He does fuck-all. So if my cat is deserving of that love, then how can I say that humans aren't?" And, Mena continues, if their friends are deserving of love, and if children are deserving of love despite never working, "then I am, too." Mena also takes inspiration from a print by Anticapitalist Love Notes, a one-woman letterpress project, that reads, "You are worth so much more than your productivity." That simple statement by a fellow printmaker opened up new ways of thinking for Mena. "I remember seeing that post on her Instagram and feeling this sort of longing in my heart," Mena said. They then began to ask themselves, "What would I need to change in order to believe that?"

The notion of an inherent dignity in all people, regardless of whether they produce anything of monetary value, leads the author and painter Sunaura Taylor to argue for a "right not to work." Taylor, who has arthrogryposis, a condition that severely limits the use of her arms and legs, notes that disabled people are just as subject as anyone to American capitalist ideals, and thus susceptible to guilt over not living up to them. Unlike Erica Mena and Patricia Nordeen, Taylor has never been able to hold an ordinary job. But she writes that she is "unusually fortunate to have been raised with a belief in my own inherent value," a belief that kept her guilt in check. "The right not to work," she writes, "is the right not to have your value determined by your productivity as a worker, by your employability or salary." It's the idea that Mena encountered in the Anticapitalist Love Notes print. It's also a reversal of the quintessentially American work ideology Booker T. Washington espoused. Washington taught that people without social recognition could acquire it through hard work; Taylor is saying that if we recognized everyone's inherent dignity ahead of time, then people could work or not "and be proud of it."[13] Their value and their freedom would be based on something else entirely.

Taylor's vision of the human good would not just liberate disabled people from the indignity and guilt of not working. It would liberate everyone. It would lower our ideals for work and justify better conditions for those who do work. It might justify a universal basic income, which would make it economically possible to exercise the right not to work. When we see illness and disability as normal parts of life, we also legitimize unpaid care for others as a normal activity, just as valid as working for pay.[14] By viewing work from the perspective of disability, we can recognize our collective vulnerability and interdependence, undermining the individualism that makes burnout always *your* problem alone, never one shared by others.

Everyone is, at best, only "temporarily abled," as Taylor mentions.[15] Regardless of our current abilities, we are all headed for disability as we age. Our illness and impairment will, sooner or later, make it impossible to work. This fact should help able-bodied workers like me see ourselves in solidarity with others who cannot work. Disability is human nature. It is in everyone's interest to see dignity in this condition and change our social arrangements so disabled people can lead lives of autonomy and meaning. Johanna Hedva calls for a radical new politics based on our common frailty: "To take seriously each other's vulnerability and fragility and precarity, and to support it, honor it, empower it. To protect each other, to enact and practice community. A radical kinship, an interdependent sociality, a politics of care."[16]

Hedva is writing about a different promise from the one at the heart of the work ethic. Instead of saying you have value only if you work, we can promise to care for each other no matter what, as Benedictine communities do. And just as we coded the old promise into our government and workplaces, we can forge institutions of care. We can adapt jobs to "the health and strength" of the people who hold them, as Leo XIII calls for.[17] There is a good chance that anyone who works today will find the reality of their job diverging from their ideals for work. In current conditions, every worker is a potential burnout. That, too, should be a source of solidarity, a spur to change those conditions and what we expect from work. We can't just throw up our hands at the problems created by the ideals of our society. We *are* society. We can change those ideals.

. . .

Then there's me. After leaving what had once been my dream job as a college professor, I followed my wife's career to Texas and tried to reassemble my working identity. It was a relief to feel the tension between my ideals and the reality of my job go slack, but I felt lost for much of my first year in the sun-blasted, concrete city that was my new home. As a newcomer, I was often asked what I did for a living. I would respond, "I'm a writer?" It felt fraudulent. I kicked around the idea of getting yet another graduate degree, or maybe a job in food service, just to have a better answer to that question. I spent long days at home, alone, waiting for someone to give me a project. I began to identify with Martin Sheen's character at the beginning of *Apocalypse Now,* the commando deteriorating in his Saigon hotel room because he didn't have a mission.

Slowly, I published more. I went to writing workshops. I charted out a new career that combined writing, speaking, and teaching. I decided I wanted to get back into a college classroom, so I emailed the director of the first-year writing program at a nearby university. She wrote back and asked if we could meet right away; she needed someone to teach a class beginning in just a few weeks.

Getting that job was a crucial step toward remaking my ability to flourish. My teaching schedule is light, just one or two classes a semester, but it imposes a structure on my days and weeks. It gives me an institution to belong to. As an adjunct, I'm on the wrong side of the fissured workplace, but my tenured faculty friends see me as a peer. Most important, I know someone is depending on me. My students rely on me to lead our class meetings, to grade their papers, to show them how to improve their paragraphs' topic sentences. That is immediate, daily validation of my labor and thus, of myself. I know how risky it is to lean on that validation, but it's nice to hear students thank me as they walk out the classroom door.

While I was working on this chapter, I took the Maslach Burnout Inventory again. I knew I wasn't burned out anymore, but I wanted scientific verification. In the four years between the two tests, I improved across all three dimensions by a surprising amount. Shortly after I quit my job, I scored in the ninety-eighth percentile for emotional exhaustion, the forty-fourth for depersonalization (or cynicism), and the seventeenth for personal accomplishment, signaling a high sense of ineffectiveness. The second time around, I scored in the thirteenth percentile for exhaustion, just the seventh for depersonalization, and the fifty-fifth for personal accomplishment.

The new scores accurately reflect my subjective sense of how I'm doing. I'm not exhausted. I wake up and feel fine. I don't dread the tasks ahead of me. Hard work, even the work of writing, which only requires I sit still and alone, is tiring. But I don't feel the constant weariness I did at the end of my full-time teaching career. Teaching takes up little of my time. I have near-total autonomy to write what I want. I'm proud of the work I do. Someone who was still burned out could not have written this book.

I think my answers reflect lower ideals for my work as a teacher. The test invited me to say how often "I feel exhilarated after working with my students." Exhilarated seems like a high bar to clear. *Should* I feel exhilarated after class? I said I did a few times a month. I'm not sure it's healthy to feel that more often. Rather than seeking euphoria in my teaching, I try to keep my emotional distance from it; I try not to let it get me too high or too low. If anything, the inventory's questions reflect too much idealism about the work of teaching. For instance, it asked me to say how frequently "I can easily create a relaxed atmosphere with my students." Easily? No. A relaxed classroom atmosphere is the result of hard emotional labor and constant attention to everything happening in the room simultaneously. There's nothing easy about it.

The frustration I feel when students don't do their reading assignments or when I find myself over-commenting on their papers is real, but it doesn't call my whole life into question, because I no longer identify so closely with that work. I'm walking around on a shorter pair of stilts; I can recover quickly when they wobble. So, at worst, I feel slightly ineffectual as a part-time instructor. I can live with that.

I preach a new vision of work better than I practice it. I'm no good at the moral austerity Thoreau links to greater self-respect. I'm bad at scheduling and get nervous when I think I haven't been productive. I struggle to take Fr. Simeon's advice and "get over it" when my work feels undone. I can't stop needing other people to validate me. I haven't picked up a drawing pencil or pulled on my hockey skates in years.

Nevertheless, I am much better off than I was in my final years as a professor. And it did take a new austerity to get to this point. In giving up my job and forging a freelance career, I took a 75 percent pay cut, which would have been impossible without my wife's income. I had to sacrifice the status that comes from having a full-time job, not to mention the academic prize of tenure. I had to give up a part of my ego. I had to give up a long-held dream. But I found a new one.

I almost hate to admit this, because I don't want to gloss over the pain of my burnout, but a part of me is grateful that I burned out as completely as I did. It was a clear signal that something was wrong, that I needed to make a significant change. If the job had been less uncomfortable, I could have persisted in it for much longer, perhaps damaging myself more severely because the harm would have been less perceptible—a slow, inexorable erosion, rather than a more spectacular collapse. Seen in this way, burnout can even be a gift.

Conclusion

Nonessential Work in a Post-Pandemic World

While I was working on this book, Covid-19 spread across the globe. Before long, I was stuck at home, with my few work routines upended and my social life utterly gone. The pace of everything around me seemed to slow. In my leafy Dallas neighborhood, I saw more people than usual out on the sidewalks at all times of day, often drinking wine or beer from a plastic cup. Dogs got more exercise. Babies got taken for longer walks in their strollers. Couples who would otherwise be at work played tennis in the park at noon on a Thursday.

The calm was only a thin mask for our national fear, anxiety, and sorrow. The virus took hundreds of thousands of lives over the course of the year. It also upended everyone's work. The unemployment rate went from a historic low to a historic high virtually overnight. Front-line workers in hospitals, nursing homes, meat-packing plants, and grocery stores faced enormous risk of infection as they labored to save lives and keep everyone fed. The distinction between "essential" and "nonessential" workers became crucial, not just economically, but ethically. Politicians and television advertisers and ordinary people banging on pots and pans all praised essential workers as "heroes," but that praise was meager compensation for the conditions those workers faced: little choice over whether to report for work, improvised protective gear, and, often, poverty wages.

Even so, essential workers did demonstrate moral heroism on the job. They saved others' lives, even at the cost of their own. Or they performed unglamorous duties that kept society from grinding to a complete halt. As New York City bus driver Frank de Jesus said in a conversation with a coworker that aired on public radio, "Through all the trials and tribulations, we do like doing what we do for New York City." The other driver, Tyrone Hampton, responded, "We do. We have a driver's heart. But now our heart is being tested." Facing the possibility of infection and seeing other drivers, their "brothers," get sick and die, these men looked to their friendship and to the nobility of their vocation to find comfort and strength. "We gonna make it through this, man," Hampton told de Jesus. "We gonna make it through."[1]

Meanwhile, millions of "nonessential" office workers began working from home, and school closures meant parents had to do their jobs while also serving as unpaid teacher's aides. In some cases, working from home meant working a lot more, because the physical barriers to work like offices and commutes became meaningless. Online networks lit up at all hours, with one virtual private network provider reporting that its US corporate users logged in for an average of three extra hours per day during the spring of 2020.[2] In short, many had no work to do; others had far too much.

The virus also exacerbated gender, racial, and other disparities in work. Women lost their jobs, or had to leave them to care for children at home, at much higher rates than men, to the point where US women's labor force participation rate dropped to its lowest level since 1988.[3] Because they disproportionately hold front-line jobs, many black workers were forced to face high risk for little monetary reward.[4] Meanwhile, undocumented workers, most of them Hispanic or Asian, could receive none of the trillions of dollars in federal funding meant to keep households and businesses solvent through the crisis.

By disrupting our work, the pandemic cut us loose from the things that order our time and give us goals to pursue. We didn't replace that order with a higher vision of what we were living for, like the Benedictine monks and sisters do. Churches, synagogues, mosques, and temples closed down. So did other sites of ritualized aspiration like gyms and yoga studios. In those first months, we organized our lives around the disease. Unless we had "essential" work to do, we aspired chiefly to avoid the virus. Everyone's highest ritual was to wash their hands. We entered a cultural null hypothesis: not a total breakdown, but not functional, either. It was terrible, without question, but it was also a rare, unanticipated breach in our culture of total work and burnout.

Some politicians and writers expressed a wish to close the breach as soon as it opened, calling for a quick end to stay-at-home orders, public health be damned. "My message is that let's get back to work," Dan Patrick, the lieutenant governor of Texas, said in a television interview. "Let's get back to living. Let's be smart about it, and those of us who are 70-plus, we'll take care of ourselves, but don't sacrifice the country."[5] Patrick's reasoning seemed to be that few younger workers would die as a result of the virus, and the country ought to accept the deaths of older ones for the sake of the economy. His words laid bare the axiom of American culture that you exist, first of all, to work. What good is health, if you're not going to use it productively? But in saying so, Patrick seemed to protest too much. By insisting on such a cruel and absurd point, he showed just how doubtful it really was. We subordinated our jobs to our health on a societal scale; we proved that we *don't* just exist to work.

. . .

Soon after most US cities went into lockdown, I posed what seemed like a taboo question to my followers on Twitter: "Is anyone enjoying this? Any parents, in particular? Are there any ways your life is better in this situation?"[6] I was surprised by the response, from more than thirty workers across the United States, Canada, and Europe. Perhaps "enjoy" was the wrong word, they fairly noted, but they did find something positive in their new reality. "I do not enjoy the forest," said Caitrin Keiper, a magazine editor and mother who lives in Virginia, "but I love my little trees." Others used the words "lovely" and "wonderful." They had stopped commuting. They were spending more time with their kids. They were getting more exercise. It was always true that we didn't all have to be in the office, plugging away on our bosses' questionable projects. The virus just made that obvious. In sweeping away our old routines and reducing our most annoying co-workers to a single tile on Zoom, the widespread quarantine freed many workers from some of the charades that make their jobs feel pointless. It revealed how much of our work really is nonessential.

One father of three young children, who works for a nonprofit in the Washington, DC, area, told me that working from home allowed for a more equitable split of domestic labor with his wife, who was also working from home. "I don't have two and a half hours of daily commute anymore. She doesn't have to cook and entertain the kids at the same time," he said. Since he was suddenly always home, he cooked every day. They each blocked out time in their schedules to take primary responsibility for their children or, as they did one day, play guitar in front of neighbors' houses so their kids could dance and sing along. In ordinary times, such whimsy might seem irresponsible, if not impossible.

The quarantine shattered the usual dilemma professional workers face between "greedy" jobs and the people they love.[7] Summer Block, a freelance writer in Los Angeles who is married with four children, told me that before the stay-at-home order, she was stretched thin with work, family, and a long list of volunteer projects, from Girl Scouts to the PTA to the Bernie Sanders campaign. "All of those things are canceled now," she said. Her kids' therapy and music lessons started happening online, so she didn't have to drive anyone around. "Usually I never feel I get enough time with my kids," Block said. "Now I finally don't have that nagging feeling of, 'I wish I saw them more.'" She even found a little more time to write.

The people I spoke with were certainly worried. Several said outright that they would much prefer a coronavirus-free, "normal" life to the conditions the pandemic imposed on everyone. "I have had daily freak-outs," said Bria Sandford, a book editor in New York City. But breaking out of her normal schedule helped her find renewed value in leisure. "Eliminating the physical stress of a commute and office environment has largely offset the stress of quarantine," she said. "I'm going for walks in the woods, eating well, hydrating, and am able to do mild exercise for the first time in years." She hoped that, once the pandemic ended, she would work more from home and maintain what she called her "no-phone-before-prayer-and-walk routine."

The workers who answered my question seemed to find a sweet spot in how they used the time they would otherwise have spent commuting. A survey of Americans working from home during the pandemic revealed that about 45 percent of that time went back into work, a quarter of it went to child care or home maintenance, and the remaining 30 percent went to leisure.[8] It isn't hard to imagine that if you had a trusting boss, then you could tilt that balance more toward family and leisure and away from labor. The workers who answered my question were not typical. Most are well-educated and have the kind of job they can do remotely. None of them said anyone in their immediate family had acquired the virus. That they experienced some positive effects of self-isolation was due partly to advantages—like job security, a decent family income, or autonomy over their schedules—that most workers do not enjoy. But that's why their experience points us beyond burnout culture. How can we remake society so that *all* workers have those advantages?

That revolution will have to entail new policies that enable jobs to meet the dignity of those who perform them. But it will equally be a moral revolution, one in which we value something higher than our work and place compassion for workers ahead of maximal productivity. The revolution was already under way during the quarantine, even as people feared for each other's lives. Erin Bishop, a university administrator in San Diego, told me that after she began working from home, her household descended into a "mayhem" of work and kids thrown together in a small space. But she still managed to find a moment that would have been impossible a few weeks before. "I just [lay] on a blanket in the backyard with my three-year-old, naming what shapes we saw in the clouds," she wrote. "It was marvelous."[9]

. . .

Early in the quarantine, I heard New York State Governor Andrew Cuomo give an interview about the challenge facing his state and the city of New York in particular. Toward the end of the interview, Cuomo issued a moral call to every New Yorker: "[E]xtend your imagination in a way you never thought and extend your ambition beyond yourself because it's not about you. It's about us, it's about the collective, it's about society. . . . Save as many lives as you can. Be responsible. Be civic-minded. Be kind. Be considerate. Think of one another."[10]

Cuomo's own behavior may not have lived up to the standard he set in that interview—many of his decisions during the crisis have subsequently drawn significant criticism, and he has also been accused of sexual harassment by numerous aides. But here, his words were inspiring.[11] He was calling for solidarity. Solidarity is the mutual recognition of dignity that motivates workers to organize so they can win working conditions that measure up to their worth. The pandemic revealed a solidarity even broader than that. We quickly learned that each of us is more intimately connected to each other than we ordinarily realize. Those connections make us vulnerable. Biologically speaking, each person is a possible vector of coronavirus. But our connections to each other are more than biological. They're economic and social and moral. The professionals who found a better routine during the pandemic could only do so because they relied on the labor of others on the front line.

The great ethical mantra during the first stages of the pandemic in the United States was "flatten the curve." The point was to slow the rate of infection so the number of sick people at any one time would not exceed the capacity of the health care system to treat them. Doctors and nurses and technicians worked to exhaustion anyway, but flattening the curve would give hospital workers a fighting chance against the disease, so their effort would be as effective as possible.

This public concern for the burden we place on medical workers was a significant departure from the norm in American society. Since long before Covid-19 arrived in the United States, the country's patients have been especially demanding, by global standards. They expect healthcare workers to be compassionate, yet they show little compassion in return, calling for expensive, risky, and often unnecessary treatments that represent additional labor for their caregivers. Among migraine sufferers, for example, Americans are three times as likely to go to the emergency room for a headache as their British counterparts. This means that Americans are more likely to put demands on some of the most-burdened workers, not only taking up time the medical staff could be spending on other patients but—in the long run, by adding to the workers' stress and burnout—actually undermining their ability to treat patients. At the same time, Americans are less likely than patients in other countries to go for routine checkups or take their prescriptions, which means that small problems aren't caught early, putting more pressure on health professionals to provide intensive treatment once their conditions get serious.[12]

Part of the problem is America's patchy and byzantine system of paying for health care. But part of it is also the lack of respect Americans show workers in general. These two factors are linked. A more reliable health care system could enable medical workers to do their best work in a sustainable way. And a more compassionate approach to being a patient would begin by recognizing the human limits of those on whose labor we depend to make us healthy. I don't mean to scold anyone for whom seeking medical care takes courage, or those who fear "being a burden" on others. Still, there is such thing as a "problem patient," those who disproportionately heap needless labor on others.[13] I can say from experience that there are "problem students," and I'll wager that in your line of work, you can identify problem customers and problem coworkers—the people who contribute more than their share to burnout. We need norms that will make these outliers' demands seem unreasonable, even unethical. To beat burnout and help others flourish, we need to lower not only our expectations for our own work but also our expectations of what others' work can do for us. We showed that compassion during the pandemic. We have it in us. Why can't we show it during "normal" times, too?

Solidarity is compassion on the societal scale. It is recognizing that my suffering and joy are linked to yours. That means my compassion for you is good for me, too. When a contagious disease strikes a society, everyone is susceptible to it. One person at risk puts an exponentially-growing number of others at risk. And each person's act of self-preservation—staying home, wearing a mask in public—also helps preserve others. Burnout is not contagious in the same way Covid-19 is, but it does share two important qualities with viral diseases. First, everyone who works is a potential burned-out case. Second, we acquire burnout through interacting with people in shared spaces and social structures. If we can acknowledge our common status as both potential victims and potential vectors, then we can reimagine those interactions, change our culture, and end the burnout epidemic.

A college professor who burns out will find it easy to blame the students and easier to blame the administrators who manage faculty workloads and give or withhold rewards. They're obvious targets. I wonder now if, when I was burning out at my teaching job, the administrators were, too. Maybe they didn't give me and my colleagues the recognition I felt we deserved because they couldn't, just as I couldn't give my students the attention they deserved. A college, like a hospital or a hardware store or a restaurant, is a network of relationships. Burnout can travel across that network in all directions, following the patterns set down by explicit rules and unwritten customs. If I'm miserable, I am more likely to make you miserable.

I sometimes imagine that a college that wanted to combat burnout would have to begin with a radically honest all-campus meeting, in which everyone acknowledges that the institution's whole way of operating was harming everyone involved, that no one really benefited from the self-destructive system. Everyone would own up to their implication in a dreary reality: how the students and faculty and staff and administrators were causing each other to burn out, but no one felt like they could admit that something was wrong, and everyone believed they had to work hard, to live up to some impossible ideal.

I want to believe that a college, or any organization, could begin building a whole new way of working, once its members recognized that everyone was in this predicament together. They might then realize that even though they all feel powerless, together they *are* the organization. And for that reason, they can remake it.

. . .

The system of meaning we have built around work—the noble lie about work as a source of dignity, character, and purpose—helps perpetuate burnout culture. The coronavirus quarantine did not dissolve that system, but it did call it into question. Obviously, your employment status had nothing to do with your worth as a person; tens of millions lost their jobs all at once, and not because they were bad workers or bad people. The US federal government greatly expanded unemployment benefits, adding $600 a week to every unemployment check, regardless of what the worker had earned before. This meant the average unemployment benefit exceeded the ordinary wages for more than half the workers who lost their jobs.[14] The benefit seemed like a step toward universal basic income at a living-wage level, and another country, Spain, did institute a version of basic income during the pandemic.[15] Some conservative politicians and business leaders in the United States even made the argument, also offered against basic income plans, that the unemployment benefits were too good, because people might choose not to work at all.[16] When protesters showed up at state capitol buildings demanding that the economy "reopen," the journalist Sarah Jaffe wrote that it was becoming clear that there was "no right to make that demand. That everyone should have the right to say no. Call it, perhaps"—echoing Sunaura Taylor—"a right not to work."[17] A universal basic income might be the only way to make that right meaningful. And along with universal recognition of human dignity, it might also be the only way to make work truly free, something people undertake with the confidence that they can quit without fear of starvation or disgrace.

Even if the virus had never appeared, the centuries-old system of meaning surrounding work was likely headed for a shakeup anyway, though from a very different source: automation. Ironically, some of the jobs that suddenly seemed socially indispensable during the pandemic—cashiers, warehouse workers, truck drivers—are the ones at greatest risk of being automated away in the next decade. There's a decent chance that machines will be able to replicate every human task by the time a child born in 2022 reaches middle age.[18] It's true that we might not actually put machines to work everywhere across the economy, but we do need to acknowledge that tremendous economic pressure is pushing in that direction. Work as we know it could disappear.

By now, you know I think that's an exciting prospect. The pandemic, for all it cost us, cleared out imaginative space for a new, more humane future. The trouble is that moments of radical change often make us less open to new ideas and more eager for the status quo ante, regardless of its proven defects. In *Radical Hope: Ethics in the Face of Cultural Devastation,* the philosopher Jonathan Lear writes that a widely-shared sense of societal vulnerability narrows our vision just when we need it to be most expansive. When our culture is under threat, we cling to familiar ideas, just like the politicians who wanted to end the quarantine and send everyone back to work. "It is as though," Lear writes, "without our insistence that our outlook is correct, the outlook itself might collapse."[19]

Lear argues that the people who succeed in a given cultural system are "the least equipped" to find solutions to the system's collapse. He wonders if "my flourishing as a member of my culture makes me *less* able to confront the challenges of a radically new future."[20] That possibility is why we need to look for inspiration at the fringes of the culture, to the people who are *not* striving and succeeding in the system as currently constituted. People like the Benedictines or the disabled artists Erica Mena and Patricia Nordeen have, to differing degrees, gotten over the work ethic. They have rejected the noble lies. They have constructed models of human flourishing on different foundations. Not on work, but on universal dignity, compassion for self and others, and a purpose discovered in freely-chosen leisure.

In an important respect, the robot revolution would solve all the problems with work's failure to deliver on the ideals we have for it. In so many industries, the ideal worker looks more and more like a machine. Machines have no need for autonomy or privacy. They have no dignity. They don't belong to a society and thus cannot be alienated from one. They have no moral character to be distorted, and they can repeat a limited set of actions forever. They don't yearn for transcendence and don't worry if they're meeting genuine human needs. And, most appealing of all to businesses, they don't expect a salary.

The fact is, work as we know it isn't worth saving. Maybe that's because work isn't inherently very good. Maybe we should just let the robots have it and figure out a way to distribute the fruits of their labor. (I admit, no small task.) Then we would be free to walk our dogs whenever we want. Play tennis at noon every day. Learn to paint. Pray without ceasing. Lie in the grass with the kids and stare up at the sky for hours.

Let the machines burn out. We have better things to do.

Notes

Introduction

1. For example, Monique Valcour, "Beating Burnout," *Harvard Business Review*, November 2016, https://hbr.org/2016/11/beating-burnout.

2. Karlyn Borysenko, "Burnout Is Now An Officially Diagnosable Condition: Here's What You Need To Know About It," *Forbes*, May 29, 2019, https://www.forbes.com/sites/karlynborysenko/2019/05/29/burnout-is-now-an-officially-diagnosable-condition-heres-what-you-need-to-know-about-it.

3. Christopher Gergen and Gregg Vanourek, "Three Ways to Beat Burnout," *Harvard Business Review*, December 1, 2008, https://hbr.org/2008/12/three-ways-to-beat-burnout.

4. United States Department of Labor Bureau of Labor Statistics, "The Employment Situation: December 2008," January 9, 2009, https://www.bls.gov/news.release/archives/empsit_01092009.pdf.

5. Rebecca Knight, "How to Overcome Burnout and Stay Motivated," *Harvard Business Review*, April 2, 2015, https://hbr.org/2015/04/how-to-overcome-burnout-and-stay-motivated; John Rampton, "8 Ways to Get Over Job Burnout (Without Quitting)," Inc.com, March 31, 2017, https://www.inc.com/john-rampton/8-ways-to-get-over-job-burnout-without-leaving.html; Tabia Robinson, "How to Spot and Stop Burnout Before You Give Up On Freelancing," *The Freelancer*, July 2, 2019, https://contently.net/2019/07/02/resources/how-to-spot-and-stop-burnout-freelancing.

6. Viviana A. Zelizer, *Pricing the Priceless Child: The Changing Social Value of Children*, reprint edition (Princeton, NJ: Princeton University Press, 1994).

7. K.J. Dell'Antonia, "Some Good News about Parental Burnout: It's Curable," *Quartz*, January 12, 2019, https://qz.com/quartzy/1521267/some-good -news-about-parental-burnout-its-curable; Jessica Grose, "How to Avoid Burnout When You Have Little Ones," *New York Times*, May 29, 2019, https:// parenting.nytimes.com/work-money/parental-burnout.

8. Two notable studies on parental burnout are Moïra Mikolajczak et al., "Exhausted Parents: Sociodemographic, Child-Related, Parent-Related, Parenting and Family-Functioning Correlates of Parental Burnout," *Journal of Child and Family Studies* 27, no. 2 (February 1, 2018): 602–14, https:// doi.org/10.1007/s10826-017-0892-4 and Isabelle Roskam, Marie-Emilie Raes, and Moïra Mikolajczak, "Exhausted Parents: Development and Preliminary Validation of the Parental Burnout Inventory," *Frontiers in Psychology* 8 (February 9, 2017), https://www.frontiersin.org/articles/10.3389/fpsyg .2017.00163/full.

Chapter 1. Everyone Is Burned Out, But No One Knows What That Means

1. Christina Maslach, *Burnout: The Cost of Caring* (Englewood Cliffs, NJ: Prentice-Hall, 1982), 90.

2. Maslach, *Burnout*, 65.

3. Maslach, *Burnout*, 134–35.

4. Ayala M. Pines and Elliot Aronson, *Career Burnout: Causes and Cures* (New York: Free Press, 1988), ix.

5. Christina Maslach and Michael P. Leiter, *The Truth About Burnout: How Organizations Cause Personal Stress and What to Do About It* (San Francisco: Jossey-Bass, 1997), 18.

6. Maslach and Leiter, *The Truth About Burnout*, 17–18.

7. Lauren Berlant, *Cruel Optimism* (Durham, NC: Duke University Press, 2011), 1.

8. "The Burden of a Stroke Call: 56% of US Neurointerventionalists Meet Criteria for Burnout," *NeuroNews International*, August 27, 2019, https:// neuronewsinternational.com/burnout-stroke-burden.

9. Tait D. Shanafelt et al., "Changes in Burnout and Satisfaction with Work-Life Integration in Physicians and the General US Working Population Between

2011 and 2017," *Mayo Clinic Proceedings* 94, no. 9 (September 2019): 1681–94, https://doi.org/10.1016/j.mayocp.2018.10.023.

10. Ben Wigert and Sangeeta Agrawal, "Employee Burnout, Part 1: The 5 Main Causes," Gallup Workplace, July 12, 2018, https://www.gallup.com/workplace/237059/employee-burnout-part-main-causes.aspx.

11. Deloitte US, "Workplace Burnout Survey," accessed October 8, 2019, https://www2.deloitte.com/us/en/pages/about-deloitte/articles/burnout-survey.html.

12. "Survey Reveals Factors Behind Millennial Burnout," *Yellowbrick Blog*, June 20, 2019, https://www.yellowbrickprogram.com/blog/survey-reveals-factors-behind-millennial-burnout.

13. Emphasis mine. See Joanne Finnegan, "A Startling 79% of Primary Care Physicians Are Burned Out, New Report Finds," *FierceHealthcare*, August 6, 2019, https://www.fiercehealthcare.com/practices/a-startling-79-primary-care-physicians-are-burned-out-new-report-finds.

14. Richard Fry, "Millennials Are Largest Generation in the US Labor Force," *Pew Research Center*, April 11, 2018, https://www.pewresearch.org/fact-tank/2018/04/11/millennials-largest-generation-us-labor-force.

15. Carolyn S. Dewa et al., "The Relationship between Physician Burnout and Quality of Healthcare in Terms of Safety and Acceptability: A Systematic Review," *BMJ Open* 7, no. 6 (June 1, 2017): e015141, https://doi.org/10.1136/bmjopen-2016-015141; Carolyn S. Dewa, Karen Nieuwenhuijsen, and Jeffrey S. Hoch, "Deciphering the Relationship Between Health Care Provider Burnout and Quality of Care," *Annals of Internal Medicine,* October 8, 2019, https://doi.org/10.7326/M19-2760.

16. Lisa S. Rotenstein et al., "Prevalence of Burnout Among Physicians: A Systematic Review," *JAMA* 320, no. 11 (September 18, 2018): 1131–50, https://doi.org/10.1001/jama.2018.12777.

17. Shanafelt et al., "Changes in Burnout and Satisfaction with Work-Life Integration in Physicians and the General US Working Population Between 2011 and 2017," 1690.

18. Colin P. West et al., "Single Item Measures of Emotional Exhaustion and Depersonalization Are Useful for Assessing Burnout in Medical Professionals," *Journal of General Internal Medicine* 24, no. 12 (December 2009): 1318–21, https://doi.org/10.1007/s11606-009-1129-z.

19. Meredith Corporation and Harris Poll, "Burnout Flashpoint," October 3, 2019, http://online.fliphtml5.com/mseh/cfmp/#p = 8.

20. Meredith Corporation and Harris Poll, "Burnout Flashpoint," 8.

21. Deloitte US, "Workplace Burnout Survey."

22. Anne Helen Petersen, "How Millennials Became the Burnout Generation," *BuzzFeed News,* January 5, 2019, https://www.buzzfeednews.com/article/annehelenpetersen/millennials-burnout-generation-debt-work.

23. Petersen, "How Millennials Became the Burnout Generation."

24. Petersen, "How Millennials Became the Burnout Generation."

25. Anne Helen Petersen, "Here's What 'Millennial Burnout' Is Like For 16 Different People," *BuzzFeed News,* January 9, 2019, https://www.buzzfeednews.com/article/annehelenpetersen/millennial-burnout-perspectives.

26. Tiana Clark, "This Is What Black Burnout Feels Like," *BuzzFeed News,* January 11, 2019, https://www.buzzfeednews.com/article/tianaclarkpoet/millennial-burnout-black-women-self-care-anxiety-depression.

27. Clark, "This Is What Black Burnout Feels Like."

28. Clark, "This Is What Black Burnout Feels Like."

29. Linda V. Heinemann and Torsten Heinemann, "Burnout Research: Emergence and Scientific Investigation of a Contested Diagnosis," *SAGE Open* 7, no. 1 (January 2017): 7, https://doi.org/10.1177/2158244017697154.

30. Pines and Aronson, *Career Burnout,* xi.

31. Linda V. Heinemann and Torsten Heinemann, "Burnout: From Work-Related Stress to a Cover-Up Diagnosis," in *Burnout, Fatigue, Exhaustion: An Interdisciplinary Perspective on a Modern Affliction,* ed. Sighard Neckel, Anna Katharina Schaffner, and Greta Wagner (Cham, Switzerland: Palgrave Macmillan, 2017), 131, 138.

32. Heinemann and Heinemann, "Burnout," 141–43.

33. Heinemann and Heinemann, "Burnout," 142.

34. Wolfgang P. Kaschka, Dieter Korczak, and Karl Broich, "Burnout: A Fashionable Diagnosis," *Deutsches Ärzteblatt International* 108, no. 46 (November 2011): 781–87, https://doi.org/10.3238/arztebl.2011.0781.

35. Johannes Bahlmann, Matthias C. Angermeyer, and Georg Schomerus, "'Burnout' statt 'Depression'—eine Strategie zur Vermeidung von Stigma?," *Psychiatrische Praxis* 40, no. 2 (March 2013): 78–82, https://doi.org/10.1055/s-0032-1332891.

36. Bernd Kramer, "Burnout Ist Eine Ausweichdiagnose," *Der Spiegel*, November 24, 2011, https://www.spiegel.de/karriere/volkskrankheit-burnout -ist-eine-ausweichdiagnose-a-799348.html. Thanks to Brian Campbell and Katherine Davies for help with this translation.

37. Lance Morrow, "The Burnout of Almost Everyone," *Time*, September 21, 1981, http://content.time.com/time/magazine/article/0,9171,953109,00.html.

38. Richard A. Friedman, "Is Burnout Real?," *New York Times*, June 3, 2019.

39. Karlyn McKell, "5 Tips to Avoid Bridesmaid Burnout (Yes, It's a Thing)," *Thrive Global*, August 28, 2019, https://thriveglobal.com/stories/avoid-brides-maid-burnout-with-these-tips/; News 4—Fox 11 Digital Team, "Local Company Looks to Help with Post-Burning Man Burnout," KRNV, September 2, 2019, https://mynews4.com/news/local/local-company-looks-to-help-with-post-burning-man-burnout; Lauren Entwistle, "Burnout in the Age of Binge-Watching," *Greatist*, October 11, 2019, https://greatist.com/live/binge-tv-burnout.

Chapter 2. Burnout: The First 2,000 Years

1. Anna Katharina Schaffner, *Exhaustion: A History* (New York: Columbia University Press, 2016), 117.

2. Eccl. 1:2–3 (New Revised Standard Version).

3. Eccl. 1:17.

4. Eccl. 9:18.

5. Eccl. 9:10.

6. Schaffner, *Exhaustion*, 17.

7. Aristotle, "Metaphysics," in *The Basic Works of Aristotle*, ed. Richard McKeon, trans. W. D. Ross (New York: Random House, 1941), 981b.

8. Evagrius Ponticus, *The Praktikos; Chapters on Prayer*, trans. John Eudes Bamberger (Spencer, Mass.: Cistercian Publications, 1970), 18–19.

9. St. John Cassian, *The Institutes*, trans. Boniface Ramsey (New York: Newman Press, 2000), 233.

10. Jennifer Radden, "From Melancholic States to Clinical Depression," in *The Nature of Melancholy: From Aristotle to Kristeva*, ed. Jennifer Radden (Oxford: Oxford University Press, 2000), 8.

11. William Shakespeare, "As You Like It," IV.i, https://shakespeare.folger .edu/shakespeares-works/as-you-like-it/act-4-scene-1.

12. Schaffner, *Exhaustion*, 58.

13. Radden, "From Melancholic States to Clinical Depression," 17–18.

14. David G. Schuster, *Neurasthenic Nation: America's Search for Health, Happiness, and Comfort, 1869–1920* (New Brunswick, NJ: Rutgers University Press, 2011), 7.

15. Julie Beck, "'Americanitis': The Disease of Living Too Fast," *The Atlantic*, March 11, 2016, https://www.theatlantic.com/health/archive/2016/03/the -history-of-neurasthenia-or-americanitis-health-happiness-and-culture/473253.

16. Quoted in Michael O'Malley, "That Busyness That Is Not Business: Nervousness and Character at the Turn of the Last Century," *Social Research* 72, no. 2 (2005): 386.

17. "Americanitis," *TIME Magazine*, April 27, 1925, 32.

18. George M. Beard, *American Nervousness: Its Causes and Consequences* (New York: Putnam, 1881), 39–52, http://archive.org/details/americanner vous00beargoog.

19. Beard, *American Nervousness*, frontispiece.

20. Schaffner, *Exhaustion*, 95.

21. Beard, *American Nervousness*, 26.

22. Beard, *American Nervousness*, 26.

23. Schaffner, *Exhaustion*, 96.

24. Beard, *American Nervousness*, 207.

25. Beard, *American Nervousness*, 126, 186; Beck, "Americanitis."

26. Beard, *American Nervousness*, 99.

27. Quoted in Schaffner, *Exhaustion*, 97–98.

28. Greg Daugherty, "The Brief History of 'Americanitis,'" *Smithsonian Magazine*, March 25, 2015, https://www.smithsonianmag.com/history/brief -history-americanitis-180954739.

29. Beck, "Americanitis."

30. Schuster, *Neurasthenic Nation*, 46–56.

31. Sears, Roebuck and Company, *Catalogue No. 112.* (Chicago: Sears, Roebuck & Co., 1902), 472, http://archive.org/details/catalogueno11200sear.

32. Schaffner, *Exhaustion*, 100, 104.

33. Schuster, *Neurasthenic Nation*, 142.

34. Kevin Aho, "Neurasthenia Revisited: On Medically Unexplained Syndromes and the Value of Hermeneutic Medicine," *Journal of Applied Hermeneutics*, April 9, 2018, 4–5, https://doi.org/10.11575/jah.v0i0.53334.

35. Schuster, *Neurasthenic Nation*, chap. 6.

36. Graham Greene, *A Burnt-Out Case* (New York: Viking, 1961), 52. Originally published 1960 by Heinemann (London).

37. Greene, *A Burnt-Out Case*, 57.

38. Greene, *A Burnt-Out Case*, 133.

39. Greene, *A Burnt-Out Case*, 111.

40. Francis X. Clines, "Village Youths Find Friend in Doctor," *The New York Times*, July 13, 1970, https://www.nytimes.com/1970/07/13/archives /village-youths-find-friend-in-doctor-village-youths-find-a-friend.html.

41. Herbert J. Freudenberger and Geraldine Richelson, *Burn-Out: The High Cost of High Achievement* (Garden City, NY: Anchor Press, 1980), xix.

42. Noel King, "When A Psychologist Succumbed To Stress, He Coined The Term 'Burnout,'" *NPR.org*, December 8, 2016, accessed May 23, 2019, https:// www.npr.org/2016/12/08/504864961/when-a-psychologist-succumbed -to-stress-he-coined-the-term-burnout.

43. H. B. Bradley, "Community-Based Treatment for Young Adult Offenders," *Crime & Delinquency* 15, no. 3 (July 1969): 366.

44. David W. Maurer, *Language of the Underworld*, ed. Allan W. Futrell and Charles B. Wordell (Lexington: University Press of Kentucky, 1981), 287; Wilmar B. Schaufeli, Michael P. Leiter, and Christina Maslach, "Burnout: 35 Years of Research and Practice," *Career Development International; Bradford* 14, no. 3 (2009): 205, http://dx.doi.org.proxy.libraries.smu.edu/10.1108 /13620430910966406.

45. Freudenberger and Richelson, *Burn-Out*, xv.

46. Freudenberger and Richelson, *Burn-Out*, xix–xx.

47. Herbert J. Freudenberger, "Staff Burn-Out," *Journal of Social Issues* 30, no. 1 (March 1974): 161, https://doi.org/10.1111/j.1540-4560.1974.tb00706.x.

48. Freudenberger, "Staff Burn-Out," 161.

49. Freudenberger, "Staff Burn-Out," 160–61.

50. Herbert J. Freudenberger, "The Staff Burn-out Syndrome in Alternative Institutions," *Psychotherapy: Theory, Research & Practice* 12, no. 1 (Spring 1975): 73, https://doi.org/10.1037/h0086411.

51. Freudenberger, "Staff Burn-Out," 160.

52. Philip Zimbardo, *The Lucifer Effect: Understanding How Good People Turn Evil* (New York: Random House, 2007), 170–71.

53. Kathleen O'Toole, "The Stanford Prison Experiment: Still Powerful after All These Years," *Stanford News*, January 8, 1997, https://news.stanford.edu/pr/97/970108prisonexp.html.

54. O'Toole, "The Stanford Prison Experiment."

55. Christina Maslach, "'Detached Concern' in Health and Social Service Professions," in *Dehumanization in Institutional Settings*, by Philip Zimbardo and Christina Maslach (Springfield, VA: National Technical Information Service, 1973), 9.

56. Maslach, "'Detached Concern' in Health and Social Service Professions," 11.

57. Maslach, "'Detached Concern' in Health and Social Service Professions," 15.

58. King, "When A Psychologist Succumbed To Stress, He Coined The Term 'Burnout.'"

59. Maslach and Leiter, *The Truth About Burnout*.

60. Schaufeli, Leiter, and Maslach, "Burnout," 206–7.

61. Ad Hoc Committee, "The Triple Revolution," *International Socialist Review*, Summer 1964, 85–89.

62. Felicia Kornbluh, "The Goals of the National Welfare Rights Movement: Why We Need Them Thirty Years Later," *Feminist Studies* 24, no. 1 (1998): 71–72, https://doi.org/10.2307/3178619; Johnnie Tillmon, "Welfare Is a Women's Issue," *Ms. Magazine*, July 1972, 111–16.

63. Nathan Heller, "Who Really Stands to Win from Universal Basic Income?," *The New Yorker*, July 2, 2018, https://www.newyorker.com/magazine/2018/07/09/who-really-stands-to-win-from-universal-basic-income; Noah J. Gordon, "The Conservative Case for a Guaranteed Basic Income," *The Atlantic*, August 6, 2014, https://www.theatlantic.com/politics/archive/2014/08/why-arent-reformicons-pushing-a-guaranteed-basic-income/375600/; James Livingston, *No More Work: Why Full Employment Is a Bad Idea* (Chapel Hill: University of North Carolina Press, 2016), 13–28.

64. Jefferson R. Cowie, *Stayin' Alive: The 1970s and the Last Days of the Working Class* (New York: The New Press, 2010), 11.

65. US Bureau of Labor Statistics, "Average Hourly Earnings of Production and Nonsupervisory Employees, Total Private," FRED, Federal Reserve Bank of St. Louis, accessed November 12, 2020, https://fred.stlouisfed.org/graph/?g=mwsh.

66. Cowie, *Stayin' Alive*, 8.

67. US Bureau of Labor Statistics, "Average Hourly Earnings of Production and Nonsupervisory Employees, Total Private."

68. Rick Perlstein, "That Seventies Show," *The Nation*, October 20, 2010, https://www.thenation.com/article/seventies-show.

69. Cowie, *Stayin' Alive*, 12.

70. Jimmy Carter, "Crisis of Confidence," July 15, 1979, https://www.pbs.org/wgbh/americanexperience/features/carter-crisis.

71. Willis J. Nordlund, *Silent Skies: The Air Traffic Controllers' Strike* (Westport, CT: Praeger, 1998), 97.

72. William Safire, "Burnout," *The New York Times*, May 23, 1982, sec. Magazine, 10.

73. Schaufeli, Leiter, and Maslach, "Burnout," 210.

74. World Health Organization, "Burn-Out," ICD-11—Mortality and Morbidity Statistics, 2019, https://icd.who.int/browse11/l-m/en#/http://id.who.int/icd/entity/129180281.

75. Maddy Savage, "Burnout Is Rising in the Land of Work-Life Balance," *BBC Worklife*, July 26, 2019, https://www.bbc.com/worklife/article/20190719-why-is-burnout-rising-in-the-land-of-work-life-balance.

76. Stela Salminen et al., "Narratives of Burnout and Recovery from an Agency Perspective: A Two-Year Longitudinal Study," *Burnout Research* 7 (December 1, 2017): 2, https://doi.org/10.1016/j.burn.2017.08.001.

77. Freudenberger and Richelson, *Burn-Out*, 4.

78. Leslie Kaufman, "Some Companies Derail the 'Burnout' Track," *The New York Times*, May 4, 1999, sec. Business, https://www.nytimes.com/1999/05/04/business/some-companies-derail-the-burnout-track.html.

79. Rebekah Iliff, "How to Grow Your Startup Without Risking Burnout," *Inc.com*, July 29, 2019, https://www.inc.com/rebekah-iliff/how-to-grow-your-startup-without-risking-burnout.html.

Chapter 3. The Burnout Spectrum

1. Crystal Hooper et al., "Compassion Satisfaction, Burnout, and Compassion Fatigue Among Emergency Nurses Compared With Nurses in Other Selected Inpatient Specialties," *Journal of Emergency Nursing* 36, no. 5 (September 1, 2010): 422, https://doi.org/10.1016/j.jen.2009.11.027.

2. Maslach and Leiter, *The Truth About Burnout,* 17–19; Pavlos Deligkaris et al., "Job Burnout and Cognitive Functioning: A Systematic Review," *Work & Stress* 28, no. 2 (April 3, 2014): 107–23, https://doi.org/10.1080/02678373.2014.909545.

3. Blake Farmer, "When Doctors Struggle With Suicide, Their Profession Often Fails Them," *NPR.org*, July 31, 2018, https://www.npr.org/sections/health-shots/2018/07/31/634217947/to-prevent-doctor-suicides-medical-industry-rethinks-how-doctors-work.

4. J. Angst and K. Merikangas, "The Depressive Spectrum: Diagnostic Classification and Course," *Journal of Affective Disorders* 45, no. 1–2 (August 1997): 32, https://doi.org/10.1016/s0165-0327(97)00057-8.

5. Angst and Merikangas, 36.

6. Angst and Merikangas, 32.

7. Barry A. Farber and Leonard David Wechsler, *Crisis in Education: Stress and Burnout in the American Teacher* (San Francisco: Jossey-Bass, 1991), 24; Wilmar Schaufeli and D. Enzmann, *The Burnout Companion To Study And Practice: A Critical Analysis* (Boca Raton, FL: CRC Press, 1998), 140.

8. Maslach and Leiter, *The Truth About Burnout,* 17.

9. Christina Maslach, "Burned-Out," *Human Behavior* 5, no. 9 (September 1976): 22.

10. Michael P. Leiter and Christina Maslach, "Latent Burnout Profiles: A New Approach to Understanding the Burnout Experience," *Burnout Research* 3, no. 4 (December 1, 2016): 89–100, https://doi.org/10.1016/j.burn.2016.09.001.

11. Sophie Berjot et al., "Burnout Risk Profiles among French Psychologists," *Burnout Research* 7 (December 1, 2017): 10–20, https://doi.org/10.1016/j.burn.2017.10.001.

12. Leiter and Maslach, "Latent Burnout Profiles"; Tamara M. Schult, David C. Mohr, and Katerine Osatuke, "Examining Burnout Profiles in Relation to Health and Well-Being in the Veterans Health Administration Employee Population," *Stress and Health* 34, no. 4 (2018): 490–99, https://doi.org/10.1002/smi.2809; Nancy J. Yanchus, Jan Beckstrand, and Katerine Osatuke, "Examining Burnout Profiles in the Veterans Administration: All Employee Survey Narrative Comments," *Burnout Research* 2, no. 4 (December 1, 2015): 97–107, https://doi.org/10.1016/j.burn.2015.07.001.

13. Julia Moeller et al., "Highly Engaged but Burned Out: Intra-Individual Profiles in the US Workforce," *Career Development International,* February 6,

2018, https://doi.org/10.1108/CDI-12-2016-0215; Jan Beckstrand, Nancy Yan-chus, and Katerine Osatuke, "Only One Burnout Estimator Is Consistently Associated with Health Care Providers' Perceptions of Job Demand and Resource Problems," *Psychology* 8, no. 7 (2017): 1019-41, https://doi.org/10.4236/psych.2017.87067.

14. Debra J. Brody, Laura A. Pratt, and Jeffery P. Hughes, "Prevalence of Depression Among Adults Aged 20 and Over: United States, 2013-2016," NCHS Data Brief (Hyattsville, MD: National Center for Health Statistics, February 2018).

15. Berjot et al., "Burnout Risk Profiles among French Psychologists," 16.

16. Leiter and Maslach, "Latent Burnout Profiles," 95-96.

17. Leiter and Maslach, "Latent Burnout Profiles," 98.

18. Schult, Mohr, and Osatuke, "Examining Burnout Profiles in Relation to Health and Well-Being in the Veterans Health Administration Employee Popu-lation," 497.

19. Shanafelt et al., "Changes in Burnout and Satisfaction with Work-Life Integration in Physicians and the General US Working Population Between 2011 and 2017."

20. Evangelia Demerouti et al., "The Job Demands-Resources Model of Burnout," *Journal of Applied Psychology* 86, no. 3 (June 2001): 501-2, https://doi.org/10.1037/0021-9010.86.3.499.

21. Nicole Maestas et al., *Working Conditions in the United States: Results of the 2015 American Working Conditions Survey* (RAND Corporation, 2017), 47-48, https://doi.org/10.7249/RR2014.

22. Schult, Mohr, and Osatuke, "Examining Burnout Profiles in Relation to Health and Well-Being in the Veterans Health Administration Employee Popu-lation."

23. Yanchus, Beckstrand, and Osatuke, "Examining Burnout Profiles in the Veterans Administration," 104.

24. Maslach, *Burnout: The Cost of Caring,* 5; Christina Maslach, Wilmar B. Schaufeli, and Michael P. Leiter, "Job Burnout," *Annual Review of Psychology* 52, no. 1 (2001): 405, https://doi.org/10.1146/annurev.psych.52.1.397.

25. Yanchus, Beckstrand, and Osatuke, "Examining Burnout Profiles in the Veterans Administration," 100, 102.

26. David Graeber, *Bullshit Jobs: A Theory* (New York: Simon and Schuster, 2018).

27. Yanchus, Beckstrand, and Osatuke, "Examining Burnout Profiles in the Veterans Administration."

28. Morrow, "The Burnout of Almost Everyone."

29. Pines and Aronson, *Career Burnout,* x.

30. Freudenberger, "Staff Burn-Out," 161.

31. Irvin Sam Schonfeld, Jay Verkuilen, and Renzo Bianchi, "Inquiry into the Correlation between Burnout and Depression," *Journal of Occupational Health Psychology* 24, no. 6 (December 2019): 604, https://doi.org/10.1037/ocp0000151.

32. Irvin Sam Schonfeld and Renzo Bianchi, "Burnout and Depression: Two Entities or One?," *Journal of Clinical Psychology* 72, no. 1 (2016): 22–37, https://doi.org/10.1002/jclp.22229.

33. Schonfeld, Verkuilen, and Bianchi, "Inquiry into the Correlation between Burnout and Depression," 611.

34. Schonfeld and Bianchi, "Burnout and Depression."

35. Quoted in Aviva Patz, "How To Tell The Difference Between Depression And Burnout," *Prevention,* November 5, 2015, https://www.prevention.com/life/a20486040/depression-or-burnout.

Chapter 4. How Jobs Have Gotten Worse in the Age of Burnout

1. Max Weber, "Science as a Vocation," in *The Vocation Lectures,* ed. David S. Owen and Tracy B. Strong, trans. Rodney Livingstone (Indianapolis: Hackett, 2004), 7.

2. Paul F. Campos, "The Real Reason College Tuition Costs So Much," *The New York Times,* April 4, 2015, https://www.nytimes.com/2015/04/05/opinion/sunday/the-real-reason-college-tuition-costs-so-much.html.

3. Colleen Flaherty, "New Report Says Many Adjuncts Make Less than $3,500 per Course and $25,000 per Year," *Inside Higher Ed,* April 20, 2020, https://www.insidehighered.com/news/2020/04/20/new-report-says-many-adjuncts-make-less-3500-course-and-25000-year.

4. Colleen Flaherty, "About Three-Quarters of All Faculty Positions Are off the Tenure Track, According to a New AAUP Analysis," *Inside Higher Ed*, October 12, 2018, https://www.insidehighered.com/news/2018/10/12/about-three-quarters-all-faculty-positions-are-tenure-track-according-new-aaup.

5. Gwynn Guilford, "The Great American Labor Paradox: Plentiful Jobs, Most of Them Bad," *Quartz*, November 21, 2019, https://qz.com/1752676/the-job-quality-index-is-the-economic-indicator-weve-been-missing.

6. Erin Hatton, *The Temp Economy: From Kelly Girls to Permatemps in Postwar America* (Philadelphia: Temple University Press, 2011), 2–4.

7. Hatton, *The Temp Economy*, 22, 39.

8. Hatton, *The Temp Economy*, 74–75.

9. Hatton, *The Temp Economy*, 93–94.

10. David Weil, *The Fissured Workplace: Why Work Became So Bad for So Many and What Can Be Done to Improve It* (Cambridge, MA: Harvard University Press, 2014), 7–8.

11. Goldie Blumenstyk, "College Leaders Are Getting Serious About Outsourcing. They Still Have Plenty of Concerns, Too," *The Chronicle of Higher Education*, March 26, 2019, http://www.chronicle.com/article/College-Leaders-Are-Getting/245978.

12. Weil, *The Fissured Workplace*, 13–14.

13. Weil, *The Fissured Workplace*, 16.

14. Lilah Burke, "The Staffing Divide," *Inside Higher Ed*, March 26, 2020, https://www.insidehighered.com/news/2020/03/26/policies-protect-college-staff-members-amid-crisis-contractors-are-left-out.

15. Zeynep Ton, *The Good Jobs Strategy: How the Smartest Companies Invest in Employees to Lower Costs and Boost Profits* (New York: Houghton Mifflin Harcourt, 2014), 158–60.

16. Shirin Ghaffary, "Uber's Baffling Claim That Its Drivers Aren't Core to Its Business, Explained," *Vox*, September 16, 2019, https://www.vox.com/recode/2019/9/16/20868916/uber-ab5-argument-legal-experts-california.

17. Alex Rosenblat, *Uberland: How Algorithms Are Rewriting the Rules of Work* (Oakland: University of California Press, 2018), 203.

18. Carrie M. Lane, *A Company of One: Insecurity, Independence, and the New World of White-Collar Unemployment* (Ithaca, NY: ILR Press, 2011); Allison J. Pugh, "What Does It Mean to Be a Man in the Age of Austerity?," *Aeon*, December 4, 2015, https://aeon.co/essays/what-does-it-mean-to-be-a-man-in-the-age-of-austerity.

19. Rosenblat, *Uberland*, 35–37.

20. Rosenblat, *Uberland*, 139.

21. Rosenblat, *Uberland*, 133–35.

22. Schaufeli, Leiter, and Maslach, "Burnout," 208.

23. US Bureau of Labor Statistics, "All Employees, Manufacturing / All Employees, Total Nonfarm," FRED, Federal Reserve Bank of St. Louis, accessed October 6, 2020, https://fred.stlouisfed.org/graph/?g = cAYh.

24. US Bureau of Labor Statistics, "All Employees, Manufacturing," FRED, Federal Reserve Bank of St. Louis, accessed December 4, 2019, https://fred.stlouisfed.org/series/MANEMP.

25. US Bureau of Labor Statistics, "Manufacturing Sector: Real Output," FRED, Federal Reserve Bank of St. Louis, accessed April 20, 2021, https://fred.stlouisfed.org/series/OUTMS.

26. US Bureau of Labor Statistics, "Charts of the Largest Occupations in Each Area, May 2018," Occupational Employment Statistics, accessed December 9, 2019, https://www.bls.gov/oes/current/area_emp_chart/area_emp_chart.htm.

27. Kathi Weeks, *The Problem with Work: Feminism, Marxism, Antiwork Politics, and Postwork Imaginaries* (Durham, NC: Duke University Press, 2011), 71.

28. Arlie Russell Hochschild, *The Managed Heart: The Commercialization of Human Feeling*, 20th anniversary ed. (Berkeley: University of California Press, 2003), 4.

29. Andrew Ross, *No-Collar: The Humane Workplace and Its Hidden Costs* (New York: Basic Books, 2003), 92.

30. Weeks, *The Problem with Work*, 73; Benjamin H. Snyder, "Dignity and the Professionalized Body: Truck Driving in the Age of Instant Gratification," *The Hedgehog Review* 14, no. 3 (Fall 2012): 8–20.

31. Weeks, *The Problem with Work*, 74–75.

32. "NUMMI 2015," *This American Life*, July 17, 2015, http://www.thisamericanlife.org/radio-archives/episode/561/nummi-2015.

33. Vicki Smith, *Crossing the Great Divide: Worker Risk and Opportunity in the New Economy* (Ithaca, NY: ILR Press, 2001), 64–65.

34. Smith, *Crossing the Great Divide*, 74.

35. Smith, *Crossing the Great Divide*, 76.

36. Smith, *Crossing the Great Divide*, 49, 38–39.

37. Da-Yee Jeung, Changsoo Kim, and Sei-Jin Chang, "Emotional Labor and Burnout: A Review of the Literature," *Yonsei Medical Journal* 59, no. 2 (March 1, 2018): 187–93, https://doi.org/10.3349/ymj.2018.59.2.187.

38. Maslach and Leiter, *The Truth About Burnout*, 38; Michael P. Leiter and Christina Maslach, "Six Areas of Worklife: A Model of the Organizational Context of Burnout," *Journal of Health and Human Services Administration* 21, no. 4 (1999): 472–89.

39. Maslach and Leiter, *The Truth About Burnout*, 2–9.

40. Organization for Economic Cooperation and Development, "Employment—Hours Worked—OECD Data," accessed July 24, 2019, https://data.oecd.org/emp/hours-worked.htm.

41. Maestas et al., *Working Conditions in the United States*, 26.

42. Jared Bernstein, "Productivity and Wages: What's the Connection?," *Washington Post*, August 14, 2018, https://www.washingtonpost.com/news/posteverything/wp/2018/08/14/productivity-and-wages-whats-the-connection.

43. Jessica Bruder, "These Workers Have a New Demand: Stop Watching Us," *The Nation*, May 27, 2015, https://www.thenation.com/article/these-workers-have-a-new-demand-stop-watching-us.

44. Emily Guendelsberger, *On the Clock: What Low-Wage Work Did to Me and How It Drives America Insane* (New York: Little, Brown and Company, 2019), 32.

45. Nelson C. Brunsting, Melissa A. Sreckovic, and Kathleen Lynne Lane, "Special Education Teacher Burnout: A Synthesis of Research from 1979 to 2013," *Education and Treatment of Children* 37, no. 4 (October 16, 2014): 681–711, https://doi.org/10.1353/etc.2014.0032.

46. Graeber, *Bullshit Jobs*, 26.

47. "Doctors Describe Harrowing Realities inside NYC Emergency Rooms: 'It's Really Hard to Understand How Bad This Is,'" *CBS News*, March 25, 2020, https://www.cbsnews.com/news/coronavirus-pandemic-doctors-describe-harrowing-realities-inside-nyc-emergency-rooms; Ellen Gabler, Zach Montague, and Grace Ashford, "During a Pandemic, an Unanticipated Problem: Out-of-Work Health Workers," *The New York Times*, April 15, 2020, https://www.nytimes.com/2020/04/03/us/politics/coronavirus-health-care-workers-layoffs.html.

48. Brian G. Arndt et al., "Tethered to the EHR: Primary Care Physician Workload Assessment Using EHR Event Log Data and Time-Motion Observations," *The Annals of Family Medicine* 15, no. 5 (September 2017): 419, https://doi.org/10.1370/afm.2121.

49. Shanafelt et al., "Changes in Burnout and Satisfaction with Work-Life Integration in Physicians and the General US Working Population Between 2011 and 2017," 1688.

50. Annalena Welp, Laurenz L. Meier, and Tanja Manser, "Emotional Exhaustion and Workload Predict Clinician-Rated and Objective Patient Safety," *Frontiers in Psychology* 5 (January 2015), https://doi.org/10.3389/fpsyg.2014.01573.

51. Danielle Ofri, "The Business of Health Care Depends on Exploiting Doctors and Nurses," *The New York Times,* June 8, 2019, https://www.nytimes.com/2019/06/08/opinion/sunday/hospitals-doctors-nurses-burnout.html.

52. Christine Sinsky et al., "Allocation of Physician Time in Ambulatory Practice: A Time and Motion Study in 4 Specialties," *Annals of Internal Medicine* 165, no. 11 (December 6, 2016): 757, https://doi.org/10.7326/M16-0961.

53. Tait D. Shanafelt et al., "Relationship Between Clerical Burden and Characteristics of the Electronic Environment With Physician Burnout and Professional Satisfaction," *Mayo Clinic Proceedings* 91, no. 7 (July 1, 2016): 845, https://doi.org/10.1016/j.mayocp.2016.05.007; Rebekah L. Gardner et al., "Physician Stress and Burnout: The Impact of Health Information Technology," *Journal of the American Medical Informatics Association* 26, no. 2 (February 1, 2019): 106–14, https://doi.org/10.1093/jamia/ocy145.

54. William Wan, "Health-Care System Causing Rampant Burnout Among Doctors, Nurses," *Washington Post*, October 23, 2019, https://www.washingtonpost.com/health/2019/10/23/broken-health-care-system-is-causing-rampant-burnout-among-doctors-nurses.

55. Ofri, "The Business of Health Care Depends on Exploiting Doctors and Nurses."

56. Atul Gawande, "Overkill," *The New Yorker,* May 11, 2015, http://www.newyorker.com/magazine/2015/05/11/overkill-atul-gawande.

57. Kevin Drum, "Join Me on a Dive down the Rabbit Hole of Health Care Admin Costs," *Mother Jones* (blog), June 15, 2019, https://www.motherjones.com/kevin-drum/2019/06/join-me-on-a-dive-down-the-rabbit-hole-of-health-care-admin-costs.

58. Schult, Mohr, and Osatuke, "Examining Burnout Profiles in Relation to Health and Well-Being in the Veterans Health Administration Employee Population," 494.

59. Arnold B. Bakker et al., "The Relationship Between the Big Five Personality Factors and Burnout: A Study Among Volunteer Counselors," *The Journal*

of Social Psychology 146, no. 1 (February 2006): 42–43. https://doi.org/10.3200/SOCP.146.1.31–50; Maslach, Schaufeli, and Leiter, "Job Burnout," 411.

60. Shanafelt et al., "Changes in Burnout and Satisfaction with Work-Life Integration in Physicians and the General US Working Population Between 2011 and 2017," 1688.

61. Jihyun Kim, Peter Youngs, and Kenneth Frank, "Burnout Contagion: Is It Due to Early Career Teachers' Social Networks or Organizational Exposure?," *Teaching and Teacher Education* 66 (August 1, 2017): 252, https://doi.org/10.1016/j.tate.2017.04.017.

62. Maslach, *Burnout: The Cost of Caring,* 60.

63. Maslach, *Burnout: The Cost of Caring,* 60.

64. Shanafelt et al., "Changes in Burnout and Satisfaction with Work-Life Integration in Physicians and the General US Working Population Between 2011 and 2017," 1688.

65. Yue-Yung Hu et al., "Discrimination, Abuse, Harassment, and Burnout in Surgical Residency Training," *New England Journal of Medicine* 381, no. 18 (October 31, 2019): 1741–52, https://doi.org/10.1056/NEJMsa1903759. Notably, residency programs varied greatly in how much mistreatment their residents reported; some programs exhibited very little.

66. Arlie Hochschild and Anne Machung, *The Second Shift: Working Families and the Revolution at Home,* Revised ed. (New York: Penguin, 2012); Kelley L. Sharp and Diane Whitaker-Worth, "Burnout of the Female Dermatologist: How Traditional Burnout Reduction Strategies Have Failed Women," *International Journal of Women's Dermatology* 6, no. 1 (January 1, 2020): 32–33, https://doi.org/10.1016/j.ijwd.2019.08.004.

67. Talisa C. Gonzalez et al., "An Examination of Resilience, Compassion Fatigue, Burnout, and Compassion Satisfaction between Men and Women among Trauma Responders," *North American Journal of Psychology* 21, no. 1 (March 1, 2019): 1–19; Radostina K. Purvanova and John P. Muros, "Gender Differences in Burnout: A Meta-Analysis," *Journal of Vocational Behavior* 77, no. 2 (October 2010): 168–85, https://doi.org/10.1016/j.jvb.2010.04.006; Maslach, Schaufeli, and Leiter, "Job Burnout," 410.

68. Purvanova and Muros, "Gender Differences in Burnout."

69. Kim Templeton et al., "Gender-Based Differences in Burnout: Issues Faced by Women Physicians," *NAM Perspectives,* May 28, 2019, 2, https://doi.org/10.31478/201905a.

70. Guy Standing, "Global Feminization Through Flexible Labor: A Theme Revisited," *World Development* 27, no. 3 (March 1999): 583, https://doi.org/10.1016/S0305-750X(98)00151-X.

71. Nina Banks, "Black Women's Labor Market History Reveals Deep-Seated Race and Gender Discrimination," *Economic Policy Institute* (blog), February 19, 2019, https://www.epi.org/blog/black-womens-labor-market-history-reveals-deep-seated-race-and-gender-discrimination.

72. Bryce Covert, "We're All Women Workers Now: How the Floor of the Economy Has Dropped for Everyone," *The Nation*, February 21, 2013, https://www.thenation.com/article/archive/were-all-women-workers-now-how-floor-economy-has-dropped-everyone.

73. Adia Harvey Wingfield, "About Those 79 Cents," *The Atlantic*, October 17, 2016, https://www.theatlantic.com/business/archive/2016/10/79-cents/504386.

74. "2020 Racial Wage Gap," *PayScale*, 2020, https://www.payscale.com/data/racial-wage-gap.

75. Clark, "This Is What Black Burnout Feels Like."

76. Elise T. Pas, Catherine P. Bradshaw, and Patricia A. Hershfeldt, "Teacher- and School-Level Predictors of Teacher Efficacy and Burnout: Identifying Potential Areas for Support," *Journal of School Psychology* 50, no. 1 (February 1, 2012): 139, https://doi.org/10.1016/j.jsp.2011.07.003; Jonathan Lent and Robert Schwartz, "The Impact of Work Setting, Demographic Characteristics, and Personality Factors Related to Burnout Among Professional Counselors," *Journal of Mental Health Counseling* 34, no. 4 (October 1, 2012): 355-72, https://doi.org/10.17744/mehc.34.4.e3k8u2k552515166.

77. Michelle P. Salyers and Gary R. Bond, "An Exploratory Analysis of Racial Factors in Staff Burnout Among Assertive Community Treatment Workers," *Community Mental Health Journal* 37, no. 5 (October 1, 2001): 393-404, https://doi.org/10.1023/A:1017575912288; Garret D. Evans et al., "Ethnic Differences in Burnout, Coping, and Intervention Acceptability Among Childcare Professionals," *Child and Youth Care Forum* 33, no. 5 (October 2004): 349-71, https://doi.org/10.1023/B:CCAR.0000043040.54270.dd.

78. Evans et al., "Ethnic Differences in Burnout, Coping, and Intervention Acceptability Among Childcare Professionals," 365.

79. Carol B. Cunradi et al., "Burnout and Alcohol Problems among Urban Transit Operators in San Francisco," *Addictive Behaviors* 28, no. 1 (January 1, 2003): 98, https://doi.org/10.1016/S0306-4603(01)00222-2.

80. Carol B. Cunradi, Meng-Jinn Chen, and Rob Lipton, "Association of Occupational and Substance Use Factors with Burnout among Urban Transit Operators," *Journal of Urban Health: Bulletin of the New York Academy of Medicine* 86, no. 4 (July 2009): 567, https://doi.org/10.1007/s11524-009-9349-4.

81. Christine Owens, "These Labor Laws Are Suppressing Black Workers," *Fortune*, September 4, 2017, https://fortune.com/2017/09/04/labor-day-2017-right-to-work-unions; Molly Kinder and Tiffany Ford, "Black Essential Workers' Lives Matter. They Deserve Real Change, Not Just Lip Service," *Brookings Institution*, June 24, 2020, https://www.brookings.edu/research/black-essential-workers-lives-matter-they-deserve-real-change-not-just-lip-service.

82. Davin L. Phoenix, *The Anger Gap: How Race Shapes Emotion in Politics* (Cambridge, UK: Cambridge University Press, 2019), 42.

83. Caroline Beaton, "Is Anxiety a White-People Thing?," *Vice*, November 9, 2017, https://www.vice.com/en_us/article/mb35b8/is-anxiety-a-white-people-thing; Melissa Pandika, "The Test We Use to Detect Depression Is Designed for White People," *Vice*, February 13, 2018, https://www.vice.com/en_us/article/vbpdym/depression-screening-not-effective-for-black-youth.

84. Ofri, "The Business of Health Care Depends on Exploiting Doctors and Nurses."

Chapter 5. Work Saints and Work Martyrs

1. Alex Williams, "Why Don't Rich People Just Stop Working?," *The New York Times,* October 18, 2019, https://www.nytimes.com/2019/10/17/style/rich-people-things.html; US Bureau of Labor Statistics, "American Time Use Survey—2019 Results," June 25, 2020, https://www.bls.gov/news.release/pdf/atus.pdf; Ruihong Liu, "Rich Teens Twice as Likely to Land Jobs as Poor Kids," *Philadelphia Magazine*, June 23, 2015, https://www.phillymag.com/business/2015/06/23/rich-poor-teen-jobs; Paula Span, "Many Americans Try Retirement, Then Change Their Minds," *The New York Times,* March 30, 2018, https://www.nytimes.com/2018/03/30/health/unretirement-work-seniors.html.

2. Pugh, "What Does It Mean to Be a Man in the Age of Austerity?"; Anne Case and Angus Deaton, "Mortality and Morbidity in the 21st Century," BPEA Conference Drafts (Brookings Institution, March 17, 2017), https://www.brookings.edu/wp-content/uploads/2017/03/6_casedeaton.pdf.

3. Eric Hopkins, "Working Hours and Conditions during the Industrial Revolution: A Re-Appraisal," *The Economic History Review* 35, no. 1 (1982): 52–66, https://doi.org/10.2307/2595103.

4. Plato, *Republic,* trans. G. M. A. Grube, 2nd ed. (Indianapolis, IN: Hackett, 1992), 414c–15.

5. Brian Kennedy and Cary Funk, "Public Interest in Science and Health Linked to Gender, Age and Personality" (Washington, DC: Pew Research Center, December 11, 2015), https://www.pewresearch.org/science/2015/12/11/personality-and-interest-in-science-health-topics.

6. John Smith, *The Generall Historie of Virginia, New England, & The Summer Isles, Together with The True Travels, Adventures, and Observations, and A Sea Grammar,* vol. 1 (New York: Macmillan, 1908), 182.

7. Livingston, *No More Work.*

8. Sonny Perdue, "The Dignity of Work and the American Dream," *Arizona Daily Star*, December 4, 2019, https://tucson.com/opinion/national/sonny-perdue-the-dignity-of-work-and-the-american-dream/article_a9109ba1-cd48-5038-b00a-41aecddd91fa.html; Jeff Spross, "You're Hired!," *Democracy Journal,* Spring 2017, http://democracyjournal.org/magazine/44/youre-hired.

9. 2 Thess. 3:10.

10. Allison J. Pugh, "The Social Meanings of Dignity at Work," *The Hedgehog Review* 14, no. 3 (Fall 2012): 30.

11. Will Durant, *The Story of Philosophy: The Lives and Opinions of the World's Greatest Philosophers,* 2nd edition (New York: Pocket Books, 1991), 76.

12. Paul E. Johnson, *A Shopkeeper's Millennium: Society and Revivals in Rochester, New York, 1815–1837,* 25th Anniversary Edition (New York: Farrar, Straus and Giroux, 2004), 57–58.

13. David Sheff, "Playboy Interview: Steve Jobs," *Playboy,* February 1985, http://reprints.longform.org/playboy-interview-steve-jobs.

14. Plato, *Republic,* 415a–c.

15. Jean Calvin, *Institutes of the Christian Religion,* trans. Henry Beveridge (Peabody, MA: Hendrickson, 2008), 472; Martin Luther, "The Gospel for the Sun-

day After Christmas: Luke 2," in *Sermons II*, ed. Hans J. Hillerbrand, trans. John J. Kunstmann, vol. 52, *Luther's Works* (Philadelphia: Fortress Press, 1974), 124.

16. Betty Friedan, *The Feminine Mystique* (1963; New York: W. W. Norton, 2001), 458.

17. Miya Tokumitsu, *Do What You Love: And Other Lies About Success & Happiness* (New York: Regan Arts, 2015); Sarah Jaffe, *Work Won't Love You Back: How Devotion to Our Jobs Keeps Us Exploited, Exhausted, and Alone* (New York: Bold Type Books, 2021).

18. Paul Ross, "Wegmans Ranked as Third Best Fortune 100 Company to Work For," WKBW, February 18, 2020, https://www.wkbw.com/news/local-news/wegmans-ranked-as-third-best-fortune-100-company-to-work-for.

19. Gallup, Inc., *State of the Global Workplace 2013: Employee Engagement Insights for Business Leaders Worldwide* (Washington, DC: Gallup, 2013), 17.

20. Gallup, Inc., *State of the Global Workplace 2013*, 199.

21. Lillian Cunningham, "New Data Show Only 30% of American Workers Engaged in Their Jobs," *Washington Post*, April 30, 2013, https://www.washingtonpost.com/news/on-leadership/wp/2013/04/30/new-data-show-only-30-of-american-workers-engaged-in-their-jobs.

22. Karlyn Borysenko, "How Much Are Your Disengaged Employees Costing You?," *Forbes*, May 2, 2019, https://www.forbes.com/sites/karlynborysenko/2019/05/02/how-much-are-your-disengaged-employees-costing-you.

23. Shaley McKeever, "3 Types of Employees: How to Spot the Silent Killer," *Recruiter.com*, January 31, 2014, https://www.recruiter.com/i/3-types-of-employees-how-to-spot-the-silent-killer.

24. Gallup, Inc., *State of the Global Workplace 2013*, 17.

25. Gallup, Inc., *State of the Global Workplace 2017* (Washington, DC: Gallup, 2017), 197; Gallup, Inc., *State of the Global Workplace 2013*, 112.

26. "Most and Least Meaningful Jobs," *PayScale*, accessed May 22, 2020, https://www.payscale.com/data-packages/most-and-least-meaningful-jobs.

27. Mihaly Csikszentmihalyi, *Flow: The Psychology of Optimal Experience* (New York: Harper & Row, 1990), 162.

28. Csikszentmihalyi, *Flow*, 151–52.

29. Jeanne Nakamura and Mihaly Csikszentmihalyi, "The Concept of Flow," in *Handbook of Positive Psychology* (New York: Oxford University Press, 2002), 89.

30. Csikszentmihalyi, *Flow*, 149.

31. Csikszentmihalyi, *Flow*, 147–48.

32. Max Weber, *The Protestant Ethic and the "Spirit" of Capitalism and Other Writings*, ed. Peter Baehr and Gordon C. Wells (New York: Penguin Books, 2002), lxx, 121.

33. Max Weber, *The Protestant Ethic and the "Spirit" of Capitalism and Other Writings*, 13.

34. Max Weber, *The Protestant Ethic and the "Spirit" of Capitalism and Other Writings*, 120–21.

35. Marianne Weber, *Max Weber: A Biography*, trans. Harry Zohn (New York: John Wiley & Sons, 1975), 243.

36. Marianne Weber, *Max Weber*, 253.

37. Marianne Weber, *Max Weber*, 263.

38. Max Weber, *The Protestant Ethic and the "Spirit" of Capitalism and Other Writings*, 76.

39. Gianpiero Petriglieri, "Is Overwork Killing You?," *Harvard Business Review*, August 31, 2015, https://hbr.org/2015/08/is-overwork-killing-you.

40. Tristen Lee, "Millennials Are Beyond Burnout Now," *The Independent*, August 13, 2019, https://www.independent.co.uk/voices/millennials-burnout-gen-z-work-life-balance-holiday-income-snap-a9055471.html.

41. Lee, "Millennials Are Beyond Burnout Now."

42. Josef Pieper, *Leisure: The Basis of Culture*, ed. James V. Schall (San Francisco: Ignatius Press, 2009), 20.

43. Pieper, *Leisure*, 53.

44. Pieper, *Leisure*, 38.

45. Karen Rinaldi, "Motherhood Isn't Sacrifice, It's Selfishness," *The New York Times*, August 4, 2017, https://www.nytimes.com/2017/08/04/opinion/sunday/motherhood-family-sexism-sacrifice.html.

46. Ian Petrie (@icpetrie), "Letter to First Grade Parents: 'It Is Important That We Start on Time. We Are Training Our Children for the Work Force,'" Twitter, September 12, 2013, https://twitter.com/icpetrie/status/378296120096468992.

47. Ellen Bara Stolzenberg et al., "The American Freshman: National Norms Fall 2017," Expanded Version (Los Angeles: Higher Education Research Institute, 2019), 36, https://www.heri.ucla.edu/monographs/The AmericanFreshman2017-Expanded.pdf.

48. Mona Simpson, "A Sister's Eulogy for Steve Jobs," *The New York Times,* October 30, 2011, https://www.nytimes.com/2011/10/30/opinion/mona -simpsons-eulogy-for-steve-jobs.html.

49. Pieper, *Leisure,* 36.

50. Pieper, *Leisure,* 49.

51. Adam Smith, *The Wealth of Nations, Books I-III,* ed. Andrew Skinner (London: Penguin Classics, 1997), 109–10.

52. Adam Smith, *The Wealth of Nations, Books IV-V,* ed. Andrew Skinner (London: Penguin Classics, 2000), 368–69.

53. Alexandra Michel, "Transcending Socialization: A Nine-Year Ethnography of the Body's Role in Organizational Control and Knowledge Workers' Transformation," *Administrative Science Quarterly* 56, no. 3 (2011): 325–68, https://doi.org/10.1177/0001839212437519.

54. Anne Li, "Despite Grueling Hours, Consulting And Finance Keep Attracting College Seniors," *WBUR Here and Now,* December 4, 2015, https://www.wbur.org/hereandnow/2015/12/04/consulting-finance-job -growth.

55. Pieper, *Leisure,* 58.

56. Booker T. Washington, *Up from Slavery,* ed. William L. Andrews, 2nd ed. (New York: W. W. Norton & Company, 1995), 71.

57. Washington, *Up from Slavery,* 72.

58. Washington, *Up from Slavery,* 38.

59. Washington, *Up from Slavery,* 68.

60. Lawrence A. Scaff, *Max Weber in America* (Princeton, NJ: Princeton University Press, 2011), 109.

61. Washington, *Up from Slavery,* 119.

62. Washington, *Up from Slavery,* 86.

63. Washington, *Up from Slavery,* 123–24.

64. Meghan McCarty Carino, "Workers Are Putting off Vacation as Pandemic Increases Stress," *Marketplace,* August 17, 2020, https://www .marketplace.org/2020/08/17/workers-putting-off-vacation-pandemic -increases-stress.

65. "Glassdoor Survey Finds Americans Forfeit Half of Their Earned Vacation/Paid Time Off," *Glassdoor,* May 24, 2017, https://www.glassdoor .com/press/glassdoor-survey-finds-americans-forfeit-earned-vacationpaid -time.

66. Kathryn Vasel, "Half of American Workers Aren't Using All Their Vacation Days," *CNNMoney*, December 19, 2016, http://money.cnn.com/2016/12/19/pf/employees-unused-paid-vacation-days/index.html.

67. Washington, *Up from Slavery*, 124.

68. Booker T. Washington, *The Story of My Life and Work* (Toronto: J. L. Nichols, 1901), 273, http://docsouth.unc.edu/neh/washstory/washin.html.

69. Pieper, *Leisure*, 35.

70. Washington, *Up from Slavery*, 83, 73.

71. Washington, *Up from Slavery*, 134.

72. Phil. 2:7–8.

73. See Jonathan Malesic, "A Kenotic Struggle for Dignity: Booker T. Washington's Theology of Work," *Journal of Religious Ethics* 44, no. 3 (2016): 416–17, https://doi.org/10.1111/jore.12147.

Chapter 6. We Can Have It All

1. *The Parking Lot Movie,* directed by Meghan Eckman (Redhouse Productions, 2010), http://www.theparkinglotmovie.com.

2. Pugh, "The Social Meanings of Dignity at Work," 30–31.

3. Arthur C. Brooks, "The Dignity Deficit," *Foreign Affairs,* February 13, 2017, https://www.foreignaffairs.com/articles/united-states/2017-02-13/dignity-deficit.

4. Perdue, "The Dignity of Work and the American Dream."

5. Bill Clinton, "Text of President Clinton's Announcement on Welfare Legislation," *The New York Times,* August 1, 1996, https://www.nytimes.com/1996/08/01/us/text-of-president-clinton-s-announcement-on-welfare-legislation.html.

6. Sherrod Brown, "The Dignity of Work Tour," accessed January 23, 2019, https://dignityofwork.com.

7. Pope Leo XIII, *Rerum Novarum,* 1891, 2, 4, http://www.vatican.va/holy_father/leo_xiii/encyclicals/documents/hf_l-xiii_enc_15051891_rerum-novarum_en.html.

8. Leo XIII, *Rerum Novarum,* 20.

9. Leo XIII, *Rerum Novarum,* 44–45.

10. Leo XIII, *Rerum Novarum,* 42. Emphasis mine.

11. Steve Siebold, "Chicago Teachers: Stop Holding the City Hostage," *The American Spectator*, October 23, 2019, https://spectator.org/chicago-teachers-stop-holding-the-city-hostage.

12. John Paul II, *Laborem Exercens,* 1981, 6, http://www.vatican.va/holy_father/john_paul_ii/encyclicals/documents/hf_jp-ii_enc_14091981_laborem-exercens_en.html.

13. Gene Sperling, *Economic Dignity* (New York: Penguin, 2020), 136.

14. Eckman, *The Parking Lot Movie.*

15. Henry David Thoreau, *Walden,* ed. J. Lyndon Shanley (Princeton, NJ: Princeton University Press, 2004), 3; Laura Dassow Walls, *Henry David Thoreau: A Life* (Chicago: University of Chicago Press, 2017), 198–99.

16. Rebecca Solnit, "Mysteries of Thoreau, Unsolved," *Orion,* May/June 2013, 18–19.

17. Walls, *Henry David Thoreau,* 194.

18. Walls, *Henry David Thoreau,* 215–16.

19. Walls, *Henry David Thoreau,* 451–53.

20. Thoreau, *Walden,* 6.

21. Thoreau, *Walden,* 6.

22. Thoreau, *Walden,* 5.

23. Thoreau, *Walden,* 7.

24. Thoreau, *Walden,* 92.

25. Thoreau, *Walden,* 7.

26. Thoreau, *Walden,* 36, 54.

27. Thoreau, *Walden,* 159.

28. Thoreau, *Walden,* 162.

29. Thoreau, *Walden,* 205.

30. Thoreau, *Walden,* 150.

31. Thoreau, *Walden,* 221–22.

32. Thoreau, *Walden,* 222.

33. Thoreau, *Walden,* 56.

34. Thoreau, *Walden,* 89.

35. Thoreau, *Walden,* 111–12.

36. Thoreau, *Walden,* 326–27.

37. Jenny Odell, *How to Do Nothing: Resisting the Attention Economy* (Brooklyn, NY: Melville House, 2019), 15.

38. Weeks, *The Problem with Work*, 109–10.

39. Mitra Toossi and Teresa L Morisi, "Women In The Workforce Before, During, And After The Great Recession," Spotlight on Statistics (Bureau of Labor Statistics, July 2017), https://www.bls.gov/spotlight/2017/women-in-the-workforce-before-during-and-after-the-great-recession/pdf/women-in-the-workforce-before-during-and-after-the-great-recession.pdf.

40. Giulia M. Dotti Sani and Judith Treas, "Educational Gradients in Parents' Child-Care Time Across Countries, 1965–2012," *Journal of Marriage and Family* 78, no. 4 (August 1, 2016): 1083–96, https://doi.org/10.1111/jomf.12305.

41. Rinaldi, "Motherhood Isn't Sacrifice, It's Selfishness."

42. Weeks, *The Problem with Work*, 8.

43. Weber, *The Protestant Ethic and the "Spirit" of Capitalism and Other Writings*, 13, 120.

44. Weeks, *The Problem with Work*, 15.

45. Weeks, *The Problem with Work*, 168.

46. Weeks, *The Problem with Work*, 34.

47. Leo XIII, *Rerum Novarum*, 13.

48. Weeks, *The Problem with Work*, 32–33.

49. Weeks, *The Problem with Work*, 232–33.

50. Eckman, *The Parking Lot Movie*.

51. Alonzo Subverbo (pseud.), "Live. Park. Die.," *Subverbo* (blog), September 10, 2016, https://alonzosubverbo.wordpress.com/2016/09/09/live-park-die.

52. Thoreau, *Walden*, 69.

53. Subverbo (pseud.), "Live. Park. Die."

Chapter 7. How Benedictines Tame the Demons of Work

1. Leslie Miller, "A Megabyte Mission: Monks Called to Put Vatican's Word on the Web," *USA Today*, November 13, 1996, sec. Life, p. 1D.

2. Deborah Baker, "Holy Web Page: In a Remote Part of New Mexico, Benedictine Monks Get on the Internet to Spread the Word," *Los Angeles Times*, December 31, 1995, http://articles.latimes.com/1995-12-31/local/me-19506_1_christian-monks.

3. Elizabeth Cohen, "21st-Century Scribes: Monks Designing Web Pages," *The New York Times*, March 17, 1996, https://www.nytimes.com/1996/03/17/us/21st-century-scribes-monks-designing-web-pages.html.

4. John L. Allen, "Monk Targets Catholic Slice of On-Line Market," *National Catholic Reporter*, April 17, 1998, 7.

5. Allen, "Monk Targets Catholic Slice of On-Line Market."

6. Ray Rivera, "Monks Put Religion on the Net," *The New Mexican*, July 27, 1997.

7. Mari Graña, *Brothers of the Desert: The Story of the Monastery of Christ in the Desert* (Santa Fe, NM: Sunstone Press, 2006), 131–32.

8. Benedicta Ward, S.L.G., trans., *The Sayings of the Desert Fathers: The Alphabetical Collection* (Kalamazoo, MI: Cistercian Publications, 1975), 5.

9. Pieper, *Leisure*, 53.

10. Philip Lawrence, O.S.B., "Abbot's Notebook for May 30, 2018," May 30, 2018, https://us11.campaign-archive.com/?e = 228db5cfa0&u = f5bb6673a3350b85b34f0d6cc&id = fc4afc0f67.

11. Mt. 4:1–11.

12. 2 Thess. 3:10.

13. Pieper, *Leisure*, 72.

14. Abraham Joshua Heschel, *The Sabbath: Its Meaning for Modern Man* (New York: Farrar, Straus and Giroux, 2005), 14.

15. Julie L. Rose, *Free Time* (Princeton, NJ: Princeton University Press, 2016), 94–95.

16. Benedict, *The Rule of St. Benedict in English*, ed. Timothy Fry (Collegeville, MN: Liturgical Press, 1982), chap. 43.3.

17. Benedict, *The Rule of St. Benedict*, chap. 43.6.

18. Jacques Le Goff, *Time, Work & Culture in the Middle Ages*, trans. Arthur Goldhammer (Chicago: University of Chicago Press, 1980), 80.

19. Allen, "Monk Targets Catholic Slice of On-Line Market."

20. Benedict, *The Rule of St. Benedict*, chap. 57.

21. Aquinas Woodworth, "AQVINAS," accessed January 14, 2020, https://www.aqvinas.com.

22. Weeks, *The Problem with Work*, 146.

23. Cary Cherniss and David L. Krantz, "The Ideological Community as an Antidote to Burnout in the Human Services," in *Stress and Burnout in the*

Human Service Professions, ed. Barry A. Farber, Pergamon General Psychology Series, PGPS-117 (New York: Pergamon Press, 1983), 198–212.

24. Benedict, *The Rule of St. Benedict*, chap. 35.

25. Stephanie Dickrell, "Benedictine Sisters Will Lead Talk on Islam, Stereotypes," *St. Cloud Times*, September 11, 2016, https://www.sctimes.com/story /news/local/immigration/2016/09/11/benedictine-sisters-lead-talk-islam -stereotypes/89776016.

26. Benedict, *The Rule of St. Benedict*, chap. 43.3.

27. Benedict, *The Rule of St. Benedict*, chap. 57.1.

28. Allison J. Pugh, *The Tumbleweed Society: Working and Caring in an Age of Insecurity* (Oxford: Oxford University Press, 2015), 18–19.

29. Benedict, *The Rule of St. Benedict*, chap. 55.18.

30. Benedict, *The Rule of St. Benedict*, chap. 48:24–25.

31. Leo XIII, *Rerum Novarum,* 42.

32. John Henry Newman, *Sermons Bearing on Subjects of the Day* (New York: Scribner, Welford, & Co., 1869), 307, http://archive.org/details /sermonsbearingooocopegoog.

33. Drew DeSilver, "More Older Americans Are Working than in Recent Years," Pew Research Center, June 20, 2016, https://www.pewresearch.org /fact-tank/2016/06/20/more-older-americans-are-working-and-working -more-than-they-used-to.

34. Span, "Many Americans Try Retirement, Then Change Their Minds."

35. Thoreau, *Walden,* 54.

36. Tomáš Janotík, "Empirical Analysis of Life Satisfaction in Female Benedictine Monasteries in Germany," *Revue Économique* 67, no. 1 (2016): 143–65.

Chapter 8. Varieties of Anti-Burnout Experience

1. Kirsti Marohn, "St. John's Kiln Firing Is Celebration of Art, Community," *Minnesota Public Radio News,* October 21, 2019, https://www.mprnews.org /story/2019/10/21/st-johns-kiln-firing-is-celebration-of-art-community.

2. Max Weber, *The Theory of Social and Economic Organization,* ed. Talcott Parsons, trans. A.M. Henderson and Talcott Parsons (New York: The Free Press, 1964), 358–59, http://archive.org/details/in.ernet.dli.2015.6054.

3. Larry M. James, *House Rules: Insights for Innovative Leaders* (Abilene, TX: Leafwood Publishers, 2018), 245.

4. James, *House Rules*, 249–50.

5. Kristin Hildenbrand, Claudia A. Sacramento, and Carmen Binnewies, "Transformational Leadership and Burnout: The Role of Thriving and Followers' Openness to Experience," *Journal of Occupational Health Psychology* 23, no. 1 (2018): 33, https://doi.org/10.1037/ocp0000051.

6. Meredith Elaine Babcock-Roberson and Oriel J. Strickland, "The Relationship Between Charismatic Leadership, Work Engagement, and Organizational Citizenship Behaviors," *The Journal of Psychology* 144, no. 3 (April 8, 2010): 313–26, https://doi.org/10.1080/00223981003648336; Anastasios Zopiatis and Panayiotis Constanti, "Leadership Styles and Burnout: Is There an Association?," *International Journal of Contemporary Hospitality Management* 22, no. 3 (January 1, 2010): 300–20, https://doi.org/10.1108/09596111011035927.

7. Hildenbrand, Sacramento, and Binnewies, "Transformational Leadership and Burnout."

8. Weber, *The Theory of Social and Economic Organization*, 363–64.

9. *Darkon*, directed by Luke Meyer and Andrew Neel (SeeThink Films, 2006), https://vimeo.com/322967237.

10. Pieper, *Leisure*, 50.

11. Erica Mena, "Tying Knots: A Language of Anxiety," April 1, 2019, https://acyborgkitty.com/2019/04/01/3792.

12. Johanna Hedva, "Sick Woman Theory," *Mask Magazine*, January 19, 2016, http://www.maskmagazine.com/not-again/struggle/sick-woman-theory.

13. Sunny Taylor, "The Right Not to Work: Power and Disability," *Monthly Review* (blog), March 1, 2004, https://monthlyreview.org/2004/03/01/the-right-not-to-work-power-and-disability.

14. Hedva, "Sick Woman Theory."

15. Taylor, "The Right Not to Work."

16. Hedva, "Sick Woman Theory."

17. Leo XIII, *Rerum Novarum*, 42.

Conclusion

1. "'We Have A Driver's Heart': New York City Bus Operators On Work And Loss During COVID-19," *StoryCorps*, April 24, 2020, https://storycorps.org/stories/we-have-a-drivers-heart-new-york-city-bus-operators-on-work-and-loss-during-covid-19.

2. Michelle F. Davis and Jeff Green, "Three Hours Longer, the Pandemic Workday Has Obliterated Work-Life Balance," *Bloomberg.com,* April 23, 2020, https://www.bloomberg.com/news/articles/2020-04-23/working-from -home-in-covid-era-means-three-more-hours-on-the-job.

3. Pallavi Gogoi, "Stuck-at-Home Moms: The Pandemic's Devastating Toll on Women," *National Public Radio,* October 28, 2020, https://www.npr.org /2020/10/28/928253674/stuck-at-home-moms-the-pandemics-devastating -toll-on-women.

4. Kinder and Ford, "Black Essential Workers' Lives Matter."

5. Manny Fernandez and David Montgomery, "Texas Tries to Balance Local Control With the Threat of a Pandemic," *The New York Times,* March 24, 2020, https://www.nytimes.com/2020/03/24/us/coronavirus-texas-patrick -abbott.html.

6. Jonathan Malesic (@JonMalesic), "I Have a Taboo Question for a Thing I'm Writing: Is Anyone Enjoying This? Any Parents, in Particular? Are There Any Ways Your Life Is Better in This Situation? If so, DM or Email Me. I Don't Have to Use Your Name, If You Don't Want Me To," Twitter, March 24, 2020, https://twitter.com/JonMalesic/status/1242511479150120968.

7. Claire Cain Miller, "Women Did Everything Right. Then Work Got 'Greedy,'" *The New York Times,* April 26, 2019, https://www.nytimes.com/2019 /04/26/upshot/women-long-hours-greedy-professions.html.

8. Jose Maria Barrero, Nicholas Bloom, and Steven Davis, "60 Million Fewer Commuting Hours per Day: How Americans Use Time Saved by Working from Home," *VoxEU,* September 23, 2020, https://voxeu.org/article /how-americans-use-time-saved-working-home.

9. Erin Bishop (@the_ebish), "@JonMalesic I Just Laid on a Blanket in the Backyard with My 3 Year Old Naming What Shapes We Saw in the Clouds. It Was Marvelous," Twitter, March 24, 2020, https://twitter.com/the_ebish /status/1242598401545392128.

10. Transcript of Andrew M. Cuomo interviewed by Michael Barbaro, March 18, 2020, https://www.governor.ny.gov/news/audio-rush-transcript -governor-cuomo-guest-daily-podcast.

11. Anna Gronewold and Erin Durkin, "Cuomo's Coronavirus Halo Begins to Fade," *Politico,* May 29, 2020, https://politi.co/2TPlGBU; Joe Sexton and Joaquin Sapien, "Two Coasts. One Virus. How New York Suffered Nearly 10 Times the Number of Deaths as California," *ProPublica,* May 16, 2020, https://

www.propublica.org/article/two-coasts-one-virus-how-new-york-suffered -nearly-10-times-the-number-of-deaths-as-california; Jesse McKinley, "Cuomo Faces New Claims of Sexual Harassment from Current Aide," *The New York Times*, March 19, 2021, https://www.nytimes.com/2021/03/19/nyregion/alyssa -mcgrath-cuomo-harassment.html; Jesse McKinley, Danny Hakim, and Alexandra Alter, "As Cuomo Sought $4 Million Book Deal, Aides Hid Damaging Death Toll," *The New York Times*, March 31, 2021, https://www.nytimes .com/2021/03/31/nyregion/cuomo-book-nursing-homes.html.

12. David H. Freedman, "The Worst Patients in the World," *The Atlantic*, June 12, 2019, https://www.theatlantic.com/magazine/archive/2019/07 /american-health-care-spending/590623.

13. Robert D. Gillette, "'Problem Patients:' A Fresh Look at an Old Vexation," *Family Practice Management* 7, no. 7 (August 2000): 57.

14. Eric Morath, "Coronavirus Relief Often Pays Workers More Than Work," *The Wall Street Journal* April 28, 2020, https://www.wsj.com/articles /coronavirus-relief-often-pays-workers-more-than-work-11588066200.

15. Carrie Arnold, "Pandemic Speeds Largest Test yet of Universal Basic Income," *Nature* 583, no. 7817 (July 10, 2020): 502–3, https://doi.org/10.1038 /d41586-020-01993-3.

16. Bess Levin, "Republicans Are Worried Coronavirus Stimulus Bill Is Too Generous to the Unemployed," *Vanity Fair*, March 25, 2020, https://www .vanityfair.com/news/2020/03/lindsey-graham-coronavirus-stimulus-bill; Andy Puzder, "Don't Extend the Cares Act's $600 Weekly Bonus," *Washington Post,* July 2, 2020, https://www.washingtonpost.com/opinions/employers-cant -find-people-to-hire-the-pandemic-bonus-is-to-blame/2020/07/02/da9b0950 -bc7d-11ea-bdaf-a129f921026f_story.html.

17. Sarah Jaffe, "The Post-Pandemic Future of Work," *The New Republic,* May 1, 2020, https://newrepublic.com/article/157504/post-pandemic-future -work.

18. Kevin Drum, "You Will Lose Your Job to a Robot—and Sooner than You Think," *Mother Jones,* December 2017, https://www.motherjones.com/politics /2017/10/you-will-lose-your-job-to-a-robot-and-sooner-than-you-think.

19. Jonathan Lear, *Radical Hope: Ethics in the Face of Cultural Devastation* (Cambridge, MA: Harvard University Press, 2008), 7.

20. Lear, *Radical Hope*, 64.

Index

Csikszentmihalyi, Mihaly, 123–24
Cuomo, Andrew, 224
Curfman, Liz, 68–69, 75, 196
cynicism and depersonalization: on
    burnout spectrum, 69, 73–74, 75,
    77; as dimension of burnout,
    20–22, 24–25; Maslach's early
    study on, 54–55; as socially
    acceptable, 82; and Stanford
    Prison Experiment, 53

Darkon (documentary), 201–2
Deloitte burnout study, 27
demonic forces, 40–41, 129–30,
    168–69, 185
depersonalization. *See* cynicism and
    depersonalization
depression: as distinct from burnout,
    32, 34, 35–36; and race, 110;
    similarities with burnout, 84–85;
    spectrum, 67–68
Desert Fathers, 168
dignity: and government policies,
    145–47; as ideal for work, 117–18;
    as inherent to the person, 148–51,
    211–12; in monastic communities,
    185–86; as term, 144–45
disability, 205–6, 207–11, 212–13. *See
    also* mental illness
doctors. *See* medical workers
Durant, Will, 118
Dürer, Albrecht, *Melancholia I,* 41–42
Dylan, Bob, 50
Dyrbye, Liselotte, 103

Ecclesiastes (biblical book), 39
Eckman, Meghan, 143
elite class, 42, 44–45
emotional labor, 94–95

engagement, 74, 120–24
Erb, Wilhelm, 46–47
errand paralysis, 29, 128
essential *vs.* nonessential workers,
    218–19
Evagrius Ponticus, 40
exhaustion: and acedia, 40–41; on
    burnout spectrum, 69, 73–74, 75,
    78; as dimension of burnout,
    20–22, 24–25; and melancholia/
    melancholy, 39–40, 41–42; and
    neurasthenia, 43–48, 60, 126; as
    socially acceptable, 81–83

fairness, 98, 111, 138
feminist liberation, 159–60
fissured workplaces, 91–92, 97,
    100–101
flight attendants, 95
flow states, 123–24
free-clinic workers, 50–52
Freudenberger, Herbert, 50–53, 55,
    59, 60, 84
Friedan, Betty, 120
Friedman, Milton, 56
Friedman, Richard, 33–34
Frissell, Hollis, 136
frustration, 75, 78–81. *See also*
    ineffectiveness

Gawande, Atul, 104
gender disparities, 106–7, 109, 219.
    See also men; women
Gilman, Charlotte Perkins, 47
government policies, 145–47
Graeber, David, 80, 101
Graña, Mari, 166
Greene, Graham, *A Burnt-Out Case,*
    48–50

Marxist feminism, 159–60
masculine ideals, 113
Maslach, Christina: early study on
    depersonalization, 54–55; on
    idealism, 19, 71–72; profiles of
    burnout, 74, 77–79; on relation-
    ships, 19–20; on six key aspects of
    workplaces, 98, 100; and Stanford
    Prison Experiment, 53; on three
    dimensions of burnout, 20–21
Maslach Burnout Inventory (MBI),
    21–22, 24, 25, 74, 77, 215
Mayo Clinic burnout studies, 25, 79
McGraw, Rene, 188
McKay, Paul, 202–3, 204
meaning and purpose, 79–80, 118–20
medical knowledge: as fluid, 37–38;
    lack of clinical definition for
    burnout, 31, 33–34, 60, 68. *See also*
    mental illness
medical workers: burnout studies
    on, 23, 24, 25–26, 79, 106–7;
    compassion for, 224–26; and
    engagement, 123; experience of
    ideals *vs.* reality, 102–4
Meiggs, Scott, 162, 163
melancholia/melancholy, 39–40,
    41–42
men: and gendered view of labor,
    90, 107–8; masculine ideals, 113.
    See also women
Mena, Erica, 205–8, 209, 211–12
mental illness: acedia, 40–41;
    melancholia/melancholy, 39–40,
    41–42; neurasthenia, 43–48, 60;
    and race, 110–11. *See also*
    depression
Meredith Corporation burnout
    study, 26–27

Merikangas, Kathleen, 67–68
merit, law of, 132–33
Merton, Thomas, 185
Michel, Alexandra, 131
Millennials, 23, 24, 26, 28, 135
Mitchell, S. Weir, 47
Monastery of Christ in the Desert
    (Abiquiú, NM): artisans, 176–77;
    digital scriptorium, 165–67, 176;
    guests and guesthouse, 174–75;
    income sources, 175–76; perspec-
    tive on prayer, 172–74; perspective
    on work, 167–69; work and prayer
    schedule, 169–71, 179
monasticism: and acedia, 40–41,
    168; avoidance of burnout,
    178–79. *See also* Monastery of
    Christ in the Desert; St. Benedict's
    Monastery; St. John's Abbey
Morrison-Lane, Janet, 199, 200
Morrow, Lance, 33, 82–83
Nakamura, Jeanne, 124

neurasthenia, 43–48, 60, 126
neuroticism, 105
Newman, John Henry, 188
Nixon, Richard, 57
"noble lie" concept, 115
nonessential *vs.* essential workers,
    218–19
nonprofits. *See* CitySquare
Nordeen, Patricia, 208–11
Norway, 122
nurses. *See* medical workers

Odell, Jenny, 157
Ofri, Danielle, 102, 103–4, 112
overextension, 75, 77–78. *See also*
    exhaustion

pandemic. *See* Covid-19 pandemic
papal writings on labor, 147–49
The Parking Lot Movie (documentary), 143, 150, 162
Patrick, Dan, 220
Paul (Saint), 117, 136, 170
Perdue, Sonny, 145
Perlstein, Rick, 58
Petersen, Anne Helen, 28–30, 128
Phoenix, Davin, 110
physicians. *See* medical workers
Pieper, Josef, 129, 130, 131–32, 168, 171–72, 202
Pines, Ayala, 20, 31–32, 83
Plato, 115, 119
potential, 162–64
poverty lawyers, 54, 71
predestination, 127
professionalism, 95–96
Prokosch, Cecelia, 180
Protestant ethic, 125–28
Proust, Marcel, 45
psychology. *See* burnout spectrum; Maslach Burnout Inventory; mental illness
Pugh, Allison, 117, 186
purpose and meaning, 79–80, 118–20

race: burnout studies on, 109–11; hierarchies and disparities, 45, 108–9; and inherited burnout, 30, 35; and pandemic impact, 219–20; and social citizenship, 117–18. *See also* black Americans
Reagan, Ronald, 59
religion: biblical models, 119, 136; hierarchies, 45; papal writings on labor, 147–49; Protestant ethic,

125–28; welcomed in work settings, 196
retirement, 113, 188–89
Rose, Julie L., 172
Rosenblat, Alex, 92

Sadler, William S., 43
Safire, William, 59
St. Benedict's Monastery (St. Joseph, MN): balance of work and prayer, 181–82, 184; history, 180–81; work of older members, 185, 187–88, 189–90
St. John's Abbey (Collegeville, MN): balance of work and prayer, 181–85; communal support in, 186–87; dignity in, 185–86; history, 180, 181; work of older members, 185, 187, 188
St. John's University (Collegeville, MN), 182–83
Sandford, Bria, 222
Satori, Jessika, 99–100
Schaffner, Anna Katharina, 38, 39, 42, 44
Schonfeld, Irvin, 84, 85
scriptural models, 119, 136
self-determination and individualism, 3–4, 133, 149, 153–54, 158, 177, 213
Shakespeare, William, *As You Like It*, 41
Siburt, John, 194, 197–98, 199
Smith, Adam, *The Wealth of Nations*, 131, 152
Smith, John, 116–17
Smith, Vicki, 96, 101
social citizenship, 117–18
social workers, 68–69

Founded in 1893,
UNIVERSITY OF CALIFORNIA PRESS
publishes bold, progressive books and journals
on topics in the arts, humanities, social sciences,
and natural sciences—with a focus on social
justice issues—that inspire thought and action
among readers worldwide.

The UC PRESS FOUNDATION
raises funds to uphold the press's vital role
as an independent, nonprofit publisher, and
receives philanthropic support from a wide
range of individuals and institutions—and from
committed readers like you. To learn more, visit
ucpress.edu/supportus.